To Coney, With Love

To Coney, With Love

MEMORIES COLLECTED BY
KATY MARK AND ROB LOWE
Foreword by Gary S. Wachs

BRITON
PUBLISHING

810 Eastgate North Dr., Suite 200
Cincinnati, Ohio 45245
www.britonpublishing.com

ISBN 978-1-956216-20-2 Hardcover
ISBN 978-1-956216-21-9 Paperback

Copyright 2024 Briton Publishing. All rights reserved.

No part of this publication may be reproduced in any form, or by any means, electronic or mechanical, including photocopying, recording, or any information browsing storage or retrieval system, without permission in writing from Briton Publishing LLC.

Briton Publishing, LLC books are distributed by Ingram Content Group and made available worldwide.

Briton Publishing would like to make a note that most of the photos in this book were taken before the digital age of photography that we now know and have become accustomed to. Therefore, the quality may not be up to the standard we normally see in our books. That said, we felt that each of these photos carry special memories and stories for not only the person who submitted them but for the readers as well. We would like to thank the reader for being understanding and enjoying these photos and the memories associated with them in the free spirit that they were intended.

A Personal Message from Rob Lowe

I would like to dedicate this book to my dad, the legendary Bob Lowe, who was Sunlite Pool's Captain of the Guards for 50 years, and to all those who passed through my life, while growing up Coney.

A special thank you to my wife, Brinka, who is also my business partner (Briton Publishing) for emotionally embracing this project. For someone who did not grow up in Cincinnati, during the editing process, she was able to grasp the importance of this project, and work at preserving these memories as if they were her own.

A Personal Message from Katy Mark

This book is dedicated to my daughters, Abby and Ellie. I wanted a place where they can be transported back to simpler summers from their childhood.

Special thanks to Ellie for her help with this project since she is the one that is a tech guru. I know I drove her crazy with my constant requests.

To my husband, Tim, thank you for your help with running the girls to and from all of the places they needed to be while I worked full time and tried to put this book together.

And finally, to those that took the time to locate family photos and submit stories — you are the reason this book exists. Thank you.

May the spirit of Coney Island live on.

*You don't stop playing because you grow old.
You grow old because you stop playing.*

From the Editor
Brinka Rauh-Lowe

An unlikely friendship was kindled between Rob Lowe and Katy Mark after the closing of the park when their lives were connected in a search for a meaningful plaque. They quickly realized there was power between the two of them with each of their unique points of view and how the park made a dent in their lives.

Rob Lowe, whose dad was Bob Lowe, "Captain of the Guards" at Coney Island's Sunlite Pool for 50 years, grew up at the park creating day-to-day memories that turned into a lifetime of love for the park. Rob is also the co-owner of Briton Publishing.

Katy Mark was one of the "full-timers" as the Coney kids called the few that worked year-round unlike the many that were seasonal. She was there the day the city came out to enjoy the amusement park rides for the last time in 2019 and also experienced the loss the day the city found out that Coney would be closing its doors forever.

Together with each of their unique perspectives, Katy and Rob set out with the hopes of bringing a city together and allowing loved ones the opportunity to relive their childhood by writing memories down so that they can live in print forever.

The pages to follow will fill your heart with memories from grandparents who rode the Island Queen to dance the night away at the locally acclaimed Moonlite Gardens, or the young Aquanaut swim team kids who spent numerous days in Coney's pool in the early morning hours. You will read the stories from married couples who met while working their first jobs at the park and have created future generations of Coney Island memory-makers, and stories about the rides that made for thrilling moments while creating memorable experiences. Several people felt such a deep connection to Coney Island that they spread their loved one's ashes there, much like Rob Lowe did with his dad's.

We know you will enjoy the beautiful tapestry of memories that is, *and always will be,* Coney Island, Cincinnati.

A Message from Katy Mark and Rob Lowe

When we heard the news of the sale and subsequent closure of Coney Island. We realized that regardless of the outcome of local citizens fighting to keep our history here in Cincinnati, there still needs to be a place for the stories to live. As the memories have flooded social media, radio, and television since the announcement of the closing of Coney Island in Cincinnati, it has become apparent that there is no one place to allow these snippets of our past to sit and just be cherished. There are books on the amazing history of this 137-year-old park that once started as an apple tree orchard on the banks of the Ohio River but there are not any books on the memories that made this place live and breathe. We are all woven into its beautiful tapestry in some way, shape, or form. Just to be a thread in its long masterpiece is an honor for us and we wanted to see those threads come together so we could pass them on to future generations. We will not let the memories of Coney Island, Moonlite Gardens, Sunlite Pool, and the amusement park be forgotten. This book is our way to keep Cincinnati's history alive. We realize that not all memories are necessarily good ones, but we chose to focus on the positive. We hope when you read this compilation, that it will inspire even more distant, and not so distant, memories.

We would like to offer our heartfelt thanks to Kathy Ryan Farro for giving our book the perfect title, *To Coney, with Love*.

We would also like to thank Michelle Shultz for submitting the beautiful photo of Coney's river entrance gate, which we used for the back cover of this book, *and finally*, in no particular order, please enjoy the following submissions!

Foreword
Gary S. Wachs
Former Vice President

Coney Island was the finest amusement park of its day, not only in the minds of its patrons but in the esteem of its peers - other park owners who held Coney Island in the highest regard. A visit by Walt Disney in 1953 seeking advice on his new dream, Disneyland, seemed to confirm the park's stature.

How did the park happen? Well, it evolved naturally as a picnic grove along an uncommonly scenic stretch of the Ohio River. Then, George Scott, an entrepreneur, came along, saw the potential of this setting, and along with six other founders incorporated Coney Island Amusement Park in 1923. The "picnic grove" was quickly augmented by the world's largest swimming pool, a ballroom, and a huge steel steamboat, the Island Queen, to transport up to 4,000 people back and forth from downtown Cincinnati, the convergence of several trolley lines from its "seven hills."

What made the park different? In my opinion, it was the spirit of George F Schott, its president and substantial owner, and my grandfather. He started "clean" in the industry. To be fair, the perception of a clean amusement park was greatly enhanced by an abundance of landscaping, one of his passions. I dare say the landscape budget at Coney Island was considerably larger than any amusement park in the United States.

My grandfather was a principled operator. He avoided, with few exceptions, concessionaires whose interests were contrary to his management philosophy. Unlike most other amusement parks, he forbade members of his family to own or operate any ride, refreshment, souvenir, or game. This type of privilege he felt would conflict with the motivation and allegiance of his trusted department managers. George Scott set a standard of safety, excellence, and class that was followed by his son Edward H Schott, President from 1935 through 1961, and his son-in-law Ralph G Wachs, President from 1961 to 1971.

As I look at the history of Coney Island during the time my family controlled it, two themes stand out. First, it was a wonderful microcosm of how we all played, the habits of our leisure time from 1925 to 1971 - from the stringent requirements in 1925 when men were required to wear tops to their bathing suits to the first bikini in 1955.

The second theme was Coney Island's amazing resilience to adversity. The park survived the depression years when the daily per capita spending was measured in cents. It barely survived the devastating 1937 Ohio River flood, the 500-year flood that caused a special meeting of the board of directors to evaluate the worth of staying in business. It provided much-needed entertainment during World War II when the United States government allowed a special exemption for the Island Queen to use valuable "Bunker C" oil to fuel its many trips carrying soldiers on furlough. (Morale was important).

After the war, the summer season saw a return to normalcy until the park's "Island Queen" blew up in Pittsburgh in September of 1947. The Queen was gone - from a welder's torch igniting that same Bunker C oil. Coney operated through the great polio scare of the early 1950s when Sunlite Pool nearly closed. Coney integrated as racial barriers came down in the 1950s and '60s for movie theaters, ballrooms, restaurants, amusement parks, and other public accommodations.

Coney Island was a survivor. The public's desire to support a first-rate amusement park has triumphed through the decades and I am fortunate to be part of that history.

This book serves to preserve a fragment of our Coney memories that will continue to forever live in all of our hearts; not just memories of Coney Island the Amusement park, but of family and friends and the times of our lives.

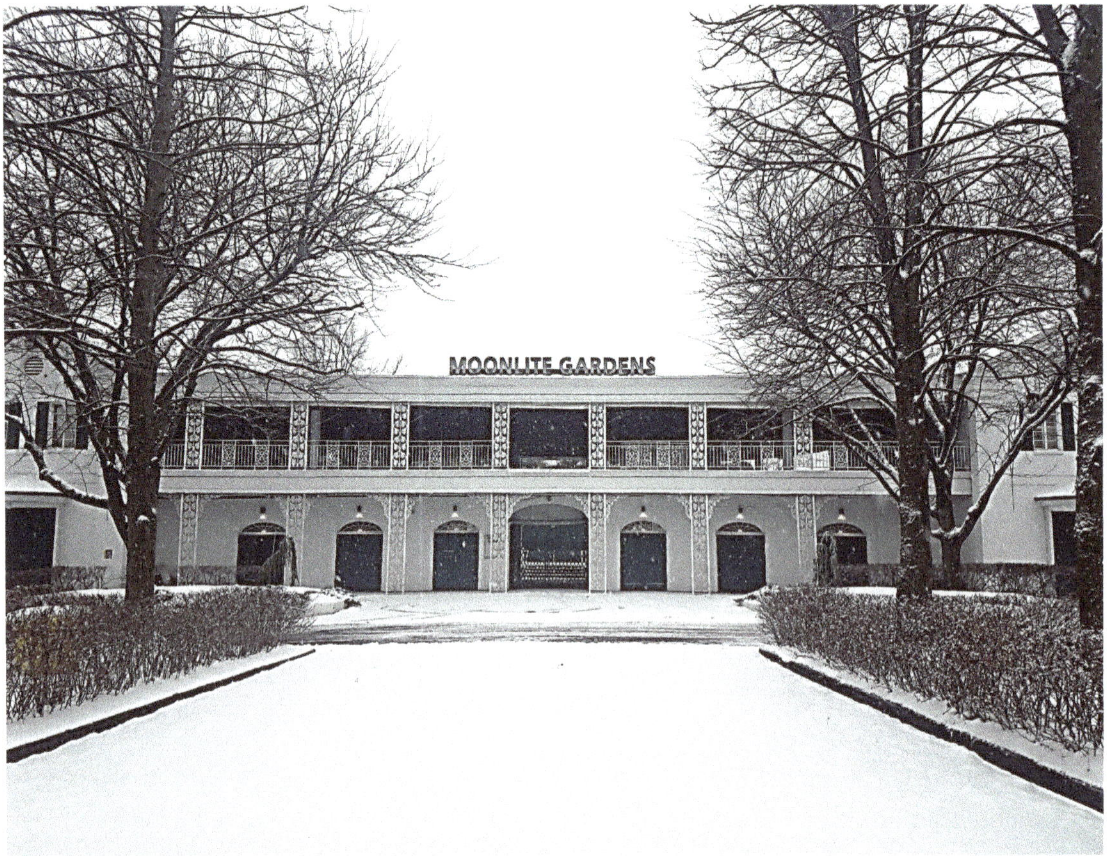
MOONLITE GARDENS

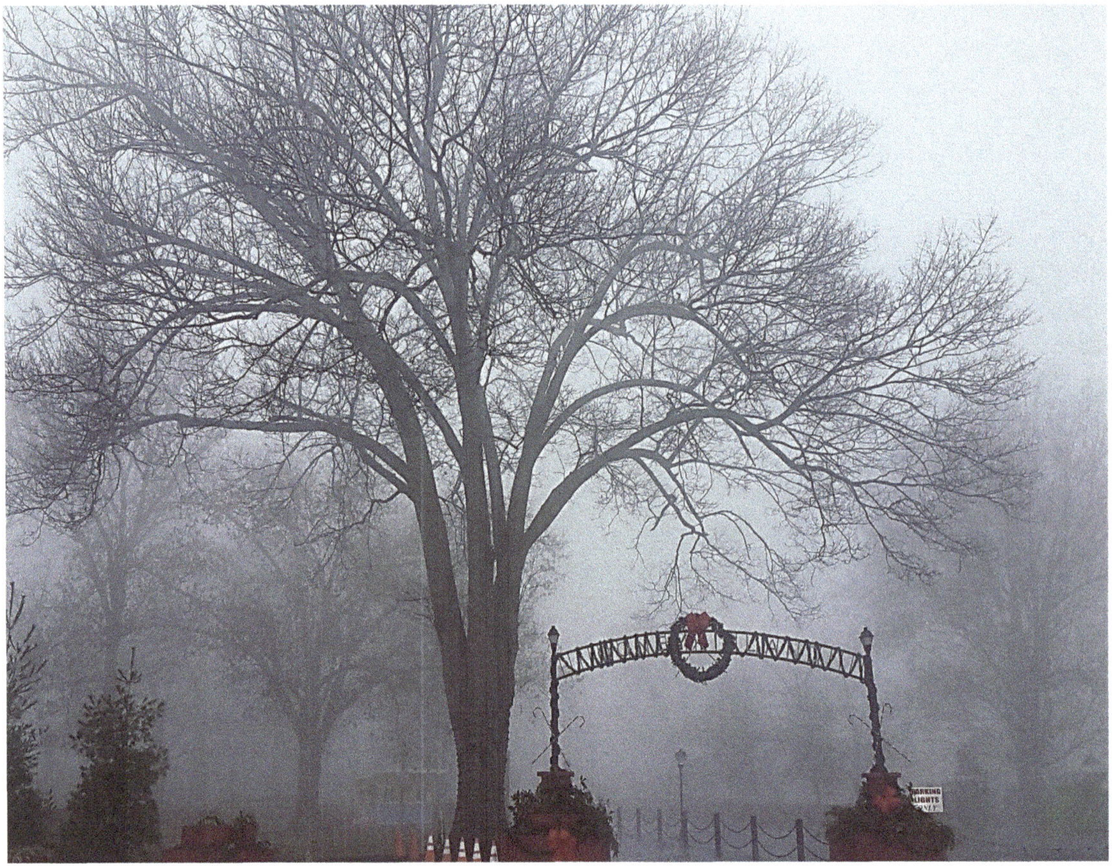

The Memories

To Coney, with Love, Ellie Mark

Coney Island's announcement that the park was closing devastated me. As the daughter of Katy Mark (co-creator of this book), I spent every waking moment somewhere in the park. I spent many cheerful days exploring the expansive landscape of the world's largest recirculating pool with friends and family. I spent multiple afternoons assisting my mom in her office as she worked hard to create an enjoyable experience for the companies who booked picnics there. I remember planning for most of my life to work with my mom and sister as soon as I met the age requirement. Whether I was shredding papers and sorting admissions tickets for my mom, racing my friends down the twister water slides, or repeatedly riding the Python coaster; there was never a dull moment at Coney. One of my favorites and most vivid memories was when my sister and I got to be the last kids to ever ride a ride at Coney Island. When staying after the park closed as my mom boxed up her belongings, we rode the drop tower countless times until we were forced to get off. It was a bittersweet memory, watching the classic Coney entrance get further and further away in the mirror. Reliving this similar experience as we left the park for the last time this past year was heartbreaking but nostalgic. I cannot express how much I will miss this park and the effect it has had on me over the years. Coney Island, you will always have a special place in my heart.

To Coney, with Love, Nancy Schroder

During the summers, I spent most of my childhood at Coney (1960-1974). I took swimming lessons every summer, which was required by my parents if I was going to spend the day at Coney. I completed lifesaving when I finally turned 18. My older brother was a lifeguard for many years, and I imagine kept an eye on me without my knowledge. So many memories and friendships made all those years. Ronnie Dale played the organ by the food area on weekends and always included our group of friends in his talent shows every summer. Mastering the different heights of diving boards and the big slide was a challenge every summer. We would play shuffleboard and ping pong in between playing in the pool. Sunday was always a family day spent at Coney with other families, taking up a large area near the shallow end. We spent much more time at the pool than the park, which was always a thrill. To this day, the smell of Coppertone always brings me back to my Coney days. What a lucky kid I was to have my summers spent at Coney Island!

To Coney, with Love, Susan M Hartung

I was a third-generation Coney Island visitor so, of course, I wanted my kids to carry on the tradition. As they got older, they would visit the rides, get hot, cool off in the pool, and repeat.

I didn't plan on giving Nathan, my oldest son, his first ice cream cone at the young age of five months. But we were at Coney one sunny day in August 1999, and it was our little family tradition to treat ourselves to a soft-serve ice cream cone every time we visited Coney. Nathan sat on my lap at the table while we were enjoying our cones. I noticed him looking at us very intently. Then he just started leaning toward my chocolate ice cream cone with his mouth wide open! It was so cute, I had to let him share, and he did! I think he had as much of that cone as I did. He's had a sweet tooth ever since.

To Coney, with Love, Wanda Engelhardt

The Shooting Star! As a child and pre-teen, one of the thrills of my life was riding The Shooting Star! How I always loved roller coasters! Unbelievably, unlike any other ride I've encountered, we were permitted to remain in our seats if we wanted to ride again! We did not have to get off and stand in line for a second time around, or a third, or a fourth. Truth is, as I distinctly recall, I had the delight of being able to stay in my seat until the thrill was gone. In my case, it was 13 times around!! What great memories! Little did I know that in 1964 while in high school, I would be singing one of our hit records at Moonlite Gardens as well. Tears Come Tumbling. Our group was The Teardrops. It was a great ride for me in more than one way, and Coney will always have a special place in my heart.

To Coney, with Love, Marianne Andrews

Mom and I went every year on a bus for Norwood Day. I remember riding the Wild Mouse and Lost River, Mom would always want the front seat, which would scare me. I also went to work picnics through the years. It was a great place to go to have fun!!

To Coney, with Love, Aleisa Yusko

This is an excerpt from my grandmother's written memoirs. Her name was Florence Bohmer Meyer (1915-2010). She titled this memoir "Coney Island-First Dance with a Boy" and photos below are of great-grandmother Mary Farfsing Bohmer and her friends at Coney Island around 1910.

Years ago, there was an amusement park called Coney Island, although it wasn't exactly an island. Besides taking a boat up the Ohio River you could also drive to get there. One time when I was about thirteen, mother arranged for us to spend the day at Coney Island. I had also been there, as I remember, when I was about six or seven years old. This time, as we pulled away from the shore, a lady with three little children came running to get on but we had already gone too far out to pick them up. I felt so sorry for them. On the way back on the Island Queen, as the boat was called, they had an orchestra playing. Mother happened to be sitting by another lady who had a son about my age. She wanted him to dance with me. Mother nodded her consent, so we danced. That was the first time I'd danced with a boy.

To Coney, with Love, Jo Ann Greene

Our family, which consisted of dad, mom, my 2 brothers and myself, went to Coney Island every 4th of July. When the Island Queen was running, we would all ride on that, I was really too young to remember that, but my brothers remember that very well and loved it, that was in the 1940s. My dad loved to ride the roller coasters, so he and my 2 brothers would ride. My dad said that he would sit in the middle of the car, my 2 brothers on either side of him and he would grab both boys' belts and hang on to them so the boys wouldn't fall out, as the coaster continued on its run. As I got a little older, in the 1950s, I remember so many good times on the rides. I loved the Wild Mouse, the little cars that I could drive around Lake Como and always, Lost River and that BIG drop off toward the end, I knew that was coming and always tensed up before the drop off and then the big splash and it was over! I also loved the merry-go-round. As a smaller child I remember the little boats I could go on. Later on, being a teenager, in the 1960s, my cousins and I went together to Coney Island. I remember one time when my cousins and I went, we got to see Nick Adams, who starred in the T.V. show, *The Rebel*. We couldn't get over the fact that we got to see a real T.V. star in person. When he said hi to us, made our whole day!! There were so many good times at Coney Island. I wish I could visit those times again.

To Coney, with Love, Maureen Baioni

I remember our parents taking our large family to Twins Day at Coney Island. We would take the ferry over from Kentucky to the park, which was fun in itself for us. My twin sister and I were pretty little at the time, so it is hard to remember too much. We probably went every year up until we were about 6 or so. We were all so excited to go because we loved the rides and the pool, but it was also so scary. We both hated the clowns! They were kind and gave us a balloon, but we were scared of them, as we were shy. I remember we waited to be tall enough to ride the Shooting Star roller coaster ride. They finally let us ride it because the ride was going away. We were really not tall enough and we were tiny, so we felt like we were going to fly out of the ride as we stayed airborne the whole ride, but we loved it! We were always glad we got the chance to ride the Shooting Star before it went away.

After we had children of our own, we took them to Coney many times and we loved it, and so did they. Until I broke my leg on the silver slide. I went down that slide so many times, so I couldn't believe I did that in my 50s! I just happened to try to jump onto the mat. The water pressure was so strong that it forced my foot into the mat. As I pulled it up, the rush and force of the water was so strong that it pushed it into the mat a second time. I had two fractures in my foot, *crazy!* I still would go down it again, I just had to keep my legs straight and slide into the water. No more trying to land on my feet. Lesson learned! My husband and sons have worked at Coney in the VIP tent. My husband has been working there for the past 20 plus years.

To Coney, with Love, Carol Metz

It was the summer of 1969. Coney Island was the popular place to go with your boyfriend. We were standing in line waiting to get on a ride when I saw a girl across from me at another ride smile and wave at me. My boyfriend asked, who is that? I said I think it's my sister! He said, *you think it is?* I had to explain to him that we were separated when I was two years old. At that time, I was 15 and she was 16. We had only seen each other a couple of times over the years. Later that day we walked past each other; she was also with her boyfriend. We smiled at each other and said "hi," then walked on. We didn't know what else to say but I remember thinking that's my sister and she is really pretty! It was a great memory! Having a fun day at Coney Island and then running into my sister who I hadn't seen in years!

To Coney, with Love, Margie Metz

One of my favorite memories of Coney were the times my dad, mom, sisters and I spent at Sunlite Pool together. We would go to Sunlite Pool for the day (even as recently as the late 2010s) my mom would pack a picnic, and we would swim the day away! My Dad would always race us in the pool to the deep end. I would feel as if we were in the ocean when crossing the deep end, with the lifeguard in their boat, and people jumping off the diving boards. We loved how deep it was. It was exhilarating and exhausting to swim the length of the pool and back. Sadly, my dad passed away in 2021, but the tradition of swimming to the deep end and having a delicious picnic my mom packed continued into the last decade with my own children. My kids would also look forward to the amusement rides that would be open for an hour in the summer after Sunlite Pool closed. Great memories that I will always treasure with my family.

To Coney, with Love, Samantha Schloss

My best memories at Coney Island were when my aunt used to take my brothers, cousins and I to Sunlite Pool during the summers. We would stay the night at my aunt and uncle's house and make lunches for our trip to Coney Island. When we got to Coney, we would ride the rides and play games and then go to Sunlite Pool and do water slides and then grab the lunch we packed (usually it was peanut butter and jelly, salami roll ups, fruit and a Capri Sun to drink). After lunch we would go back to the water slides. It was always a fun time at Coney Island!

To Coney, with Love, Ethan D Flexner

One of my very best Coney Island memories is going there every summer. I would go multiple times during the season with my grandma and my cousins. I really loved going there and going down the slides with my cousin (mainly the purple one) whether I had to go alone or wait for my sister and cousin.

Coney Island really was such a great place, and I have made so many memories here for as long as I can remember. I LOVED getting on the bumper cars until they removed them, or just walking around the pool during the summertime. Swimming laps in the pool with my cousins and sister was one of the most fun things to do, but very tiring. Also, jumping from the island in the middle of the pool into the deep end, going down the metal slide in the middle of the pool. I learned about the history of the park from my grandma, and really just being there was the best memory of all. I am just so happy I got to experience Coney Island while it was open.

To Coney, with Love, Logan Meredith

Remembering back to the days of my childhood and the long car rides from Wilmington, Ohio, to Coney Island. My grandparents always set aside special time for their grandkids every summer for a fun filled day at Coney Island. Too many quarters were spent at the arcade with my grandfather trying to teach us the patience of the Roller Bowler. The hours we spent watching the live performances when things got a little too hot. I will never forget those moments and the feeling of walking around Coney Island with my family. The time we spent at Coney will forever remain a part of my childhood and always in my heart.

To Coney, with Love, Amber Spicer

Coney Island — *Where do I even start?!* It holds such a special place in my heart. I've grown up at Coney, raised my adult children at Coney, and my youngest who's 6, at Coney. We had so many more memories to make there! I spent countless hours there in high school bathing in the sun, not a care in the world! My Senior Prom was held at Moonlite Gardens. Then when I had my boys, I introduced them to Coney! So many hours of playing and splashing carefree and riding the rides (the Ferris wheel being my favorite); paddling the boats on the lake, and never getting them to go in the right direction. Enjoying putt-putt golf, and LaRosa's Pizza. Midnight Swim was always a hit!

Coney's pool is one of a kind, a real gem! The layout has changed over the years, but our love for it has grown! My youngest participated in swim lessons and which built up his confidence 100%. Such an amazing program! Being a teacher, I work hard all school year dreaming about summer days at Coney with our Coney family! I love how the pool starts out shallow, which is wonderful for everyone! Floating along the rope soaking in the rays, it doesn't get better than that! Tossing the ball in the water, diving for rings, racing down the slides! Memories! I loved my Coney Community where everyone is welcomed!

To Coney, with Love, Sue Martin

When we were dating, my now husband of 60 years and I went to Moonlite Gardens almost every weekend to dance or for a concert. I saw my first ever concert there (Wayne Newton). During intermissions, we would go out to the games, and mainly played Skee Ball! By the end of each summer, we would have thousands of tickets, which got us little keepsake prizes! It was our absolutely favorite date place, and we have so many great memories!

To Coney, with Love, Judy Doyle

If it weren't for Coney Island, I might have never been born. My father helped pay his way through college by running the Merry Go Round and my mother enjoyed swimming at the pool. They met there, dated, married, and produced me.

My grandfather, Wilbur Harmon, was office manager at Coney Island for 23 years. He was a dapper dresser, always wearing a shirt, tie and suit, topped by a wide brimmed hat. His staff loved him, and many called him "Dad" Harmon. Every year, he received a Father's Day card from his crew, expressing their affection for him. He treasured those cards and saved them.

Since my father was deployed during WWII, my grandfather was the first "Dad" I knew. He spoiled me with cherry pie from the Coney cafeteria and arranged my birthday parties, giving ride tickets to all my friends. Some of my happiest childhood days were spent at Coney Island and with my grandfather.

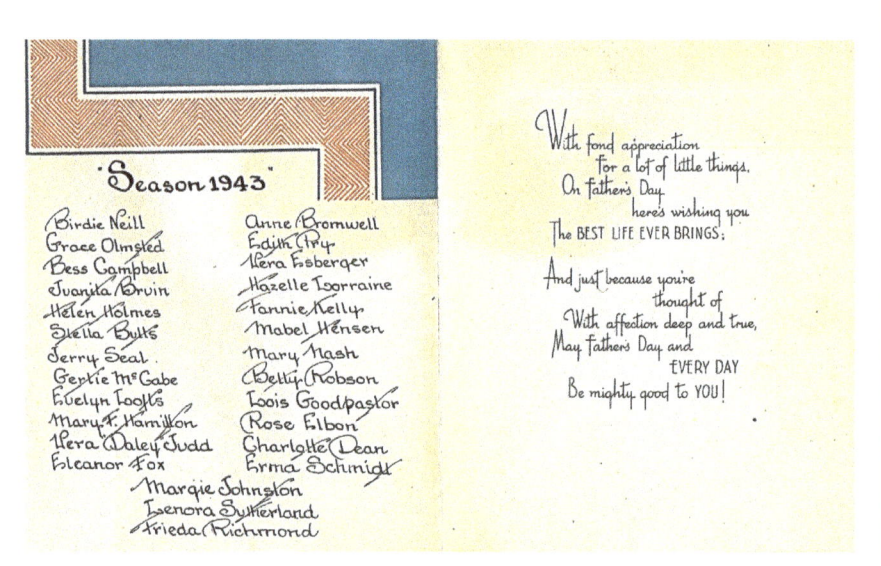

To Coney, with Love, Patricia Parks

We lived in Boone County, way out in the country and it was such a treat to go to Coney Island to swim and ride rides. My sister and I are two years apart in age. This picture had always been one of my mother's favorite pictures. She had us in identical outfits both of us with this wild natural curly hair, but this picture always made me kind of laugh I wondered what I was so mad at, and my sister was so happy with at the same time!

To Coney, with Love, Kathy Farro Ryan

Thousands of Cincinnatians hold cherished memories of their days at Coney Island, which are almost invariably about their first kiss on the Lost River, or going down the slide in Sunlite Pool. My childhood summers were certainly dominated by pool time and rides, but some of the sweetest memories of my life were made elsewhere. In 1998, I was 15 and needed to get my first summer job. My high school friends and I applied at Coney, excited to work together all summer. I wondered which department we would all be in. The swim shop? Sunlite Grill? Guest relations? Who knows! The application had a spot where you could put down your top three choices. I picked those three, just like my friends did.

My friends had their interviews and got their jobs. It was finally my turn. I spoke briefly with the manager and then he placed my paperwork down on the table, pulled out a ballpoint pen and as he wrote he said, "we are going to put you in the grove." I stared at the word "GROVE" scribbled on the application. I didn't even know what that meant. I thought of Grover from Sesame Street. The what? I was 15 years old and too nervous to ask. This clearly was not going how I thought it would.

On my first day, a Coney employee led me to the back of the park, through the gravel and the tall 200-year-old trees, to a large shelter that had a kitchen in it. I spent little to no time in this area of the park as a kid and didn't realize there was a kitchen back there. In the kitchen there was a large stainless-steel table with employees gathered around it. It was "prep day." I was told to slice tomatoes with this tall lanky kid Kenton who, 26 years later, is my best friend. I sliced what felt like the most tomatoes I've ever seen in my life, and then I sliced more. And more. I still wasn't sure what we were doing. Again, I was 15 and too afraid to ask. I didn't think that Sunlite Grill needed this many tomatoes for a weekend, did they? What exactly are we doing here?

The second day I cried when my dad dropped me off at the front gate. I wanted to quit. The family scandal of 1996 stood out in my mind. It was when my cousin Mary quit her first job at the Holidome after the first day. The horror! I could just hear my older relatives: "Kathy quit after one day, too. Kids these days just don't want to work." I couldn't meet the same fate. I will not. By the time I arrived back in the grove, I had dried my tears and resolved to suffer through the summer and complete one season to save face, and to save my generation's reputation. I did so even though getting through even a single other day of slicing thousands of tomatoes felt like hell, and September felt like it was years away. A grove manager sent me to a shelter where I would man the frozen lemonade stand for the day. As I watched the other employees set up buffet lines and dessert tables throughout the day, I realized what we were doing. This is a PICNIC grove! People are having company picnics! As the summer went on, I made friends and got to know the job, and I really loved it. I would go home covered in beer and baked beans, and it made me happy. Suddenly, September felt like it was coming up way too fast.

Later in the season, we stood in the commissary watching the chef Scott make a giant fruit and cheese board on a mirrored tray, in the days before the word "charcuterie" was in our regular vocabularies. As my coworker watched him put it together and cut strawberries into fancy shapes, she said, "wow... you know, you should really go into catering." Scott stopped mid-strawberry slicing and looked at her. "What do you think we are doing here, exactly?"

That summed up everything about working at Coney for me for seven seasons. It never really felt like a job, and it was easy to forget that it was. We worked long days and worked hard; labor laws be damned. It was no small task to wrangle a bunch of unwitting fifteen-year-olds into an operation that might feed 10,000 people in a single day. But we did it, over and over again.

I felt sorry for my friends working soul-sucking retail jobs under fluorescent lighting at Eastgate Mall and the like. I would arrive at the grove in the early morning when the fog of the river hung low, and it was slightly cool and very quiet. I would end the day sweaty and cleaning up Shelter 3 while a bunch of drunk, sunburnt picnic-goers berated whatever poor 15-year-old we assigned to evening bingo that day.

The picnic grove was Coney Island's underdog. Coney Island began as a picnic grove and operated that way for 58 years before Sunlite Pool opened. It brought thousands of people every weekend of every summer, even in the rain. It made the park money, and the picnic grove employees carried an air of being the misfits in the back of the park. Other park employees would look at us and tell us they have, "no idea what you do back there."

I will miss Coney and the picnic grove forever. I wish for every kid that they can have a first job that brought me the joy that mine did, and create the lifelong friendships and memories that I experienced. The grove was not flashy. It was so unassuming, in fact, that you could work a full first day there without even knowing what was going on. When I was a little girl in Mt. Washington, I thought I might work at Coney when I was a teenager, as many did. Coming of age for seven summers amongst a few worn tents and picnic shelters, watching how crazy people can get after a day of free beer and eight hours in the sun, was not how I saw this going. But I wouldn't have it any other way. I can thank the picnic grove for some of my most cherished memories. And thank you, Mary, for quitting the Holidome after one day. Without that, I don't know that I would have stuck it out long enough to have this part of my life.

To Coney, with Love, Megan Bettle

I am not one of those who have years and years of Coney Island memories, but the memories I do have are amazing. In August of 2015, we got tickets to a Coney Island company picnic. My kids, approximately 2, 4 and 12 at the time, were so excited. They had never been to an amusement park or even ridden any kind of ride, even at the fair. While reminiscing I found an old Facebook post from the morning of our first visit, my 4-year-old asked, "What day is it, Mom? What day is Coney Island?" and I was happy to reply, "Today is the day little man, today is the day." We stayed from open to close and rode as much as we could in that time. My oldest daughter rode some of the more thrilling rides, while the 2 little ones rode some smaller rides, and we rode several as a family. They had so much fun running from ride to ride jumping and smiling, and my husband and I knew we had to come back.

We ended up getting Coney Island season passes for the 2016 season and hiding a copy of them in their Easter baskets. Little did I know what special memories we would make. The first big memory is we all five rode the Serpent roller coaster, our first coaster as a family, this is the moment we became roller coaster enthusiasts! Another great memory was when the park randomly selected two families to be the first down the Typhoon Tower! It was an amazing event, and I am so glad we were chosen to do that. At the Typhoon Tower Preview Party, they were photographed with Ronald McDonald, which made their day. I still have the sunglasses they got that day on display in my house and I got each of my kids a Typhoon Tower t-shirt to remember the day. We also really loved the Balloon Glow event for the 4th of July, it was definitely memorable because it poured down rain the whole day and even during the fireworks.

My husband wound up being in the hospital a lot the 2016 summer. He ended up having a major surgery and had to stay in the hospital for weeks. In between hospital visits and doctor's appointments I tried to find things to keep the kids busy and occupied. We ended up spending several days at the park just so I could keep my mind off everything going on. We would throw food and drinks into a cooler and have a big picnic before spending the day riding rides and swimming. In what was a hard time in my life, we were still able to make so many good memories.

To Coney, with Love, Katharine Robinson

We spent our first summer after moving to Cincinnati at Coney Island. My kids loved the water slides, the food, and the high dive. We moved after the rides closed, so the water activities were always our favorite part. My younger son learned to swim by taking lessons at Coney. We enjoyed visiting as a family and with friends. We will miss the fun atmosphere and vacation vibes that are unique to Coney!

To Coney, with Love, Dwayne Stanfill

My earliest memories were when my parents took me there at about two years old. I remember the fireworks scared me. As I grew older, they did not bother me anymore. I was in the Goshen High School marching band, and we were invited to march for the closing of Coney. That was quite the honor. Another honor was when we also marched for the opening of Kings Island. My picture is of the souvenir they gave the band members for marching at the opening.

To Coney, with Love, Denise Fitzpatrick Long

During my college summers, I had the best job in Cincinnati. My girlfriend, Nancy, and I were in charge of running the Accessory Shop at Coney Island Sunlite Pool. The area was small but was packed with anything you needed for the summer sun, from lip gloss to jock straps. Yes, you read that correctly! In the 60s and 70s, the style was for men to wear short, tight-fitting swim trunks. When one of them would forget and leave that precious item at home, another could be purchased at the Accessory Shop. Of course, we had to ask the size that was needed: Small, Medium, or Large. Of course, they ALWAYS answered "Large!" Little did they know it merely meant the waist size! And, of course, there were no returns!!

For so many decades, people in the tri-state have been waking up, anticipating the Saturday on Memorial weekend when Sunlite Pool would open. Getting the summer bag ready, trying on old and new bathing suits, and anticipating seeing old friends once again, but not this year or ever again.

All you have to is drive down 52 and see piles of clumped concrete instead of that pristine pool of water. It takes me back to the very early 70s when I worked at the pool in my college summer years. The parking was in the same area but you had to walk back around the pool to the entrance to attain entrance to the pool. There you were greeted with cashiers, workers dressed in the red and white striped culotte jumpers with zipper up the front, handing you a locker key and small Coney towel. These needed to be turned in at the end of your stay. Then you would wind through lockers, showers, dressing rooms. In the women's area, there were mirrors where ladies would apply make-up and do their hair for the numerous big band dances at Moonlite Gardens. I remember that as a child, looking in awe! Many lasting friendships were made among workers and patrons. So many great memories that we need to keep, as this is the end of a great era. This will be a somber summer as we remember joining our friends that turned into lifetime friends. Thank you, Coney, for this gift.

To Coney, with Love, Marian Barton

I grew up in Anderson Township, so I have many memories of Coney Island. My mother worked in the locker room around 1958. You got a key for a locker and a towel when you went in. The captain of the lifeguards taught me how to dive and float on my back. I think his name was Bob Lowe. I am 85 years old now so that was probably around 1955. I remember going downtown on a bus with my mother and getting on the Island Queen to go to Coney. I can still hear the calliope. I loved it. My Dad would come after work, and we would have a picnic and then ride the rides. That was what we considered our vacation once a year. My most memorable memory was when I almost lost my life as I knew it. We were a one car family of six.

My sister and I were close in age and in the late fifties we would borrow Dad's car and go to Ladies Night at Moonlite Gardens. On one such occasion we met some boys who had just bought a convertible and at intermission we went for a ride. When we got back to Coney it was closed and the gates were padlocked. We were horrified. Dad needed that car to go to work the next day. We were dead ducks if we didn't get the car out. After we freaked out, we decided to climb the fence, in our dresses no less. We didn't even think about how we would get the car out. A guard came over to the fence and asked us what we thought we were doing. In a panic we started crying and begging him to let us get the car out while explaining we couldn't face our dad without the car. At the least we would be grounded for life with no car. Thank heaven he was understanding and unlocked the gate. God Bless him. My son got married at Moonlite Gardens in 1992. It was the perfect spot. Beautiful.

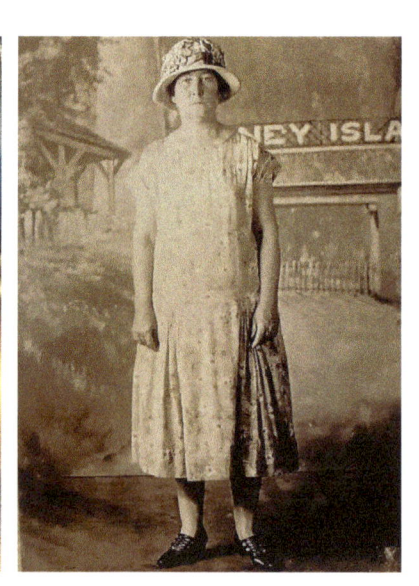

To Coney, with Love, Amanda Cowell

My husband and I and our 8 kids all grew up going to Coney Island every day, every summer. It was the one place everyone in the family would agree to go to! My 7-year-old daughter (6 at the time) had a 4th degree burn across her leg last year and as much pain as she was in, she cried saying "now I can't go to coney" because she wasn't able to get it wet. Well, we took her anyway and saran wrapped her leg and let her have the fun she wanted. My grandkids loved Coney as much as all my kids. 40 years of memories!

To Coney, with Love, Rob Lowe

My story for Coney Island could go on for a lifetime. My dad was Bob Lowe. He was captain of the lifeguards at Sunlite Pool for 50 years. I grew up at Coney. My parents were divorced at an early age and I saw my father every Saturday and 2 weeks every summer.

The two weeks that I spent with him every summer were always the most memorable of my life. At a very young age, he would bring me to work with him and I would take naps underneath his guard stand.

As I grew older, I was able to explore everything that Coney had to offer on my own. Since everyone at Coney knew my dad, everyone seemed to know me. I can remember walking in the park and playing all the games that they had. Every time I would walk by the restaurant, I would say hi to Chef Tony and he would make sure I was fed. Happy the Clown would ride me around in his car.

In the evening, if there was someone at Moonlite Gardens my dad would take me there to see the bands. My earliest memory of that is when the star of the T.V. show *The Rebel*, Nick Adams was there. He took me on my first Ferris wheel ride.

As time went on, I spent more time at the pool with my dad. We would spend endless days laughing and telling stories and meeting all the most interesting people. I think if I have to say what I remember most is the generations of people who I grew up with. They took care of me, played with me, and made me feel like I was a part of their lives. If any of those friends are reading my story, I thank you from the bottom of my heart for making my life a part of yours. At that time, I think my dad was synonymous with Coney Island. When he passed away, at the ripe age of 92, we sprinkled his ashes at the pool and Moonlite Gardens. That's what he wanted and that's what seemed appropriate.

While Coney Island is now gone, the life that it created for me made me who I am today. The wonderful memories and stories that linger in my mind always bring me joy and happiness. One memory that I always think fondly of is watching my dad dive. In his younger days, he qualified for the Olympics as a diver and I would see him do all of these wonderful acrobatic dives wishing I could do them, which I never could. I spent my younger days trying to swim across the deep end without having to stop and rest. So many people that I remember and so many that I would like to thank but if I mentioned every name, it would be a book on its own. Thank you, Coney Island, and thank you to everyone who created a great life for me.

*You are the light that shines on me
You always were, and you'll always be
So I had to let you know, just this once
Just this once before I go, -Love Robbie*

To Coney, with Love, Deborah Stahlhut

While money was tight, my mom made sure to take us four kids to Coney at least two times each summer. Once to swim all day and once to enjoy the rides. Special "extra" days we might go were Dot Food Day (lots of prizes), Nickel Day (all ride tickets a nickel), Coke Day (every ticket bought came with a free small glass bottle of coke). One year on Coke Day, we had so many bottles of coca cola, we stored some in my littlest sister's baby buggy. I still can remember the smells of Coney, a combination of popcorn and other carnival foods, as well as the smell of the grease and oil from the rides, especially the Dodgem, the Whip, and the Cuddle-up, as well as the unique sound of the Tumble Bug. My favorite rides from my younger years were the Teddy Bear, the pony rides, and the kiddie hand cars. The ferry rides to and from the park were almost exciting as any ride, and the challenge of getting on the last ferry back to Kentucky or "we'd have to walk home", added a bit of daring adventure to the end of our day at Coney.

Every year we would stand by the big metal giant welcoming us to the Land of Oz, after we walked up the hill from the ferry, with the mark showing how high the water got during the 1937 flood. Each time our imaginations would go wild thinking about how much destruction the flood waters caused, how much cleanup was involved in getting Coney ready for another year, and a great appreciation for all that was done to keep our beloved Coney Island up and running. It was a rite of passage to be finally tall enough to drive the cars in the turnpike out over Lake Como, and to go out on the canoes and paddleboats by ourselves. When we became teenagers, we saved our money and were allowed to go to Coney without our parents' supervision. By then, there was a pay one price admission, and you could ride all day, all rides. There were no cell phones then, so right before the park closed, we would find a pay phone, call home and ask our dad to meet us on the Kentucky side of the ferry landing. I remember the feeling of freedom and independence on that first solo trip to Coney.

No trip to Coney was complete, without a time or two at the fish pond. We never won anything big, but any trinket was a treasure, and I wish now I would have saved one of them as a lasting souvenir from good old Coney Island. My grandparents, Hazel and Robert Burns, were married in 1921, in Vevay,

Indiana, and came to Newport to live. Their honeymoon was a trip on the Island Queen to Coney Island for a day. Enclosed find a picture of them from their special trip as newlyweds. Three generations from my family had the privilege of enjoying Coney Island. I am grateful for all the happy memories.

To Coney, with Love, Mildred Partin

My husband and I had our first date at Coney Island. It was where my husband's work had their picnic every year. One of my favorite pictures is one of myself and my wonderful husband Bob who is in heaven now. Here is a picture of us and our firstborn daughter on the 4th of July 1960. She was born June the 27th, 1960 so she was only a few days old. Just the start of us with our girls. We shared so many wonderful times there and I still do with my daughter and grandchildren. Makes me cry to think I will never get to go again.

To Coney, with Love, Alicia Vargas

    I was born and raised here in Cincinnati, Ohio. One thing I've always loved about Cincinnati has been Coney Island. I've visited Coney Island so many times throughout my life. I've attended the Balloon Glow event on multiple occasions. It has always been something I've enjoyed and looked forward to. I took my daughter to the event back in 2013 and my son and my partner just last year, 2023. Such a fun time! Another favorite event that I've always loved has been Summer Fair. I enjoyed seeing all the talented people and their crafts. And yes, I have bought many things throughout the years. I remember one year Coney hosted the Home and Garden show. That was a blast. And another fond memory is when my partner and I danced at Moonlite Gardens during a Cinco De Mayo event. Coney Island holds many wonderful memories that I will always cherish. I'm so happy my kids also had an opportunity to experience Coney Island as well. From my son swimming at Sunlite Pool with my sister to my daughter spending her summer as a Slide Dispatcher just last summer, 2023. Coney Island will always be in our hearts and we're so sad to see it go.

To Coney, with Love, Sophia Ramundo

I began my journey at Coney Island as a season pass holder for many years of my childhood. My summers there were spent meeting up with cousins and friends, jumping off diving boards, and countless twister races. Then, my mom, Nicole Ramundo, was finally ready to get back into merchandising after 10 years of being a stay-at-home mom and became a "full-timer" at Coney, running the Island Shop and developing merchandise. Once when I was 15 about to turn 16, I was so eager to work at Coney, but I was unable to due to a scheduled spinal surgery that summer. So, my mom brought me in to work with her before my surgery, pricing items and helping set up the Island Shop. Once January 2021 rolled around, I applied to work in the Island Shop as quickly as possible, but HR told my mom I was not able to work under her. So, I reluctantly applied to work in the admissions department because I thought to myself, *at least that job had the option to be in air conditioning.*

I had shown up for my interview with J.T. in March, not knowing that this job was going to have such a great impact on my life. My first summer, I caught the "Coney Bug" and absolutely fell in love with the place and the people, so much so that I asked J.T. to consider me for a manager position for the following summer. The next summer, working in the pool office was even better than the previous year at the guest services booth and gates. I met so many incredible people from other departments that I shared the office with pool managers, lifeguard supervisors, and first aid. Additionally, being promoted to manager gave me an outlet for my control freak personality, and when the opportunity to take over the scheduling role became available mid-summer, of course, I would offer to take it over. This led me to be more involved in Coney for summer 2023; I wanted to make major changes to the admissions department and scheduling to make things run smoother. I had worked on this plan throughout the year when I had free time while away at school- it had helped me get through an awful second semester of college, knowing that in a few short months, I would be back at my favorite place with my favorite people.

The day after I took my last final exam and moved out of my dorm, I was back at Coney preparing for the season, working in both admissions and helping in the Island Shop with Olivia, who had taken over my mom's role. I was finally happy again, with my people doing what I love. Summer 2023 was full of late nights, the creation of the "Women in STEM," water balloon fights, chats in the back of the Island Shop, inside jokes, friendship bracelets, conspiring in first aid, a Taylor Swift-themed Employee Cafe case, working the cash room for concerts, the annual bowling party (that happened to fall on my birthday), 45 hour weeks, a work "family," cabana hunting, a car accident and a concussion the day of Midnight Swim, and living every second of the summer to the fullest up to the very last second. On Labor Day, after the pool had cleared out, a group of supervisors and managers stayed after work to say goodbye to summer in the best way possible. We jumped off of the crow's nest, went down the slides, and hung out in the deep end of the pool, "Lake Cumberland style," on lifeguard and twister tubes. I didn't know it at the time, but we were the last people to swim in Sunlite Pool after its 123-year history-and that is one of my favorite Coney memories and one that I will forever cherish.

After transferring to UC, I was fortunate enough to be able to help close down the Island Shop in the postseason and then have the opportunity to work Nights of Lights — setting up the lights and working the cocoa and admissions booths. In 2023, I was also incredibly grateful to be the last to receive the Ceil Burke Award in the Admissions Department and to also be nominated for the Jim Babb Award for my dedication to Coney. I feel as though words cannot describe what Coney Island truly means to me; my heart swells just thinking about the memories, laughs, and friendships that Coney gave me in my few short years of working there. Coney Island, thank you for changing my life — I will love you forever.

To Coney, with Love, Ronda Carter

My favorite memory at Coney Island was our high school prom, 1979 Norwood High School. The park was lit up magically and the music and atmosphere brought all the good feelings. It was a beautiful memory and although I'd spent many summer nights at the pool and riding all the rides and many Christmases driving through the Christmas light display, I'll never forget prom night with the love of my life. Thank you, Coney Island, for a lifetime of unforgettable memories.

To Coney, with Love, Heather Wyland

Our family moved to the Cincinnati area in 2009 and went to Coney Island every year for the Kroger Company picnic. Our girls loved Coney for canoeing on the lake, the bumper cars, the Ferris wheel and so much more. On Kroger Day, we would ride all the rides first until we got too hot, then head to the Sunlite Pool to cool off and finish off the day with a round of putt-putt golf. One of our most memorable visits to Coney ended with some surprise visitors on the last hole of the putt-putt course. It was getting dark as we headed to the 18th hole, when suddenly a mama skunk and several of her babies came walking down the green! We hung back and watched them go by until they disappeared under a nearby bush. We decided it might not be safe to play the 18th hole without making mama skunk uneasy so we ended up turning in our clubs without a final score, but we still felt like winners since we escaped a smelly encounter with our skunk friends!

To Coney, with Love, Regina Barth

    This would have been our 25th summer. I love water and oh the deep end, I could tread for hours. My daughter and her young family, along with my daughter-in-law and her babies, plus our Coney friends would set up camp every day but Saturday or Sunday. So many friends! My "grands" could go from one umbrella to the others. We felt so safe with our summer friends. Some of our friends would be invited to the Kentucky side for parties. I just can't believe it's over. So many memories and not enough words.

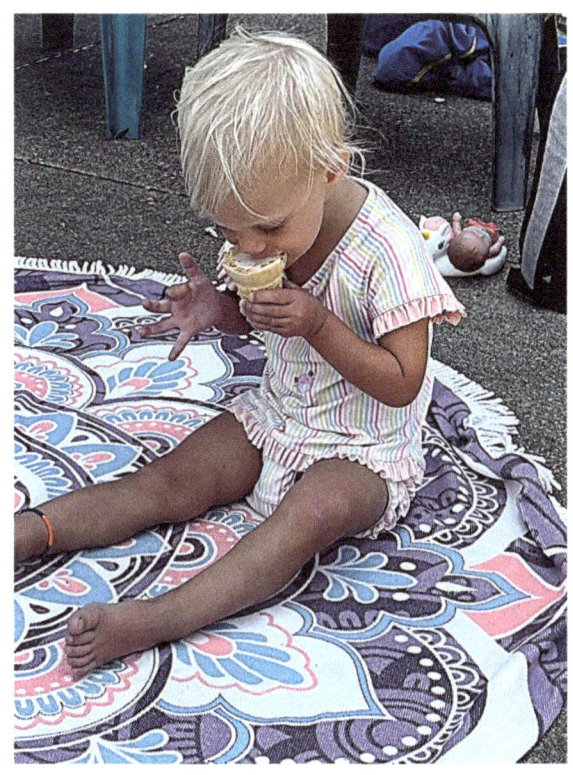

To Coney, with Love, Maria Bjonnes

Not only was I a member of Coney for many years, I also was an employee. I worked in food service and loved my job. I went from LaRosa's to Cincy favorites to Stand 20 and my last position (2023) was at the employee cafe where I served the employees. I served them all; the part timers, lifeguards, full-timers, etc. I looked forward every day to go to work. My bosses, Jason Reid and Chris Anderson were awesome, and my co-workers were the best. Loved my full-timers, and I looked forward to cooking for them daily. It was a fun job for close to 14 years.

To Coney, with Love, Victoria Vogelgesang

I had my first kiss at Coney Island and my first date, with my first boyfriend. But none of that compares to the afternoon in this picture with my parents, sister and nephews. I almost didn't join them that day, thinking there's a million more times to go in the future. But there weren't. My nephews love Coney Island almost as much as they love Xavier's Blue Blob mascot! This picture is the reason I've been fighting to save Sunlite. My oldest nephew was 3 at the time the news of the closure broke. I always point out Coney Island when we drive past. The other day he asked me, "Are you trying to open Coney Island?" "Yes, I am," I said. "Why?" He predictably asked. "Because I love you!"

To Coney, with Love, Mary Rosen Meiners

As a child, Dad's vacation included a trip to Coney Island and the Zoo. I remember picnics (with wafer cookies, grapes and sandwiches) sitting in Coney's on the river picnic area and watching and listening to Coney's Shooting Star roller coaster. After picnicking, the family rode rides and late in the day went swimming in Sunlite Pool. What a treat! The sounds, the picnic conversations and walks through Coney Island, were a vacation day treat I will always remember, and those memories continue today with my family.

To Coney, with Love, Bella Jaynes

Coney Island was one of the biggest parts of my childhood and my sister's childhood. For many years, we had season passes because we only lived about 15 minutes from Coney Island, and it allowed us to keep busy during the summer. Our dad drove us there often. While we were having fun, he was working. It was a win-win. Often times, we got to use our "bring your friend" passes and friends came with us. Our Nana also took us there as well. I will never forget how excited we were when they announced the opening of Typhoon Tower. The best part of the Sunlite Pool for sure. The Python was the first roller coaster that we had ever been on. There are a few rides that we rode pretty much chronically though. Those were the Scream Machine and the Flying Bobs. We would ride them several times in row. On the Flying Bobs, we would wait to get on and let the person behind us go so that we could get on a ride that was going backwards. The Flying Bobs were definitely our favorite ride to get on at Coney Island. We both will miss Coney Island very much as this is a place we planned on taking our kids to together.

To Coney, with Love, Aline Vargas

Coney Island was the "event" that we (8 brothers and sisters) waited for as school was coming to an end. It was an affordable amusement park for large families of the "baby boom" generation. My dad was a teacher at Xavier University, so he had the whole summer off. That way, we could go more than once during the summer months to Sunlite Pool. My favorite "ride" was the Turnpike. Maybe that's where I developed my love for driving. My daughters hold many good memories of having had great times at Coney. My granddaughter worked at Sunlite Pool last summer. She's sad, not to be able to work at Coney Island this coming summer. It's sad not to be able to continue this "tradition" for future generations. I am grateful for all the great times I had at such a unique amusement park.

To Coney, with Love, Karen Hirtzel Kiefel

When I was growing up in the 50s and 60s, we went to Coney several times every summer. The best day was Mt. Adams Day, which was the Holy Cross School picnic. They passed out Coney Island coloring books at school. Ride tickets were sold at school for half price. I remember going on a bus from school a couple years. My mom would get me a new outfit to wear. The day ranked right up there with Christmas!! Roos' Bakery in Mt. Adams would take special orders for their buns since so many families wanted them to make their sandwiches to take. When we got to Coney we would leave our food at the picnic area by the river. Then we would spend the whole day at the pool. I can remember the locker rooms and the smell of sun lotion. We ate lunch at the pool restaurant. When my dad got to Coney after work we would go eat our picnic supper. Then it was time for the rides.

Early on I loved kiddie land and the friendly giant at the entry. The Teddy Bear was my favorite. As I got older my favorite rides were the Whip, the Cuddle Up, the Tumble Bug and the Flying Scooters. My dad taught me how to whip the chains on the Flying Scooters. I wasn't brave enough to ride the Shooting Star until the year after the Wildcat closed. That was too bad because my mom and uncle always loved the Wildcat. I rode the Shooting Star with my friend's father the first time. I kept my eyes closed for the whole ride. As soon as it stopped, I was ready to go again. I can still remember the cars climbing that first hill, the small dip at the top with a view of the Ohio River. I also loved the Penny Arcade with the gypsy fortune teller. Most often I played Skee Ball. I still have some prizes, including a hideous fringed velvet pillow cover that I got on the last day I went to Coney before it closed. It's in a box somewhere, I only got it for the sentimental value.

My grandma loved to go on the special days, like Dot Food Days. It was more crowded, and she loved to play Tango and Fascination. The more people that played the higher the winnings. She loved the fireworks, too. My mom always talked about going to Coney on the Island Queen, something I wish had been around in my time. I did join Coney's pool when my oldest son was three. He took swimming lessons there. So at least another of the next generation of my family got to spend time there. Some of the happiest days of my childhood were spent at Coney.

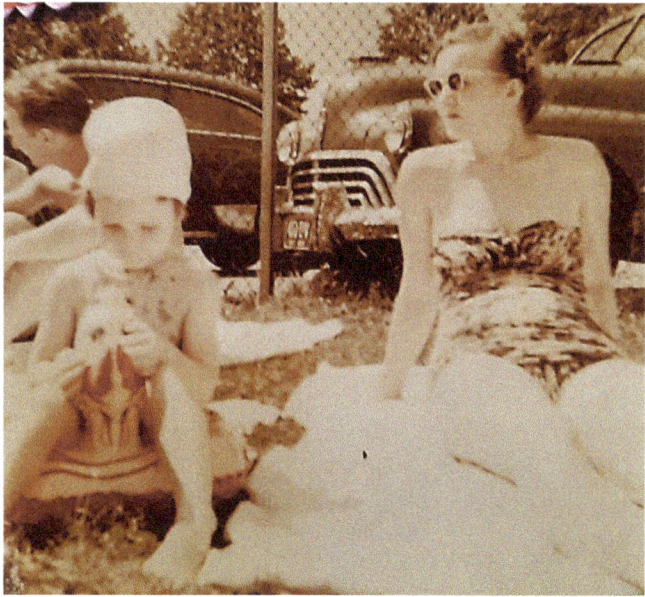

To Coney, with Love, Joshua Blake

I remember my father talking about the wonderful time he and his family had growing up going at Coney Island throughout the 1950s and 1960s. He had vivid memories of getting to a ride pony, the Shooting Star roller coaster, and swimming at Sunlite Pool. Little did I know that several years later, I would be working at the park. I began working for Kings Island in 1995 as a games associate where I stayed for three seasons. I was then offered a position at Americana in 1999 and at the time the park was owned by the same family that owned Coney Island. After Americana closed for good, a select few of us were offered positions at Coney. I worked as a games and merchandise area manager and assisted the bank employees with Riverbend concerts. I remember them saying that our restructuring of the games merchandise department was something they had not seen since the park closed in 1971 and I was very proud to be a part of that team. I think what I cherished most about that park was that even without world-class rollercoasters, we still drew large crowds and had the time of our lives working with one another. It was a breath of fresh air. After leaving Kings Island I realized that it's the people that make these memories, not the rides and attractions. But I am very sad that the property will yet again get a facelift, and that era has come to a close.

To Coney, with Love, Mary Siefert Zander

We had an annual tradition of going to Coney Island with our girls from the time our oldest was about 4 or 5 and loved going every year! We only went to Kings Island when we had passes (which was only twice in the girls' lives), but Coney every year.

We loved the traditional rides, and the shows, and the way we could just easily be ourselves there. It was an amusement park, for sure, but there was so much for anyone to do, and it was not so huge that it was exhausting for the young or old. We actually never went to the pools there. Just the park. And it was perfect. One of our favorite spots was where the little mini town was. Just a simple space with about a half dozen wooden buildings in old country/west style and we spent probably an hour there at least every time we came. When the "town" came down, we were sad. It had been such fun!

We also attended for company picnics, which were a blast! We came before we had kids, spending time with friends and then also when we had kids and sharing the park with them – *all such wonderful times and great memories, in a very special place.*

We also went to the Warbirds World War II style dance every Memorial Day weekend at Moonlite Gardens. It was a huge part of our tradition, too. I actually had wanted to go for years before I could due to another conflict, but when I finally could go, I went every year. And my girls with me! And other family members, too! It was such an important part of the fabric of our family — I am not sure what we are going to do this coming year!

We also came to the fireworks contest one year, and it was fabulous. We attended the Fall-O-Ween with the kids one year, too, and loved that great experience!!

When we learned it was closing, ugh, it was devastating. My youngest was never going to be able to go! It closed before she was old enough to ride even the kiddie rides. We kept hoping someone would buy the place, or the rides, or they would change their mind, or the classic rides would show up at Kings Island. So, a huge part of our family history was ended, and a major chapter closed. We didn't live close enough to be season pass holders, but it was an integral part of our family, extended family, going with my parents, and hearing about their experiences at Coney with their families before us. A huge loss for our community. Coney Island, you will be missed!

To Coney, with Love, Linda Mason

Growing up in Anderson Township, Coney Island was my summer vacation destination. We didn't take many trips, but my mother would make sure we got to go to Coney Island. She would save all year, a little out of her monthly budget, enough to get us to the amusement park and pool. She didn't drive so we'd take a taxi to the pool and in the evening on his way home from working downtown, my father would join us for a swim. After swimming, we would sometimes go into the park for dinner and rides. I felt so special when I was big enough to ride the carousel by myself and get to personally hand my ticket to the carousel operator collecting them. It was a big thrill for a five-year-old.

In 1971, I was 10 years old. It was the last day the pool was open for the season, and several Coney regulars, Richard, Tilley and others dressed up like the Wizard of Oz characters and marched around the pool singing and being silly. The final night the amusement park was open, I recall sitting with my family by the lake waiting for the fireworks. When the announcers came on the speakers, I knew even at a young age what a sad moment it was. This would be the last time Coney Island as I knew it would be the same, *no more amusement rides*.

Thankfully, that wouldn't be the last day we'd get to swim in Coney's Pool. My grandparents, parents, my children, and grandchildren have all gotten to enjoy a piece of Coney Island and hope to for many more years to come. My love for Coney, and its history has led me to help co-administer the Coney Island (pre-1971) page on Facebook. I've gotten to hear some amazing stories that were never printed, interview employees, and see some wonderful photos and films.

To Coney, with Love, Rick Springmeier

I grew up as a kid going to Coney Island. I remember going there on Italian Day and I also went when they had German Day. For German Day, there was a tribute to the Beatles in German.

To Coney, with Love, Jo-Anne Thomas

My first date was to Moonlite Gardens. Wednesday night was Ladies' night. I was 16 years old when a group of us from Kentucky took the ferry across the Ohio River from Brent to Coney Island. We danced the night away to live big band music.

To Coney, with Love, Paul Martinez

1. The world's longest cheese Coney dog hosted by Rich King (former WKRC AM Radio disc jockey). It stretched the length of Sunlite Pool...on the sideline of the pool of course.
2. I was 3 or 4 years old at Sunlite Pool with my mother & friends. My mother asked her good friend to watch me while I was in the pool. I disappeared under the water in the shallow end. I was drowning but no one knew it. Someone pulled me out to save me. I'm 72 years old now, and can't believe I actually remember this incident.

To Coney, with Love, Ashley Varol

I lived up the street near Salem/Sutton growing up — and Coney was our pool. My mom took us regularly and I have so many memories growing up there. From the random music that would come on, to trying to jump the most times off the island. Watching the lifeguard in the paddle boat go in circles. Fixing swimsuits after being shot down the slides. It's where I learned to swim, it's where I'd meet my friends, it's where I'd listen to sound checks from the bands I loved. I also got to work at Coney for 3 years in the picnic grove and have friends (and a scar on my leg!) from my time there. Seeing so many families and colleagues coming through, having a great time, and just enjoying company (pre-cell phone times) while my teenage friends and I ran frantically around with hot dogs, burgers, baked beans and fruit salad will forever be etched in my memory (I still cut my fruit the same way to this day). I can say I learned a lot of transferable skills from that job, time and event management being at the top of the list. It was so nice when Coney and Riverbend would work together, and they'd let us fill in during some of the busier concerts in the concessions. I don't miss the knee length khaki shorts, but that place was special.

Now, as a parent of three living in Anderson, I appreciate Coney so much more. I was one of the people that was ok with the loss of the rides/games, as it helped us stay in one spot and enjoy family time. We are Kings Island members, but don't generally go to their water park as it's just too big and spread out, and I always feel like I'm going to lose a kid — Coney didn't make me feel that way at all. I loved the addition of the diving well and the obstacle course, and the space was huge, but also comfy, making it great for my family. My kids learned to swim here, with the same instructors I had over 25 years ago. They learned to be brave here, jumping off both the lower and higher diving boards. I could sit with a chair and let them ride the slides over and over and over, and over again. We'd pack snacks, meet friends and family and be at Coney all day long. My dad would be embarrassed to know I sent the picture with him and my son, but when I was a kid, he worked a lot and wouldn't come down — but as a grandpa, he was in the water and that was everything to us. I have no idea how I have that last final picture from Coney on the last weekend and how maybe I knew I needed it, but Coney is nostalgia and present day all at the same time.

To Coney, with Love, Laurie Kotha

My daughters were on the Coney Island Swim team from 1995 to 2013. Both of them swam from 5 to 18 years old. I was the team mom for 10 years. It was not summer without Coney. Dear friends and many memories were made. Families returned year after year! Coaches returned year after year. Both worked at Coney as well. Nicole, now 28, and building a career in clinical research, worked some weekends through 2023. I asked why, as she worked full time. She said she just loved Coney and the friends she continued to work with in the Island Shop. We are all so devastated for the end of Coney. My girls grew up there!! Summers meant Coney and special summer friends!!

To Coney, with Love, Roseann Powell

When I was a very little girl, my father worked for Ohio National Life Insurance Company and every summer his company would give the employees a day of relaxation at Coney Island, including the whole family. As my parents mingled with fellow employees, us kiddos spent the day swimming and riding all the rides in the park. Sadly, my father passed away when I was 11, so the fun ended for our family, but the previous years were fantastic, spending our day of fun at Coney Island. I continued to take my children there for most of their childhood. I will miss the events and pool for my grandchildren to be able to enjoy.

To Coney, with Love, Gabby Cooper

Growing up, the Cooper and Weigel family religiously drove to Cincinnati from Batesville, Indiana every summer to go to Coney Island. Half the day was spent at the pool and the other half was spent riding rides. We were all big fans of the Frog Hopper.

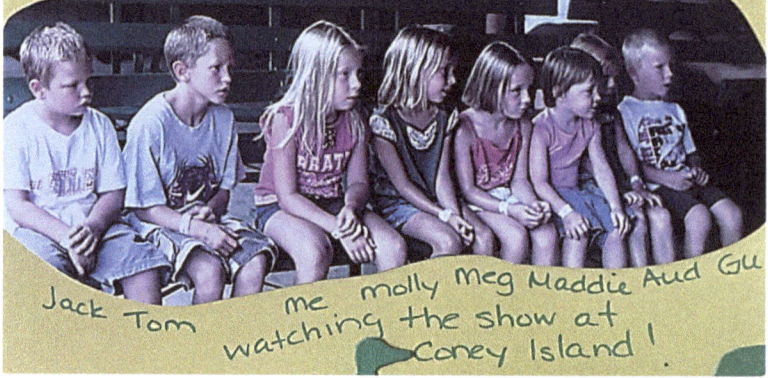

To Coney, with Love, Robbie Zerhusen

I started working at Coney in 2002 as a ride operator as my first job. I thought that I would only stay one season before leaving. I ended up working there 20 seasons, and was a rides manager from 2010 until the rides were removed at the end of the 2019 season. This was my part time gig as I work full time at an architecture firm. My favorite ride to run was the Ferris wheel. Once I was even a manager, and I would head out and run that thing. I had my engagement pictures taken at Coney and have fond memories of taking my son on his first Ferris wheel ride. The hours were long, and the pay was paltry, but seeing kids with smiles on their faces as they were riding the rides made it all worth it. I am sad that future generations (and the rest of my kids) will never get to experience the Coney that I knew.

To Coney, with Love, Dawn Singleton

My Dad, Ronald Singleton was the captain of the Ski Ballers team in the early 60s. He was one of the men on the bottom of the pyramids. He skied through rings of fire and skied under a huge kite in their shows. This was also the time that he and my mom met. So, Coney played a big part in the beginning of their relationship. Mom and dad's cousin, who they met through, used to go watch dad in the shows. Mom said between the shows they would run around the park and ride the rides. They had so much fun and made many memories there. At one time they wanted my mom to become part of the show, but she was too afraid of the water. She told me about how they used to practice for their shows in Hamilton on the river and that there was a special dock put in for them to practice there. I wish we had pictures to share but the one we did have has sadly been misplaced. It was of him flying with the kite being pulled by the boat. I am so happy their story will be a part of this book. My Dad is very ill now, and his memories have faded but my mom shares them with me and I love it! Again, it was a huge part of their "courting" as it was called in those days.

To Coney, with Love, Faith Kuschel

    I have so many memories over the years at Sunlite Pool. I started going as a young kid. My Mom would take us almost every day over the summer. I grew up with 8 siblings so I'm sure the pool was a lifeline for my mother. As I got older and had two children of my own, I would save a special day in the summer for Coney until I finally bought season passes. My most favorite memory to tell my children is how my dad, who rarely came with us and self-proclaims to not be a great swimmer, taught me one summer evening how to doggy paddle all the way to the island. That memory sits so very vividly in my head that I could never walk to the center of the pool or the island without the flashback. This past summer, 2023, my dad at age 71, came again for a pool day. The grandkids had so much fun watching him try all the slides and especially the obstacle course. He jokingly said that day that he can't wait to see what will change when he comes back again in 20 years. I'm so thankful fate brought him last summer to make that memory with us.

To Coney, with Love, Gina Schroder Cameron

My summers at Coney Island are my fondest memories from my childhood! My family was fortunate enough to be members from the time I was born until adulthood. We went down to Coney Island Monday through Friday from Memorial Day to Labor Day. My brothers taught me to swim and when I was five, I can remember them taking me to the middle of the deep end and telling me to swim to the side and I earned an ice cream cone for my efforts! They bribed me the same way to get me to jump and dive off the 10-foot board!

Many hours were spent swimming with friends over the years. We would check in with our mom for lunch and a snack! We had a designated spot where we sat at the pool, and a table we always sat at to eat our packed lunch and snack! That way friends always knew where to look for us! We bought a soft drink and occasionally purchased those yummy fries or an ice cream! I was on the diving team for a few summers when I was about the age of 10-13! I remember the early morning practices with my friends that were on swim team. We would laugh and carry on in between dives and swims! The meets were always exciting and an excuse to extend our days well into the evening! We rode the rides, slides and played putt-putt endlessly!

We came of age at Coney and spent many hours scoping out the hot boys!! And there were a lot of those to be had! As a teen I took the kids I babysat along with us and enjoyed watching them learn to swim! *Bonus, I got paid for it to boot!!* As an adult, my own children learned to swim and dive at my favorite place in the world! They spent hours running amuck the same way I did in my youth!

The full amusement park sadly closed when I was 7 but I do remember riding the rides and playing the games a couple times a season! We always looked forward to those days! I can remember the countdown board out in Lake Como and watched the number of days sadly dwindle away! I also spent a lot of time at the tennis courts taking lessons with friends! We spent a few years volunteering to be ball girls for the Western and Southern Tennis Tournaments! I got to see greats like Jimmy Connors and Harold Solomon play matches! We spent hours in the stands watching the greats of the time play! Not a bad way to spend an afternoon or evening! I hated to see it go up to Kings Island but am glad it was successful and relieved to learn it will remain in Cincinnati! I was sad to learn of Coney Island closing this year and mourned the fact that the current and future children of Cincinnati won't get to experience the kind of childhood I was blessed to have! Thanks for memories Coney and goodbye!

This is my parents with friends at Moonlite Gardens. From left-to-right Anne Campbell Schroder, Joseph Schroder, unknown, Joe Sauter, Jim Murphy, Ruth Jester. They always went on the Island Queen from downtown as they were from Northern Kentucky. She always remembered those trips fondly.

To Coney, with Love, Amanda Iannitti-Sherman

I worked at Coney from 1999 to 2004. I started in rides, moved to Guest Relations/Memberships in 2001, and then to the cash room in 2002. I enjoyed all of my roles, but managing the cash room was my favorite. Late nights with the best team, walking concerts at Riverbend, and seeing the park fun from open to close! Those were my favorite summers — working hard and making lasting memories! One memory that sticks in my mind is the year of the cicadas (2004?) and someone from the picnic grove sent a "present" of cicadas in a money bag! My favorite memories are from working concerts and seeing so many big names up close! The best ones were Dave Matthews, any country concert, and MOST OF ALL Jimmy Buffett!! Though Coney will be gone (for now) and I only got to take my daughter a few times, the memories and stories will live on in those who worked and played there, and the books/pictures that keep them going!

To Coney, with Love, Sara Walton

My mom told us that my dad and her, and their friends, loved spending summer days at Coney. They look so happy in this picture!

To Coney, with Love, Maddie Sonnenberg

I have far too many Coney Island memories to only pick one. I grew up at Sunlite Pool, going every day during the summer and eventually working there. From the childhood picnics and swims to the late-night pool deck conversations with co-workers, Coney Island was like no other. There were Lifeguard training classes, listening to concerts, late nights on the Twister, the booze cruise, bonfires and so much more. The friendships Coney Island brought us will forever be cherished. There was not one person who didn't love working at Sunlite Pool. Everyone who worked there played a huge role in making Coney what it is.

One specific memory I love talking about was an employee night swim. All of us racing down Twister together like our life depended on it. Hanging out in the deep end with the twister tubes, all just talking about life. We spent hours together to soak in the last little bit of summer we had left. That is something that will never be taken away from us; the friendships and memories we have together. We all share a bond that we love, *Coney*. Words will never be able to describe the impact each and every person had on one another. To Coney Island Sunlite Water Adventure, we love you.

To Coney, with Love, Bob and Marilyn Smith

Marilyn Smith's Story

My story began in 1969 at the age of 16 living in Silver Grove, Kentucky. I would drive 2-3 miles to ride the passenger ferry across the Ohio River to work at Coney Island in the refreshment department. In 1970, I worked there as my summer job running an ice cream stand and popcorn wagon. That resulted in my boyfriend's family referring to me as the "popcorn girl" and meeting my now husband there, as he was a "litter getter". So of course I had the cleanest spot in the park! The 275 bridge did not exist back then, but it eventually put the ferry out of business as no ferry could be within 2 miles of a bridge. Bob was from Amelia, Ohio and back then, that was 1 hour distance by car. Meeting at Coney Island was and still is a major highlight of our life. It was a special place for us. Every time we cross the 275 bridge we remember our meeting place. We were married 3 years later in 1973 and celebrated our 50th anniversary, October 2023. In September 2023 we were welcomed by Katy Mark. She graciously met us in the park and drove us around to various spots in the park to take photos to rekindle our precious memories. Her excitement for us and our story was special for both of us. We took our grandchildren around 2018 when some of the rides were still there. We are so glad to share our story and the history of our special place with anyone that is interested in hearing it. We have so many memories as Bob and I loved playing Skee Ball and riding rides after work. I also remember using tickets to ride the rides then buying a wrist band for $4 that allowed you to ride for the whole day! Was sad when the Coney location was moved to Kings Island in Mason. The new location was far away, a lot bigger and we could no longer work there as we had now graduated from high school. Coney Island was a great place to work and has given us lifelong memories.

Bob Smith Story

My story at Coney Island began in the summer of 1969 when I worked in the parking lot. My father would drop me off at the top of the hill in Mt Washington and I would ride my bike down the hill to the park each day. At the end of the day, we would take the bike back up to a friend's house to store for the next day. The next year I "graduated" to the maintenance crew to see that the park remained one of the top parks in the country, voted the cleanest. It was in that summer I met the girl from Kentucky who sold popcorn and ice cream with her southern smile to all who needed a refreshment. Naturally I kept her area exceptionally clean all the time. My family would have annual picnics in the grove area, and I got to introduce her to them as they fondly referred to her as the "Popcorn Girl". There were times when we both finished our work for the day and would go throughout the park riding various rides and playing some of the challenging games. One of our favorites was the Lost River where you could sneak a kiss before screaming down the slide into the water below. We had many friends that we met during our time there and remained in contact for years after our time working there. Our first "real" date was to a Cincinnati Reds ballgame at riverfront stadium. Since we lived in 2 different states we decided to meet at Coney Island, so I met my future wife of 50 years at the top of the Ferry boat ramp. All I remember that day is that it rained all the way along Columbia Parkway to the game. I really don't remember who won the game as I was excited to go with my new best friend. There never has been or will ever be a place like Coney Island for the two of us. Our memories were quickly recalled for both of us as we went back on our 50th wedding anniversary to once again seal the recollection of where it all began for us. The park may change over the time, but we will always know that Coney Island is and was that special place for us.

To Coney, with Love, Emily Burton

Coney Island was a gem to the Cincinnati/NKY area. The park was totally walkable without being overwhelming to those with littles ones. It had the charm of smaller rides that still offered big fun! Sunlite Pool was one of a kind, and a treat in the summer to visit.

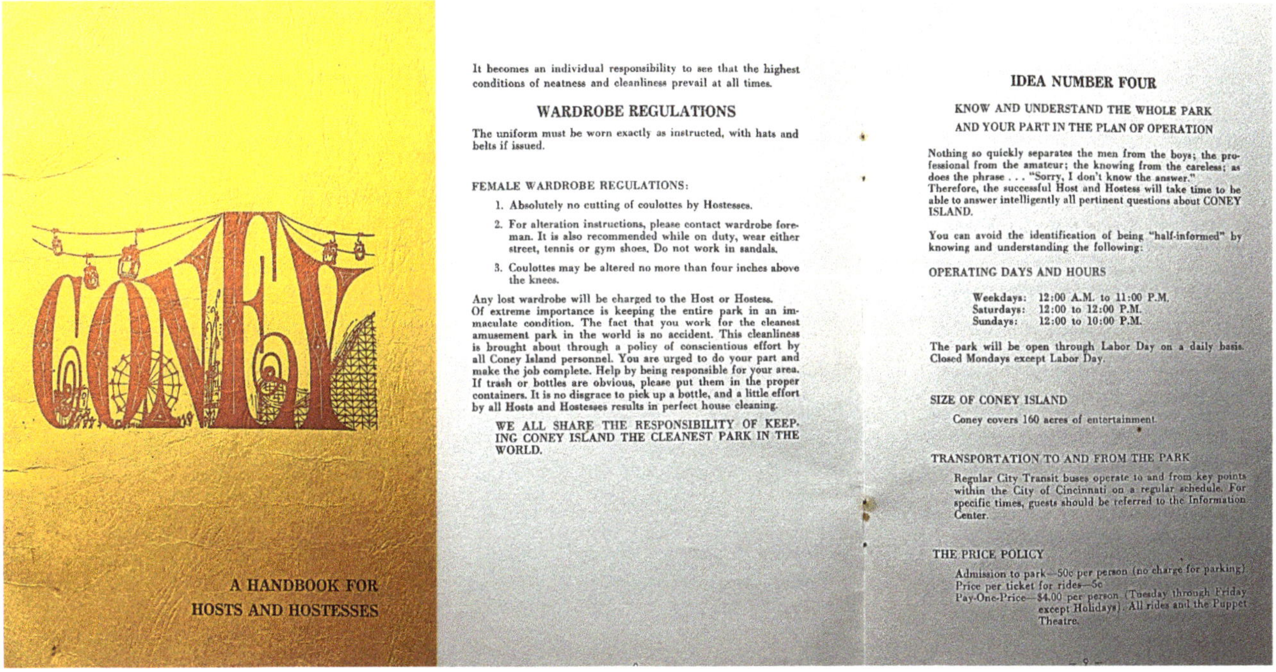

With the different events and festivals that were held at the park, it was as if it reinvented itself with each change of the seasons. It offered space for smaller concerts and for events like my senior prom in 1996. However, the park will always hold a space in my heart because of the times I would spend there with those that I loved.

It was a brisk afternoon, October 5, 2014, the first time that my husband (John Burton), our 3-year-old son (Lucas), and myself went to Coney Island for the Fall-O-Ween (first time we ever visited the park as a family, too!). We went with my parents, Derek and Beverly Hastings, as we were visiting from Georgia, and we were always looking for memory making moments since we didn't get to visit as often. It would be the first time Lucas rode a roller coaster, bumper cars, or even the giant slide!

He giggled and his eyes were full of delight at every ride or the other things the park had to offer; like the haunted hayride, the trick-or-treating, or discovering the mini village decorated with ghosts.

Despite the weather getting colder as night fell, we continued to enjoy all of the festivities, the lights, and riding the rides at night. It was a moment that will be cherished with warm memories, as the next time we would be visiting Coney in 2017, it would be without my husband who died of service-connected illness from his service in the US Army. When we moved back to the area in 2017, we made it a point to go to the Fall-O-Ween every year with some of his cousins until the owners of the park decided to cancel it.

Since we were living closer now, we became season pass holders and would often come to the pool in the summer, making a day of it with other friends with children my sons' age. Despite the frigid temperatures of the splash pad, Lucas loved it no matter how old he got, I would find him in there at some point during our visit. It was wonderful to be able to enjoy some time at the pool into the early afternoon, and then head over for some amusement park rides, putt-putt, and the arcade!

Lucas and I even made fun Christmas memories sitting in the long line of cars to see the Christmas lights. We did it all at Coney and will miss those traditions of visiting the park from his early childhood years.

Before I end this, I will forever leave a part of us behind. In the bottom of Lake Como sits an iPhone with a teal and orange case on it. My phone had slipped out of my pocket just as we had started to paddle off one October afternoon. When I realized what had happened, I was distraught, as it had photos on it from that visit that didn't make their way to "the cloud" and there were also sentimental things on my phone like voicemails from my late husband. An amazing staffer named Mitch (who was also a lifeguard) offered to wade into the cold lake after the park closed for the day to try to find it. Security came and they eventually made him get out of the water, but not after he had given his best effort to locate my phone in the murky water. I hadn't even given him an inkling of why I was so upset until he had offered to get in the water. Later, I found out that the reason he was so dedicated to trying to find my phone was because he had lost his father not long before and someone had stolen his phone.

A few days passed and after contacting my friend Katy Mark, who was an employee at Coney at the time, we were granted permission for one afternoon only to come with some mutual friends of mine that were experienced divers to try to find it. While my phone was never found. There were several phones that were, among other things. Ever since then, I would pass the lake, say hello to my phone, and wonder if it would ever be found one day.

To Coney, with Love, Kyle McInturf

I worked at Coney Island for 25 years. I started in parking and ended as the personal manager in 2016. The main thing that strikes me about working at Coney Island is the nature of how Coney Island always felt like a giant family. When I started at Coney, I was hired in the parking department by Jim Robinson. Jim and John Callebs (AKA JC) both worked at New Richmond High School with my dad. My dad had worked out a deal with Jim to get me a job at Coney Island.

I started on a Friday night. It was the first night of Appalachian Festival and I worked until 10:30pm. I was exhausted that first day and I remember vividly that I was due back at 8:00am on Saturday and was supposed to be working until around 6pm. I was young, working my first job. I thought to myself, *what did I get myself into here? This job seems harder than I expected.*

After working the first year, I got used to working and how it was to be in the workforce. At the end of the first year, I was a bit on the fence about year two. I was wondering if I should find something else to do. I ended up returning, and then again in year three, but I was looking for other jobs and got a job working at McDonalds. That year I worked from 4 am to 1 pm at McDonalds and would come to work the concert parking at 5 pm at Coney. I had weeks in that timeframe where I had no days off and was exhausted in general. But what kept me close to Coney? The family feel. Jim and JC had both treated me great, and for the most part, I stayed out of trouble. And I enjoyed the money I was making ($3.75 per hour).

During the off-season of my third going into my fourth, I got a call from Jerri Young. Jerri was the Personal Manager and was interested in interviewing me for her assistant. Now, I knew nothing about that. But it sounded like more money and the idea of not working two jobs was appealing.

I got that job and was offered 5.25/hour. I took it. I started as the personnel assistant and that really raised my profile in the park. Now I was interacting with President Vic Nolting, controller Linda Layton, VP of food operations Tom Rhein, VP of sales and marketing Mary Schumacher and VP of Operations John Ellison and then Keith Henize.

When we had the flood of 1997, it was all hands-on deck and guess where I was? Right there, shoulder to shoulder with Vic and Keith. These were my first experiences with Chuck Rempe (head of maintenance), Ron Harrison (electrician) Gary Marlow (maintenance foreman), Bob Adams (carpenter), and Tom Chase (ride mechanic). Every single one of them was looking at this young college guy thinking, *boy he looks like a fish outta water*. You see, I was an office guy. My theory was to get through college so I could get an office job and NOT have to ever work in that type of setting again. But having the Chucks, Garys, and Rons of world out there, made the collective of a giant family where everybody does their part for the greater whole.

During the 1997 season something happened, and Jerri Young quit. I remember getting a call from Linda Layton at my house letting me know that Jerri had quit, and she needed me to cover. I had no idea what that meant, but seeing as I had no other jobs, I was willing to just wait and see. I was due to graduate from NKU that fall already so I figured I'd wait and see if this could turn into a permanent job.

That summer I went to school full time and covered the entire personnel department. I was doing all the employment paperwork and all the timecards weekly. I was working 6 days a week at Coney and going to school 5 days a week, but I knew there was a chance I could get this personal manager job. So, I waited. In the fall of 1997, I was offered $23,000 a year to be full time at Coney. I had no other leads for jobs, so I took it. I was due to become full-time in January 1998.

Now, I'm working full-time at Coney, and I knew very early that we needed people, and a lot of them, and what had happened previously was not working as not enough people returned from year to year. So, I devised a plan to recruit from the high schools.

I started to contact every school that appeared close to Coney that an average high school student could get to the job by driving there. I went to just about every local high school I could get to in the months of March and April of 1998 and 1999. Meanwhile, back at Coney we had built a strong core of full-time people ready to help this new crop of high school students. Jim Christmann, a McNicholas grad, was running the gardens and pavilion. Aaron Weaver, a Walnut Hills grad, was running the Grove. Mike Howard (New Richmond), Mike Morris (Amelia) and Rob Morrison (Batavia) were running the operations, maintenance, and security. Brian Silz (Highlands) was Pool 1. We had key operators representing several local schools and I wanted to tap into that. When we did, that helped us keep people as well.

As time went on, it was obvious that none of us were here for the money we made. But we were all here for the kinship and friendship that developed. We worked floods together. We worked picnics in the Grove together and concerts together. We ran the park as a small family-owned amusement park. We all knew what it was capable of. I can remember being asked to work the cash room, but not *in* the cash room. Just as a person that carried the money bags. There are countless people that I worked with in the cash room. For a time, we had Andrea Horn (New Richmond), then Jennifer Verdin (New Richmond), then Albert Boehmer (Roger Bacon) running the cash room as a full-time person. Even Controller Linda Layton worked in the cash room on bigger concerts. The cash room group was a family, too. I remember working in the grove for bigger picnics. I generally did the grilling. I even once fell onto a grill that was on. That gave me a scar on my arm for a year.

By the early and mid-2000s I was married to Mindy (St Ursula) who was working in group sales with Susan Whitaker, Cathy Murray, Amy Pass, Mary Schumacher, and Jim Christmann. When my daughters Gina and Sydney were born, we took them to the park several times a week. We even had both my brothers-in-law (Steven and Dustin Edwards) working at Coney. As well as, my mother (in the Island shop) and my mother-in-law (bartender at Moonlite Gardens and Riverbend) were there, too.

I had great friends, like JT Wilson, Madeline Brown, Lisa Peters, and Julie Saylor. We went to lunch together almost every day all summer and some days we would head up to Beechmont Ave. and eat at Butterbees. We had a fantasy football league that had Aaron Weaver, Jim Christmann, Rob Morrison, Mike Howard, Jason Ried, Luke Burger, Mike Morris, Chris Luginbuhl (among others) as members. We were all great friends that have proven to be hard to find in jobs I have had since.

As time went forward, I learned a lot of skills I would otherwise not know how to do like how to fix the time clocks. How to order and uniform 1000 people in 18 departments. How to staff the park.

How do taxes work when half the park is in the city and the other half is in the county. I also had to figure out all the ins and outs of Workers Compensation. I learned how to write and rewrite the employee handbook. I had the opportunity to set up and run Super Staffer dinners and at times the manager outings. The list goes on and on! I also need to mention that I was able to broaden my horizons by hiring assistants. I had several people that ended up being impactful to me and need to be mentioned here. Bill Haines, Bob Geis, and Ron Siry are all three retirees that I hired to be my assistants. I found that having a person older than myself was a great way to learn. Ron Siry was with me longest. He was a retired University of Cincinnati professor — he was also the public address announcer for Highland's football for years as well. Ron worked with me for about 10 years (give or take) and I enjoyed his college professor absent minded approach to everything. There was nothing that went on that stressed him out. Somebody missing a paycheck? Nope. Not having a 2XL tee shirt and an Anderson high school football player standing there needing a shirt didn't worry Ron at all. His "don't sweat small stuff approach" has come in handy as I got older.

I left Coney Island in 2016, right around the September Fire up the Night event. I felt conflicted about leaving at all. I believe that I could set up a meetup for next week and I could get a lot of those former full-time people I mentioned above to get together. Many of those mentioned above I no longer see regularly, but they are all still family to me. To that, I will always be thankful to Coney Island!

To Coney, with Love, Vic Nolting, President (1984-2015)

My first memories of Coney Island go back to the 1960s when the school I attended treated the junior high students to a day at Coney. Obviously, it was the most anticipated day of the year and as it got closer you could feel the excitement in the air. Everyone was on their best behavior to ensure they would make the trip and not be left behind due to a lapse in good conduct.

Those outings were simply magic… experiencing my first rides on practically everything, finally mustering up the courage to ride the Shooting Star and putting my arm around a girl in the Lost River; while my buddies ran around inside like wild men jumping from boat to boat. Luckily, none were caught.

These were days of tremendous fun, new experiences, smells, flavors and sights to behold when the sun went down, and the dazzlingly beautiful lights appeared. Those times were over in a flash, but Coney was with me for years… remembering date nights, spring dances, and concerts at Moonlite Gardens. What treasured moments I had in a magical place.

Then in 1972 it was gone, but not forgotten. Who knew? Certainly not me… that I would move back to Cincinnati and spend over 30 years being part of a team dedicated to give a new generation of Coney visitors their own "Coney Moments."

The "icing on the cake" for me was watching my daughter and son frolic through the park experiencing its rides, swimming in Sunlite Pool, and enjoying the many special events. Seeing them have the same enjoyment were moments to treasure. Later, like thousands of other area teens, they got their first jobs at Coney. I was able to watch them grow and develop their strong work ethic and willingness to go above and beyond.

My daughter's wedding reception at Moonlite Gardens was yet another unforgettable night. A few years later, the visits to the park by the next generation my grandsons provided me with delight and pure joy.

Over the years, millions of guests from all over the area visited the park for various reasons. There was Sunlite Pool, park rides, area-wide special events, group picnics, concerts or events and private parties at Moonlite Gardens. Millions of dollars were spent on upkeep, maintenance and providing new rides and experiences for its patrons.

Walt Disney came to Coney Island when he was planning Disneyland to learn from and observe park operations management. He came because of Coney's reputation of cleanliness and the quality of its facilities, staff, and operations. That outstanding legacy is the basis for the success of Disney, Kings Island, and its sister Cedar Fair parks.

Coney has given me far more than I have given her. For over 130 years, under different owners and managers, and with diverse ingredients and components, Coney Island was a special place for fun, excitement, wonder, scenic beauty and sometimes romance.

The only way all of this happened was by the unimaginable hard work, imagination, and dedication of the park's full-time and seasonal employees. Their commitment and pride in their work made it all happen and that is what I remember today. The tremendous pride I felt being part of an extraordinary team who day after day, rain or shine, gave it their best shot to make Coney a place where lasting memories were made. Coney Island has certainly earned its legacy and warm soft spot in Cincinnati's heart.

History of Coney Island Events from 1984…

One of the more important aspects of the park's business was its impressive list of annual special events. These events brought a wide range of customers to the park from a very wide geographic area and were critical in re-introducing the park to the Greater Cincinnati area.

Moonlite Gardens, numerous weddings, reunions, corporate events and public dances like Hot Wax Hops and Big Band Dances

Appalachian Fest, the region's largest assemblage of Appalachian arts, crafts, music and food

Summerfair, the largest juried art show in the Midwest, music, food and performing arts

Cincinnati Flower Show, the largest display of floral designs, landscaping, and related products

Balloonfest, hot air balloon race, which evolved into Balloonglow, a field of tethered balloons, park rides followed by a spectacular firework show

Fire-Up-the-Night, a one-of-a-kind international fireworks competition choreographed to music followed by a grand finale from Rozzi's Famous Fireworks

Falloween, a family friendly event with rides, shows, hay bale mazes, Trick or Treat Trail and petting zoo

AFL-CIO Family Picnic, the largest gathering of unions in the country which brought with it visits from three Presidents: Bill Clinton as a candidate, Joe Biden as Vice-President, and Barack Obama as a seated President

In addition, every season the park staged a number of other smaller events: Kid's Camps, Ladies Nites, Paddlefest, Kid's Club and Cruiseapalooza, a regional classic car show.

In the early days, the park hosted the Greater Cincinnati Dog Show, The Van Dells Rock 'n Roll Review, WVXU's Jazzfest in Parkers Grove, the Bob Hart Outdoor Show. At Sunlite Pool, the World's Longest Cheese Coney with Skyline Chili, The Fabulous Wallendas Thrill Show, a kazoo concert with Carmen DeLeon of the Cincinnati Pops, a high dive exhibition, synchronized swimming and a jet ski show.

Finally, an impressive list of one-time events:

- National Governor's Convention Family Party with Dick Clark's Rock 'n Roll Review
- The sponsor's party as part of the 1989 Major League Baseball All-Star Game
- The P&G International Sales Awards Banquet
- A "Celebration of the Millennium" featuring the Fabulous Wallendas, a human cannonball, trapeze acts, and other top-notch circus performers

In addition, Coney's staff had to park cars for hundreds of thousands of concert goers and operate all of the Riverbend concessions at an average of 50+ concerts annually… then be ready to operate the pool and all its rides shows and events the next morning.

Floods

Between 1984 and 2023, the park experienced 18 floods. Some were just an annoyance, a few were a lot of work, a couple were very damaging, and 1997 was a disaster. At 64.7 feet, it was 12.7

feet above flood stage which put over 8 feet of water over the highest part of the park. Sunlite Pool and the Main Gate were 14+ feet under water.

Old Man River brought with it an unimaginable amount of debris and mud. The total area was covered in mud and there was extensive damage and loss of equipment. In total, the cost to get the park back on its feet was $1.5 million.

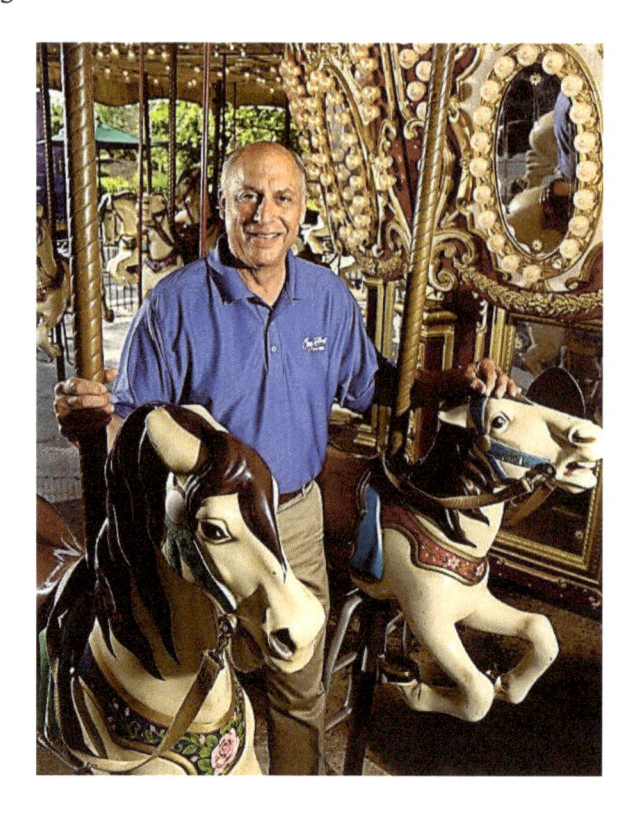

To Coney, with Love, Sally Voth

My family became Coney Island pass holders in the early 1980s. It's where the three of us kids all learned to swim. The swim lessons were VERY comprehensive. In the final year, we had to swim four lengths each of all five strokes: the crawl, breaststroke, backstroke, elementary backstroke and sidestroke. We also had to retrieve a brick from the deep end and learned to make pants and long-sleeved shirts into flotation devices. I also remember having to tread water with only our legs, keeping our arms raised in the air. The result was I developed into a very strong swimmer.

After lessons, we would play with our friends in the pool all day long. Our mom packed lunch in a cooler every day and we ate it at the picnic tables. I remember my friend Cresta and I making our moms watch our synchronized swimming "routines." I loved riding the Zoom Flume, and wished I could try to ride it standing up like the lifeguards did. I was a little scared of the Zip because you would get airborne on the second hill. I enjoyed the silver slide but was always slightly afraid I'd fall off the ladder or the platform at the top. The rules were slightly less stringent in those days, so we could go down the silver slide backwards, on our belly, etc., and a couple of us could go down the Zoom Flume at once. We also liked going off the diving boards. When I was a kid, there were three levels — the low dive, the medium dive and the high dive. I also thought it was so cool that the deep end was so big, that they needed to have a lifeguard in a rowboat. I remember there was always a crew of old people soaking up the sun and socializing on the pool deck. I have always been amazed at the skill and professionalism of the lifeguards at Coney. In the many years that I've gone to the pool, as recently as summer 2023, I've often heard the long whistle, which meant a guard was jumping in to save someone and other guards would race from the office area, usually with one carrying a backboard. I've been dismayed when I go to other public pools and see lifeguards not paying attention, and not constantly surveilling the water.

I always loved the music I'd hear in the afternoons at Coney in the 80s and early 90s. When some of those songs come on the radio today, it takes me right back to those warm afternoons when life was so much more carefree.

My first job was at Coney. I worked in the concession stands at Riverbend for two summers in high school. We didn't have cash registers, so had to add sales up in our heads. We had a cup counting system to see what we should end up with at the end of the night. Some of the concerts that took place when I worked there were Chris Isaak, Elton John, and, of course, Jimmy Buffett. When family and friends would visit from out of town, and even out of the country, if it was summertime, we'd take them to Coney Island. In addition to the pool, we'd also play putt-putt, ride the pedal boats, go on the rides, and sometimes play some of the games and eat LaRosa's pizza.

Now that I have kids of my own, we are sure to come out for a week every summer. My parents would usually get two of us season passes so we could combine our guest passes and go to Coney four or five times. They loved riding the rides with their cousins and watching the shows. The pool was always the highlight. My older daughter would do her own thing swimming all over the pool, while my younger daughter loved the diving boards and Typhoon Tower. When they heard Coney was closing, my older daughter, Macy asked, "But, what will we do when we go to Cincinnati?" My younger daughter, Josie, and I participated in one of the protests in front of Coney this past winter.

To Coney, with Love, Barb Tyler

I remember being there when I was a little girl. The merry-go-round was a memory that stood out the most. Years passed and my very first job at 16 years old was working at Coney Island. I kept the cafeteria eating area tidy and bused the tables.

I also got to know the famous lifeguard, Bob Lowe. My mother and I cleaned his house, and also did his laundry.

As more years passed, more memories were still being made. We would share old stories at the pool and the Tiki Bar with family and friends, all the while making new memories. Whenever I would go, I would always bump into an old friend. It was a great meeting place; *everyone knew where Coney was!* I always felt like I was on vacation when I was there. I looked forward to taking some of the little ones to the kiddy area. The bell would go off, and the water would pour down. I loved watching the little ones, as they laughed and ran when the water poured down on them. It was such a joy.

To Coney, with Love, Stephanie Bloemer

Growing up in the 70s, my family had our own pool. But all our neighbors and friends went to Coney, so I begged my mom to buy me a 12-swim pass which was offered back then. I went to Sunlite Pool as a child and then with my friends when I was a teenager. I can still remember lying in the grass covered in baby oil and sometimes mixing in a bit of iodine. It was a safe and wonderful place to hang out with friends and no parents!

Fast forward to the 90s. I left my job to be a stay-at-home mom. On my very first day at home with my four kids, we piled into the car, and I took them to Coney. To keep them from getting too excited, we would either play the quiet game with the winner earning a quarter, or they would count the horses that were out at River Downs. What a great place for little kids to learn to love the water as they could comfortably play on the side and gradually wade into deeper waters as they grew up. All four of my kids took swim lessons every year, three of them took lifeguard lessons and one took diving lessons. I taught swim lessons for a few years and my middle school kids were my helpers. I love everything about the pool... the Island, the Zoom Flume, the Silver Bullet, the Cyclone and the many diving boards. I truly treasure these memories of this magical place.

To Coney, with Love, Elaine Huber

When I was little, my grandma and grandpa had a house up from Coney Island. My brothers and I would sit and watch people come and go from Coney Island. When I was older, I got to go myself and it was so fun. Then as a grandparent I lived long enough to take my grandchildren to Coney. We started out always sitting by Typhoon Tower and as they grew, we sat by the deep end of the pool! What fun to see them enjoying themselves and with their friends. Will miss it so much but will always have fond memories.

To Coney, with Love, Shawna Shouse

I'm a Gen X, and started visiting Coney Island (Cincinnati, Ohio) in the 1980s. My first memory of this summer paradise is going with my best friend and her family for Pepsi Cola days. You could get in for a discounted rate with pop bottle caps. The park was different back then. That's when the locker room and shower house ran along Kellogg Avenue. The pool had several diving boards, including the high dive, that later was removed. I remember jumping off the diving board and thought it would be cool to swim to the cement island that separated the shallow end from the deep end. As I stood there on the diving board, measuring the distance, I was sure I could make it. Besides, if I couldn't, the lifeguard who sat in the boat out in the middle of the deep end was there. I plunged into the 10-foot water on that summer day and began my trek to the cement island. At first, I was fine, but soon realized that I misjudged the distance to get there and quickly became restless. Before I knew it, I was going underwater and couldn't get myself to the island. As I realized I was in a bad situation, someone grabbed me and took me to the cement island. I never tried that again!

The Zoom Flume was always lots of fun until your bathing suit bottom gave you a wedgie and it felt like you could shoot right out of the slide! As I became a young adult, Coney Island adventures would continue. I worked for Western Southern, and we had our annual company picnic at the Land of Oz shelter. This is when the amusement park rides were still in full operation. I spent all day in the sun at Sunlite Pool having some beers with friends and coworkers and then late afternoon, we headed over to the picnic shelter to enjoy a picnic style lunch and more beer! Those were the days! We had so much fun! As the years went by, I enjoyed Coney Island on several occasions.

My mom and I, being the sun worshipers we were, spent quality time at Sunlite Pool soaking up the rays. As I became a mother, I took my son to this place I grew to love so much. We zipped down the Silver Bullet after climbing the tall metal steps that were barely wide enough for adult feet.

We got soft serve ice cream cones to cool off from the hot sun. In 2022, I became a season pass holder so I could enjoy my oasis anytime I wanted. My aunt and uncle were also season pass holders and we often spent Sundays at the pool enjoying the regulars dancing the conga line. Sunday "fundays", as we called it, were special times for us.

I often took my friends with me for a day at the pool. Who was going to be the lucky friend to get my guest pass? We had so many good times there. Often on Fridays when I worked from home, if I had a light day, I would take my laptop and phone and move my office to my happy place, a lounge chair in the grass by Cannonball Cove! I would tell my mom, "I'm at my other office!" My mom passed away last year and in honor of her and our love for Coney Island, I wanted to get her a memorial brick placed, but unfortunately, they were no longer doing that. Did they know the demise was imminent?

Coney Island was my therapy. I often went there to relax and get away from the stressors of life. I enjoyed quality time with family and friends there and I made lots of memories over 4 decades at this Cincinnati treasure. Coney Island wasn't just an amusement park and pool, but I attended several of the events hosted there; Summer Fair, Holiday in Lights, Appalachian Festival, Light Up the Night. I remember standing in the drained pool for Light Up the Night and thought it was the coolest thing. I am so saddened to see this Cincinnati gem close. I truly don't understand the rationale behind the finality of a historical treasure. It brought so many, so much happiness and a place to make memories.

I will forever cherish Coney Island and the memories I made there. I feel like a piece of me will be lost without it. Thank you for all the great times and memories I'll share for years to come!

To Coney, with Love, Leah Carballoso

It was some years ago, but I remember the message clear as day... my best friend asked me to attend her work's summer cookout, held at the Moonlite Pavilion at Coney. It was a beautiful afternoon, and we enjoyed the music, games, and food; but the standout was the entertainment. They had brought in palm readers, tarot card readers, and a caricature artist. We sat for the caricature, hearing of how we seemed like two halves of the same coin, how she wanted to draw both of us together, instead of just focusing on one. Then it was time to have our cards read. I don't remember the name of the woman reading the cards, but I remember the message: your first love will be the one you marry. At the time, we weren't able to be together, so I laughed at the woman reading my cards. But sure enough, we are celebrating 5 beautiful years of being married. That reading gave me hope and a reason to hold on, it just happened to be something that happened at Coney.

To Coney, with Love, Diane Brown Hershberger

I have many wonderful memories of Coney. After driving to Coney, we felt such excitement as soon as Coney came into view. My dad would drop my brother and I off so we could swim all day at Sunlite Pool and then meet the rest of the family to enjoy the rides. As a teen, I would go with my friends. We had so much fun jumping off that high diving board (never did dive from that board). We would finish off our day riding the Shooting Star. As I got older, the BEST date night was Moonlite Gardens. As an adult, I was lucky enough to introduce my children to several fun days at Sunlite Pool and even once I took a couple of my grandkids, they loved the slide that took them right into the pool. Perhaps now you can understand just how many memories I have enjoyed, over several generations, and what I have included is not even all of them!

To Coney, with Love, Lois Vallandingham

My first date with Richard Vallandingham was at the iconic Coney Island on July 3, 1964. We had our photo taken of us sitting together on Coney's impressive "Moon Slice" It's a beautiful and lasting memory for us. We married in September of 1970, and we were blessed to celebrate our 50th wedding anniversary in 2020. Attached photos: Lois and Richard Vallandingham's first date at Coney 1964 and celebrating their 50th wedding anniversary Sept. 19th, 2020.

To Coney, with Love, TJ Weil

Fall-O-Ween 2017 and 2018!

To Coney, with Love, Katy Zerhusen

I spent most of my summers at Coney when I was young; mid to late 90s. Whenever I saw the arch entrance when coming down Sutton, I knew we were almost at Coney. I learned how to swim there. My favorite part of my day at Coney was going down the Zoom Flume many times in a row. That was my favorite slide. When I got older, we stopped going for a few years. Then in 2006, I got a job working as a pool cashier, then eventually a cashier foreman (2006-2013). I made many friends and made new memories working there. Most of all, Coney is where I met my husband, Andy Zerhusen. He started off working in rides, then switched over to the pool as a porter, then a pool manager. Never did I think the guy who came in and out of the pool area gates with a big dumpster collecting trash would someday be my husband. I always dreamed that my daughter would also learn how to swim there and spend her summers there like I did, but that dream will never come to be. Coney will always have a special place in my heart, and I will always cherish the wonderful memories I have there.

To Coney, with Love, Vickie Reder

Our memories of Coney Island reach back to the 1940s when our mom and our Granny would go to Moonlite Gardens to hear the big bands and dance the night away! Mama's love of Moonlite Gardens never wavered, and we were so fortunate to celebrate her birthday at her favorite place, dancing to music provided by the Pete Wagner Band. Classic tunes by Glen Miller, Harry James and many others filled the place! She shared stories and memories of her girlfriends (and a few boyfriends) enjoying nights under the stars. Her reminiscences took her back to those days and we all enjoyed going back in time with her, while also celebrating the present moment, making new memories. We love Moonlite Gardens because she did. My husband and I saw Sha Sha Na, a fabulous '50s style band and man, that evening was a blast from the past! I'm sure we're among many in this mutual admiration society and will miss being able to share with future generations. Thank you, Coney Island, Sunlite Pool and Moonlite Gardens!

To Coney, with Love, Lani Amann

Coney has always been a special place. As a kid I remember swimming and running around with friends and then I got a summer job there when I was 17 and have spent every summer working there since! I spent 34 summers there working in various spots and have made best friends forever! I met my husband there while he was working first aid, and I was in food service. We got married on the patio of Moonlite Gardens. Our 2 kids grew up as Coney babies and learned how to swim like fish there! The closing of Coney has my heart broken. Lots of wonderful memories and great friends! Working at Coney has taught me lots of life skills!

To Coney, with Love, Ashley Clark

As the sun sets on an era we bid farewell to a beloved landmark, Coney Island. For generations, this enchanting amusement park has been a part of my family's story. From my great aunt and uncle's romantic engagement on the tranquil waters of Lake Como to my grandma's leisurely swims and relaxation, the island holds a special place in our family history. Growing up, Coney Island became synonymous with weekends filled with laughter, adventure, and camaraderie. After my great aunt and grandma passed, I passed on my life of Coney with my little cousins. Not only that, but for many years I got to visit the park alongside former coworkers turned lifelong friends, we reveled in the nostalgia of paddle boat rides and enjoyed soaking in the sun catching up on daily lives. The memories created within its gates will forever be cherished, but the prospect of saying goodbye still feels unreal.

To Coney, with Love, Maria DuPont

My family had annual memberships to Coney Island. Coney was so special to us. So many of our personal memories were created there, as well as knowing and appreciating the wider historical significance of this Cincinnati icon. Both of my parents were history teachers, and my dad, Mike Hils, especially embraced the history of Coney Island and Sunlite Pool. I remember taking walks all the way back through the amusement park rides to the Ohio River, and he would tell us stories about the Island Queen, Moonlite Gardens, Civil Rights, and the generations of people who got to enjoy this treasure that also served as our summer home.

When anyone mentions "summer," the first thing I think of is the one-and-only Sunlite Pool. This place had so much to offer to all types of people and personalities. It was a place to have a blast with friends, a deep talk with your mom, or even to mellow out all by yourself.

Some of my most memorable birthday parties were spent at the pool with my cousins. I was so proud to show them every piece of it that I found the most fun. Running up the endless stairs of the Zoom Flume, challenging each other to the best cannonball off the Island, laughing at the "squirt" that shot water at your feet near the Silver Bullet... Just to name a few favorite spots!

Most of the time, especially in recent years, Coney Island has been the place where my dad and I could get away from the world. In the summers, he cut grass to make some extra cash. When he would get home after a long, hot morning, he'd say, "Wanna go to Coney?" And off we went! Even though Coney was often so crowded, we introverts loved to find a spot for ourselves where we could hide behind a newspaper or a good book. He always pointed out the Marian Spencer plaque on the lifeguard chair that sat in front of our typical spot. We'd people-watch and talk about all kinds of things, like preparing for the upcoming school year, current events and politics, and old family stories. Then, when we'd start to burn in the sun, we'd get up and dive off the pool wall into the deep end!

Every single time we would swim in the deep end together, which would be most days out of the week, he would say: "I just love this place," as he gratefully took a look around, and then floated on his back. I would giggle out of breath treading water, both because of this ritual and the fact that neither one of us is amazing at swimming. We might have done a couple of laps here and there as a little workout, but really, we would just see how long we could hang in the 9-foot area until we got tired... You can't really swim freely like that anywhere else. Most other pools don't let you just chill and tread water as long as you'd like in an area that is more than 5-feet deep. Many public pools have a "deep end" that is reserved for taking quick turns on their diving boards, but you have to get out of the way for others as soon as possible... We just loved this unique feature of Sunlite Pool!

My mom, Dawn Hils, preferred the shallow end, and we would walk back and forth around the shallow perimeter with her when she would join our Coney Island adventures. We'd smile at the babies and remember how my first steps were actually taken right there in Sunlite Pool. We reminisced about how my siblings and I learned how to swim there, which was very safe due to that nice and easy flow from the shallow to deeper ends (along with the very attentive lifeguards). We'd also laugh about how on many occasions, my brother and sister and I would play catch with a little ball over dozens of people's heads across the pool. Several times a year, my grandparents would come with us and carefully walk down the ramp to float on an inflatable in the middle of the pool (Nana would float; Pa would gently push her around). Sunlite Pool was such an incredible experience for all of us, at all of our stages of life!

My dad and I tried so hard to save Sunlite to the bitter end. My dad was a very dedicated "Save Coney Islander," attending meetings and staying in-the-loop through multiple communication strands. We went to fundraisers, peaceful protests, and even spoke up at the last Anderson Township town hall meeting together. We are so sad and mad about the destruction of our paradise, but we are so joyful for the memories we will hold in our hearts for years and years to come. We will tell our stories forever!

To Coney, with Love, Becky Atkins Lasita

It was the summer of 1981. My parents took my little baby sister and me to Coney Island for a day of fun at Sunlite Pool. I was just 3 years old and had been swimming on my own, without "swimmies," all day. I remember getting out of the pool and walking over to our blanketed picnic area that mom had set up underneath a perfect shading tree.

My dad had started towards the high dive and I, not realizing this, quickly took my drink and ran to trail behind him. As he started climbing the ladder, I knew we were about to do something wild, and as we climbed and passed the people climbing next to us as they reached their diving boards, I knew we were about to do something very risky. It was right at the time that I had reached the highest diving board known to man and watched as my dad jumped that I knew I had possibly made a very large mistake in thinking I knew what I was about to do.

I reached the diving board and made my slow walk to the edge, *man, this is high!* I thought to myself. It was like looking into a fish aquarium, the depth was hard to measure. All I knew was that I had to jump, and I was not about to waste any time overthinking this and have people notice that I had no clue what I was doing up there. I had too much pride even at three years old, it was time to make my move.

I remember looking down at the people and it was then that I had noticed my mother having an absolute hysterical fit down below. She was yelling my name and pointing at me to get my father's attention who had just come up for air after his big moment. I looked down with a giant smile on my face, counted to three in my head, leaped in the air and let gravity do the rest. I remember holding my breath and my nose and then having to let go to take another breath, thinking, *man, this is taking longer than I thought.* Splash!!!! I hit the water and my little legs started kicking wildly. As soon as my head popped out of the water, my dad grabbed me laughing with pride, "You did it!!! You did it!!!" The little daredevil inside of me, had never been prouder. "I did it!!", I yelled! My mom had finally recovered from her mild heart attack, and we continued our adventure at Coney Island's Sunlite Pool. Thank you for the memories!

To Coney, with Love, Dawn Hils

For five generations, our extended Shields family, originally from Mt. Adams and Covington, spent many summer days at Coney Island. Way back in the day, my great-grandma, Addie Shields (pictured in black and white around the late 1950s-early 1960s) was once crowned the Queen of Coney Island! She would board the Island Queen steamboat at the Cincinnati public landing at the foot of Broadway, as would my Grandma Blanche (Kenney) Shields, as well. In her later years, Grandma Blanche would mention how tired she was as a young girl after a long day at Coney, taking the boat back to Cincinnati and then still needing to get back over the Suspension Bridge to her home in Covington. Always a long but special day!

A fun memory for me as a young mom was taking our Granny Blanche (pictured in the orange shirt in 2008) back to Coney for family birthday parties in the late summer. My grandma would reminisce, stating she'd been coming to Coney since '25 (as in 1925)! One time, under those statuesque trees, on a beautiful sunny day in the grassy area by the pool, my 95-year-old grandma announced that she wanted to see if she could still SKIP! I guess she was enjoying watching her great-grandkids frolic around her and thought she'd join in the fun, too! By golly, with just a little help, she got up and skipped there in the grass, alongside that famous pool she swam in so many years ago!

Another sweet Coney memory with my siblings in the 1980s, is that our mom, an elementary school teacher, would bring all five of the kids nearly every day to Sunlite Pool, and while we'd swim and race down the silver bullet slide, Zoom Flume, and The Zip, she would sit under the beautiful trees and do her graduate work. My dad would join us after work for a packed picnic dinner in the early evenings, and sometimes other relatives would join in, too. Eventually the teens in the family would work in the Sunlite Grill and Riverbend. Fun memories of hot, sweaty, long days!

As time went on, some of the next generation would lifeguard and teach swim lessons at Sunlite Pool, as well. Whether there to participate on the swim team, work, or just play in the pool, several family members were truly Coney lifers, for sure! My 81, and 82-year-old parents just loved to still float around the pool and read under those old shade trees all these years later!

Our parents had fun experiences at Coney Island as young kids, and my own first memories (aided by old photos) take me back to my toddler years in the late 1960s and early 70s when we would board the Brent's Landing Ferry on the Kentucky side of the Ohio River and make our short way toward the iconic stone Coney Island welcome sign and lighthouse on the other side. Also pictured is of me boarding in 1969 and again on the ferry with my dad and little sister the following year. There is even a picture of us inside the ferry! Sweet memories of some amusement park rides that even my own children enjoyed 30 years later!

Soon after my husband and I got married and started a family, we made sure to secure our own annual Coney passes. In fact, a day or two before our first child was born, we swam in the pool and then headed to an Elton John concert right there at Riverbend. A sweet final hurrah before our little world changed! Funny enough, that new baby girl took her very first steps in Sunlite Pool the next year on her first birthday!

Raising kids at Coney was a natural thing for our entire extended family to do, and all these decades later, it's hard to believe that it's all over! No more birthday parties in the picnic area, no more diving contests (or who's the fastest on the slide), no more long walks around the world's largest circulating pool, no more racing to get an open lounge chair, no more checking on the mainstay older generations to see if they indeed survived the winter, and, among a million other traditions, no more closing down the pool on the last day. Goodbye, Coney. You will always have our hearts!

To Coney, with Love, Megan Hughes

July 12th is the anniversary of my dad's death. I was 9 years old when he passed away suddenly of a viral infection in his heart. He was only 34. Every year my family and I would go to Coney Island to celebrate his life because my mom told us how much he loved going to Coney! She said it was one of his favorite places to go and so we made it a tradition to go at least once a year on or around the day of his anniversary. We always had so much fun and started bringing all of our kids there too! We were all so sad to hear the news of the closing and we truly hoped it somehow can stay open! Whenever we went there, we could feel my dad's joy and love, and we would look forward to going every year!

To Coney, with Love, the McMahon Family

Coney changed the path of my life. It's been part of my soul for 45 years.

My name is Cathy McMahon, and my story starts the summer of 1980. I was working at a YMCA when a fellow guard left to work at Sunlite Pool. He told me they needed swim instructors. I replied, saying, "I don't want to work there! The pool is open while you teach and that pool is too big to lifeguard!" I ended up guarding at the pool for five years. The year 2024 would have been my 45th teaching swimming.

At Coney, I met my husband, Tim, who had joined Coney with his family when he was 11. As a kid, he was on the swim and dive team, and then he became a lifeguard at 18 and coached the dive team. He was a collegiate diver at Ohio University. He was 19 and I was 21 when we met. Coney had seven diving boards then: one three-meter-high board, two five-foot, and four one-meters. We also had a 44-foot platform that was closed to the public, but, starting at 14 years old, Tim opened and closed the pool for the season by doing a 1 ½ off this tower.

We were married in 1983 and had our wedding reception at Coney's Moonlite Pavilion.

In the summer of 1989, after teaching two classes a day for nine weeks every summer for nine summers, I had taught a family of 13 children. One day, the 17-year-old walked me to my car with my two toddlers to tell me unhealthy things were happening in her home. I had to report the parents. Child Protective Services came to Coney to remove five girls from the home — I brought three home, and another Coney mom took two. They became our foster daughters. Their ages were 9, 11, and 17.

In addition to our three foster daughters, we had five children. We lived on the west-side without air conditioning. All five children came to Coney every day, playing and helping me with swim lessons. Coney let me teach one class to earn a family pass for the summer. We stayed all day, sometimes from open to close. Our family dog was named Coney so my kids could "have Coney all year round."

Our sons, Nick and Jimmy, both lifeguarded there for five years, which helped them pay their way through college. Our daughter Shannon (a lifeguard at a west-side pool) took her engagement photos at Coney in 2013. My son Timmy's thing was putt-putt golf over by the rides. Our youngest, Sean, loved the diving boards so much that, at four years old, he saw a board that had been put out for the garbage and asked if we could bring it home. Coney management let him have it! My husband put that 14-foot diving board on his Dodge Durango and drove it all the way to the west side, where the kids laid it in the grass and played on it all day. Now, it is mounted on a fence next to the pool we built in 2023, serving as our "dive bar."

It seems that, every year for the last ten years, I've considered not teaching. But each year, I would teach the first day, get home, and say, "oh my gosh, I have the cutest kids in lessons!" I loved teaching swimming. I even had private lessons that were extremely rewarding experiences.

Coney is a soulful place — a place people call their "happy place." A place that, for three months of the year, the world was a good place. A place with sunshine, beautiful water, and good people to be around. There were a lot of members that started in January counting down the days until Coney opened — including my children!

I remember a member from the 1980s named Carl. Carl was an older man who had survived the Holocaust (pictured below, next to the picture of Bob Lowe, the legendary lifeguard). He came to Coney every day with his chess board, playing chess with the guards and other members and always bringing a bag of hard candy to hand out to the guards. It was his safe place.

I am a lucky girl to have worked at Coney, filling my heart with thousands of children and beautiful people. I cried for four days when they announced the closing, the ending of an era, but I am forever grateful for everything and everyone that Coney brought to my life. Thank you, Coney — you brought love to my life, the gifts of water and sun, the gifts of children, the gifts of good friends, and memories in my soul. Those things cannot ever be lost or taken. I will be sad for a long time, but forever grateful.

To Coney, with Love, Lauren Hackney

Hello! Our names are Christine Darling and Lauren Hackney Darling. We are mother and daughter, and both Coney Lifeguard Alumni! We are so sad about the loss of a piece of Cincinnati history and a place that gave us such amazing memories, friends, and experiences we will never forget.

My brother Kevin Darling was also a guard about 4 years after me! We also swam together on the swim team. And yes, Coach Robin. We always touched the island even if you could not see that far from the diving board. When Lauren became a Coney Guard, it was so fun to connect and share Guard Stories!

Over the years, things had changed some but the experience of spending summers in guard chairs looking across the World's Largest Recirculating Pool at the crowds of people, some who knew how to swim, and some who didn't but tried! We were always watching, wondering if people would make it across the deep end side of the island or if it was time to blow the whistle and go in after them! If we were in Chair One, ringing the bell as we went into the water, to alert the other guards to head over to meet us! An amazing first job with amazing people!! Thank you to all who gave me a chance! Gave my brother a chance, and then years later gave Lauren a chance! It was fun that we all worked with some of the same people! Somehow, Lauren earned the Quietest Lifeguard Award one year. She remembers learning during a storm that the mats on Pipeline Plunge became kites in the wind as she carried four left by patrons at the top, down the stairs!

There was never a dull day at Coney! The Park will always have a special place in our family's hearts. Thank you, Coney!

To Coney, with Love, Morgan Brondhaver

I grew up at Coney Island from day one. My dad and pappy were parking managers, so I remember being there all summer, whether it was swimming, riding rides, or handing out brochures in the parking booth. Once I turned 16, I was officially a Coney Island employee, but it wasn't anything new since I had been "working" there my whole life. Coney is in my blood, and I will forever cherish the memories of the place I lived for the first 23 summers of my life.

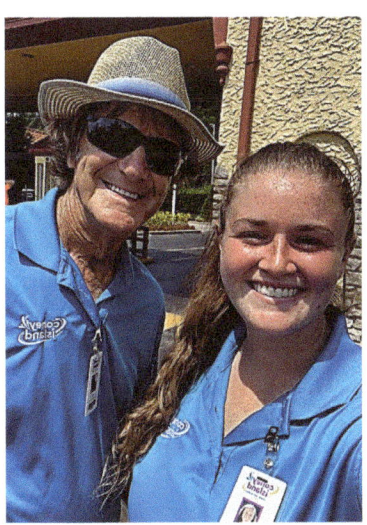

To Coney, with Love, Donna Reece Smith

I have many memories of Coney Island, from early childhood until now. I grew up in Mt Washington and when I was young, we would go to Coney several times a summer. I remember the anticipation and excitement building as we would drive down Sutton hill, and when we could finally see the entrance...well there was nothing like it. As a matter of fact, I still get that feeling, although more subdued, daily when going to Coney.

We started getting season passes when I was 14 and I have had one almost every year since, even when I lived in Price Hill, I would bring my stepdaughters almost daily to swim and ride the rides. Then I would bring my own daughter and most recently my granddaughters, who are now 8 and 10, and are devastated about the closing of Coney. They all took swim lessons, loved the silver bullet slide and of course the island. They loved the rides also. We spent hours and hours with them jumping off the island, and most recently the high board in the new dive pool.

We had many family picnics at Coney. My entire extended family came every year for the annual Italian day picnic in August. Relatives came from neighboring states to attend and reunite with family and friends at this exciting place, that had something for everyone.

I have many photos taken at Coney. One of the photos included here is of me in 1960 at Coney Island and another photo of me in 2015 with my granddaughter at the same age. It's sad to think that we won't be spending our summers at Sunlite Pool anymore.

I cannot believe this era is over. I wish I could have known, so I could have taken more pictures to remember this wonderful place. I am heartbroken.

To Coney, with Love, Sophia Raines

After I had spent many summers at Coney with endless memories, good and bad, I felt safe and sound, surrounded and guarded by what felt like the best lifeguards. After spending many summers there and gaining the infamous nickname of "Coney Rat," I realized I was desperate for a job to earn money for myself. But I also wanted to spend my days like every other summer, in my second home. After debating the strenuous job, I decided to say, "Forget it." This "Forget it" led to 589 hours, four lives saved, two near deaths, and a group of lifelong friends.

I had spent almost every waking moment within the gates of the pool that summer. One of many summers, and I planned to be a part of for many years to come.

It all started with the training classes, May 2023. The most exhausting days of my life. I was the first one there. My nerves I had all week and anticipated embarrassment had finally happened. Four boring hours in the place I had been so familiar with suddenly felt so intimidating and unfamiliar. First, a video that scared the life out of me, it was a video of a child drowning for twenty minutes in a pool. After that, CPR. *Breathe rise and fall, breathe rise and fall,* three hours of repeating those words to save the life of a lifeless rubber dummy. I felt so stupid, as I didn't know what I was doing. I was also the youngest there so my already existing anxiety had risen to its highest when I had to go perform CPR in front of 35 people. The next two days were arguably the two most physically demanding days of my life. Swimming 500 meters in freezing water at six in the morning, as well as pulling 300 pounds out of the pool countless times. I hadn't exactly made friends at this point, because I was super shy and timid. But I did have a familiar face there. My ex-classmate from elementary school. That was an old connection that was rekindled that summer.

I have had many Coney friends at this point, but Capture the Flag night was the best for seeing them all together. We had no responsibilities except to find the flags. That night was so memorable after hurt feelings, bruises, and a concussion. But this was the last time I would see my friends before I left for a month abroad. I was devastated to leave my friends, so upset I almost canceled my trip. Although I'm glad I didn't, I still feel like I missed out on many opportunities to become closer with my work friends. After I came back, it was a blur of a short 3 weeks until the season was over, and everyone was starting to get burned out. We held on for an extra four hours after we closed on the last day just because we wanted to spend as much time as possible together.

Our last memory of the season was the Luke Bryan concert. It's almost a Coney tradition to go to the show because he comes here so often. I remember that night so vividly, but also as a blur. Shoving my way through the lawn trying to get up close with my friends, right at the barricade. I have never pushed harder and walked through such disturbing things in my life. But I knew it was all worth it when we all locked arms and sang the most repeated song at Coney, "Sunrise, Sunburn, Sunsets," because it was our song. We were across the lot from our place, with our people, and our song. It was our song because we had spent countless sunrises, sunburns, and sunsets together.

To Coney, with Love, Steve Hais

Grandpa taught me to swim and dive, but walking on water came naturally.

To Coney, with Love, Greg "Chubbs" Cunningham

I spent the majority of my life at Coney. My family was like the "Lt. Dan Family" from the movie *Forest Gump*. They were a generational military family, and we were a generational Coney family.

All of my stories about Coney are because of my grandma. My grandma Rita, aka "the purple lady" (she loved the color purple), spent every day of summer at Coney from when she was little until her death. She had her "spot" on the north side, right in front of the ramp and under the umbrella. Grandma would watch us kids every day, so we also got to enjoy Coney.

I was on the swim team when I was 5 until I was 17. Every day we were at Coney from 8am - 3pm. Grandma would come in with us, walk her bags down to her spot and then hangout in the bathhouse till 10am when the pool opened. Just so she would have a head start from the other members. My siblings and I were Coney brats. Always running amuck and causing problems. Being there so often, like a lot of coney brats, eventually we would end up working there.

My grandma worked at Summerfair and my mom taught swim lessons for years. All of us kids worked there as lifeguards or porters. I started that adventure in 1999 at 14 as a junior lifeguard, at age 15 I became a porter, at 16 a lifeguard, at age 17 to 19 I went back to being a porter. However, since I was always there, I wound up working in every department at Coney to help out when short staffed.

My favorite job when being a porter, was cleaning the pool. We would fill the pool around April and the iron and dirt in the water would settle to the bottom. We would use the trash pump to vacuum it all up. In the deep end we would wear a full-face mask hooked up to an air compressor and we would be down there for hours. The water was always cold, and the wetsuits Coney had had holes in them.

The other scary but favorite job was cleaning the pre-filter baskets. These were in place to grab all the loose debris (grass, ride bracelets, money, hygiene products, etc.) The pool had 2, the Zoom Flume had one and the Pipeline Plunge had one. You would mask up without a weight belt. The basket for the pipeline was in a pit that you had to squeeze into. It was covered and had one opening 2' x 2' and was full of water. It was about 15' deep, about 20' long 8' wide. It was completely dark in there and if you touched any of the pipes the rust would come off, making visibility to zero. You would take the basket off the inlet pipe and rope hoist it to the outside to be cleaned off. It was about 18" wide and 18" deep. The pool's pre-filter basket one was a lot bigger, at about 3' wide x 2' long and weighed close to 40 lbs. The basket was 30' under water and in a pit about 10' x 10' You would go down in this pit with a ladder attached to the wall, it was scary, cold and the bottom was covered in paint chips and rust. You would rest your knees under the basket to lift it up so you could unscrew the 4 bolts and then tie a rope to it. Give 3 wanks of the rope and the guys would hoist it up, clean it, then send it back down. I loved changing the baskets and cleaning the pool.

In 2005, I left for the Army and in 2013 came back to Cincinnati. That summer I applied again at Coney. I only wanted to clean the pool. However, they made me a pool manager. I loved being back at Coney. That post season I was hired full time to become a ride mechanic. The ride mechanics were in charge of the rides, slides, and the fleet of equipment for Coney. I knew some mechanics, but during that time I learned so much more. Especially from the lead ride mechanic, Tom Chase. Tom started in the early 90s and knew everything. I learned so much from him and he was one of the greatest bosses and mentors someone could have had.

Unfortunately, Tom passed away in October 2023. He will forever be missed. Every morning, the mechanics climbed in, under, over, and on top of every ride to ensure it was safe to operate. After that, we hung out until we were needed.

To pass time, the mechanics, referred to as "the mean girls" would work on carts but we would prank the other maintenance departments for fun. From putting a horn on a golf cart so when it goes in reverse it would go off, occasionally we would fill someone's locker with Styrofoam chips, or we would wrap a cart in plastic, the list goes on and on. But that's what made Coney the greatest, all the employees at Coney are family. I even had my name stenciled on the Red Barron plane. There wasn't a happier feeling than to have my name on my favorite ride as a child. I left coney in 2018 and moved to Germany. But I miss my time at Coney every day and still talk to friends I met at Coney 20 years ago.

My first steps, my first swim, my first date, my first kiss, my first love, my first heart break, my first job, my first great boss, my first beer, and my first true friendships, all happened at Coney.

That cannot be taken from me.

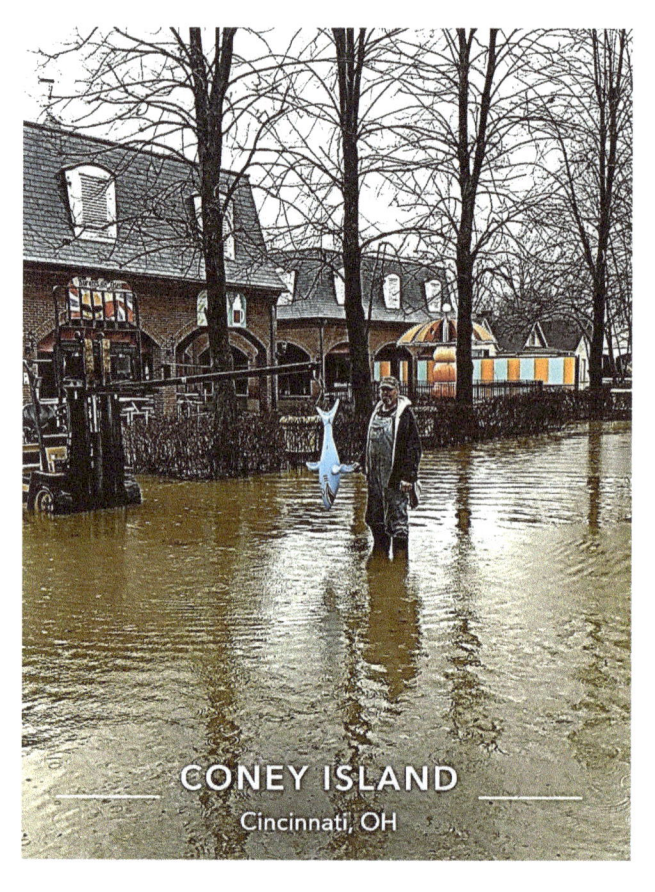

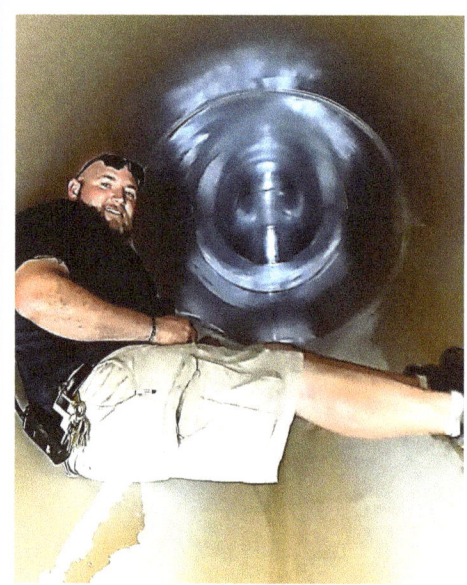

To Coney, with Love, Susan Whitaker

Coney Island has been an integral part of my life for as long as I remember. In the 1970s-'80s, my mom and our family of 5 kids spent our summers swimming, diving and riding the Zoom Flume with friends and neighbors at Sunlite Pool. Swim lessons and packed lunches fill my memories of those great days growing up!

In 1985, when I was 16, I got my first job as a locker room attendant at Coney. It definitely wasn't glamourous, but it certainly taught me so many lessons. I met amazing people who opened my eyes about true work ethic and working with the public. I really didn't enjoy that first year and my dad said I couldn't quit unless I found another job. Well, I ended up staying at Coney all summer and then many, many more after that. Years later, we laughed when my dad said he didn't mean I could NEVER quit working at Coney!

My Coney story over the years included various jobs: pool cashier and cashier trainer; Sunlite Pool manager (what a huge honor to be one of the first women in this position); cash room girl (not our official title, but that's what we were called); Riverbend beer server, and a group sales account executive (20 amazing years in this position). That's a lot of memories in the workplace that I called home for so long!

A few of my highlight memories include:

- Employee parties in the 80s. One year we created a huge train of employees all riding down the Zoom Flume at once (not safe, but definitely fun!). Another year for the employee party skits, the cash room girls' rendition of "Money" by Pink Floyd had everyone laughing!
- Working as a Sunlite Pool cashier during the Grateful Dead concert at Riverbend in 1986. So many deadheads were trying to sneak into the pool just to take a shower! I met some great people with very interesting stories.
- A million walkie-talkie radio calls were made over the years, but my favorite was one day when it was slow in the cash room, we decided to take a quick ride on the Scrambler (this wasn't allowed, but I figured that I was past the time for getting written up for it). As we were spinning, we got a call on the radio: "What is your location?" We were laughing all the way around and saying, *sssccccrrraaammmbblleeerrr!*
- Five sold out Jimmy Buffett concerts in a row in 1993, and many other Buffet shows before and after that year. Wow, we made a lot of margaritas!
- Getting to bring my kids to work with me when they went to Coney's summer camps. Fishing camp was a favorite… there are some huge fish in Lake Como!
- Being on a Coney radio spot as a "Coney mom". Also, my kids filming a Coney commercial with their friends as extras. They rode the Scream Machine over 50 times that day. Needless to say, that ride wasn't requested for a while after that!
- Watching the amazing Rozzi fireworks for Balloon Glow in the best seats in the park in Moonlite Gardens.
- Countless company picnics with customers from so many great companies around the city. Each organization showing appreciation to their employees by planning a day of fun for their families. It fills my heart with pride thinking about all of those times that were created by our Coney team parking, grilling, setting up buffet lines, counting tickets, putting on tablecloths, blowing up balloons, calling bingo, moving cornhole boards, fork lifting, employee giveaways, and walking thousands of steps around the park. It couldn't have all happened without the very best team of people all working together.

I'm so proud to say that my daughter Morgan followed in my footsteps and also started working at Coney Island when she was 16. Her summers included working in rides, recreation, pool food service, and many years at Riverbend. Serving the concert crowds definitely taught her some very important lessons about work ethic and working with the public, just like her mom learned at that age. My husband and boys each spent a summer or two working at Coney, of course they did; it was like our second home for so many years.

Most of what I remember about working at Coney Island is the people. There are too many to name, but I remember each and every one of their faces and how they impacted my life. I made some of my best friends who are truly friends for life. My family is so grateful for the people, moments and lessons that we learned at that beautiful amusement park on the river.

The Floods

63
62
61
60
59
58
57
56
55
54
53
52
Floods
Come In All
Sizes!
They Begin Here.

The Events

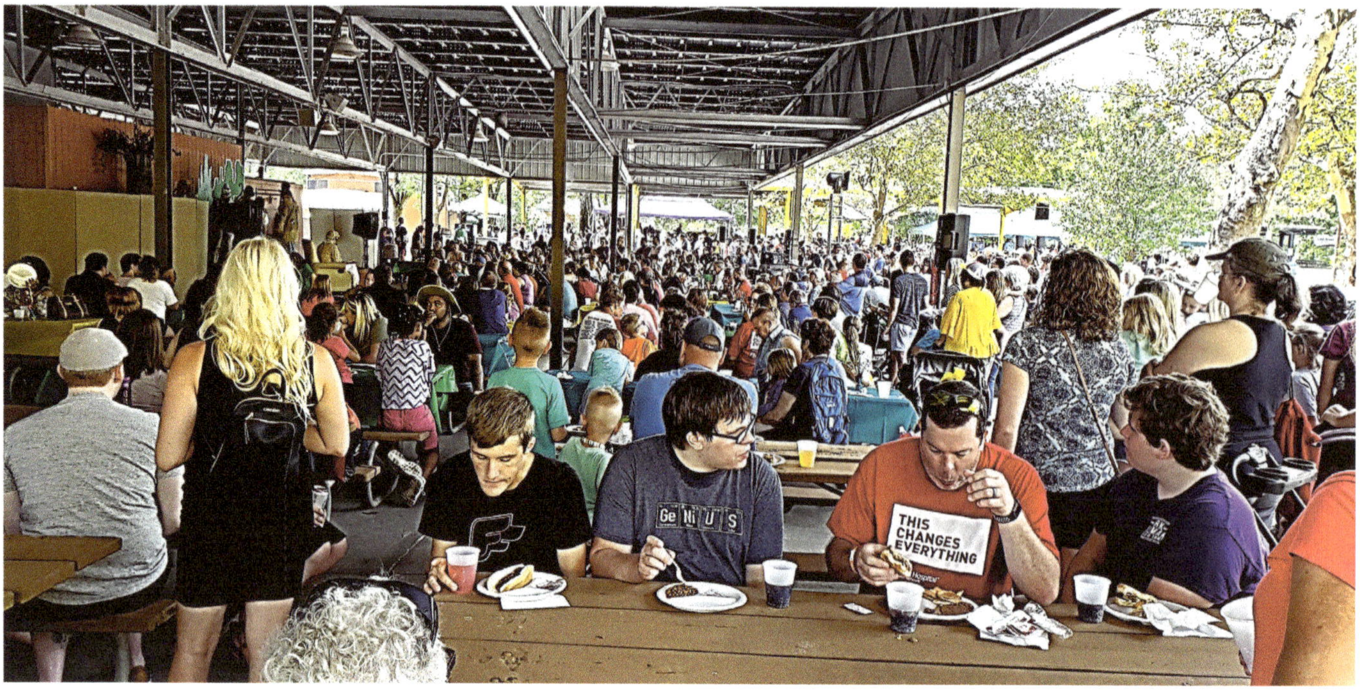
THIS
CHANGES
EVERYTHING

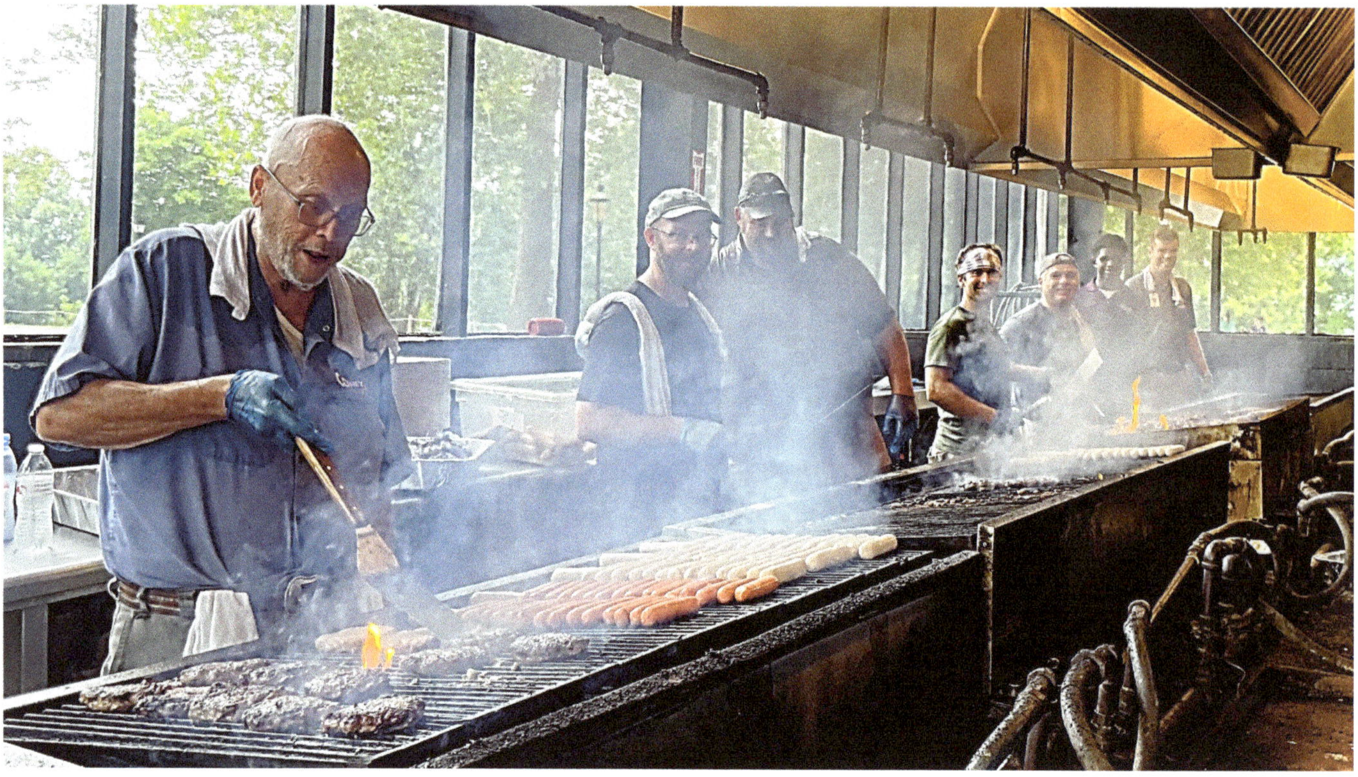

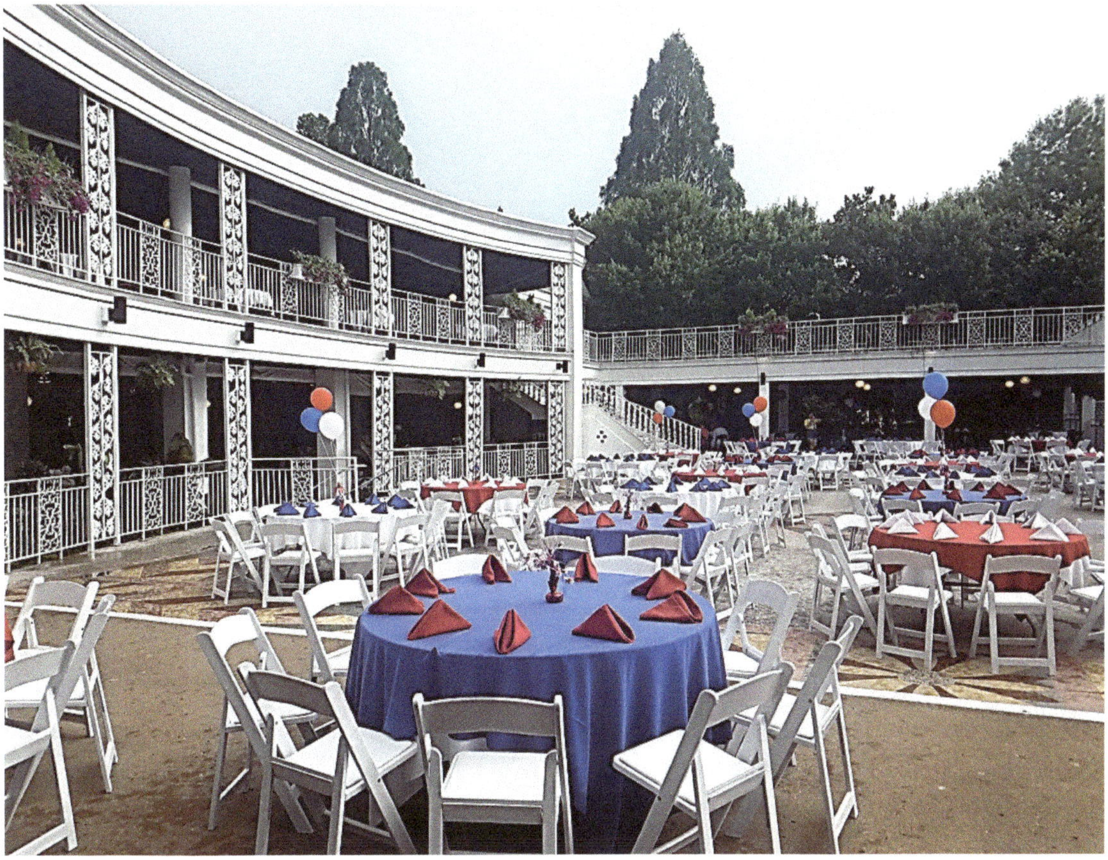

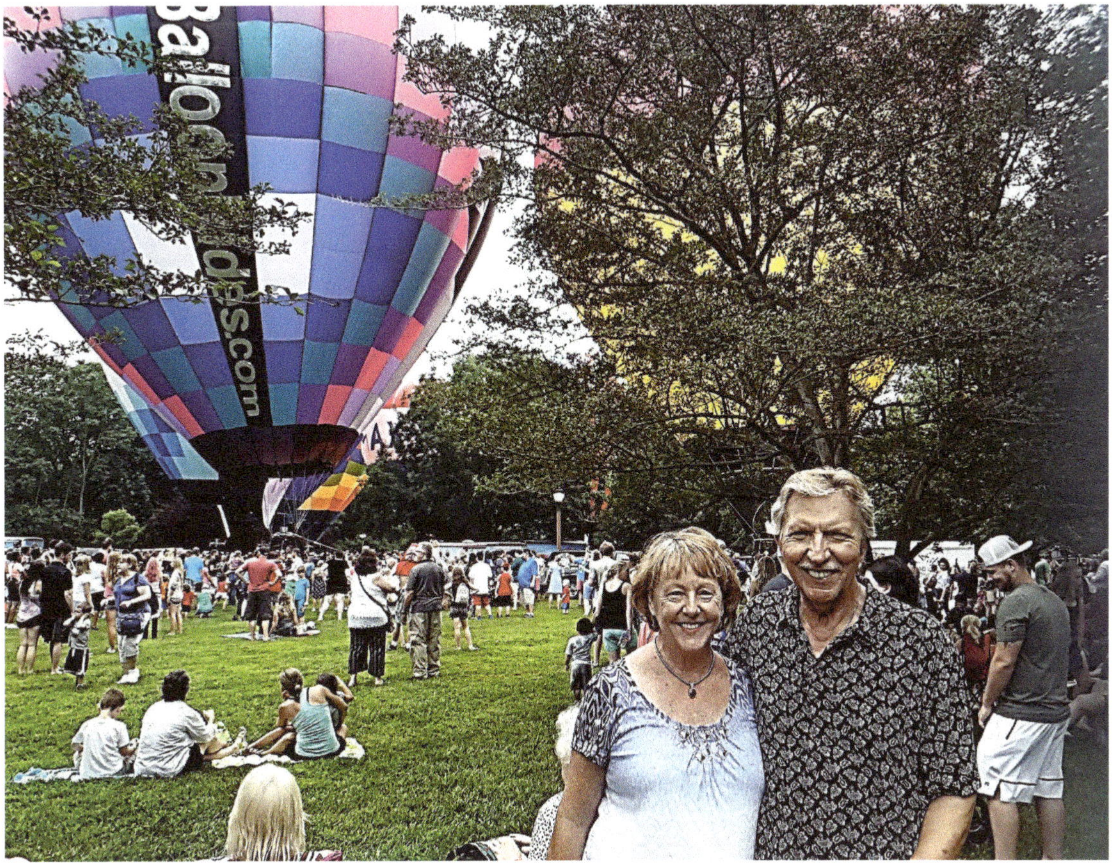

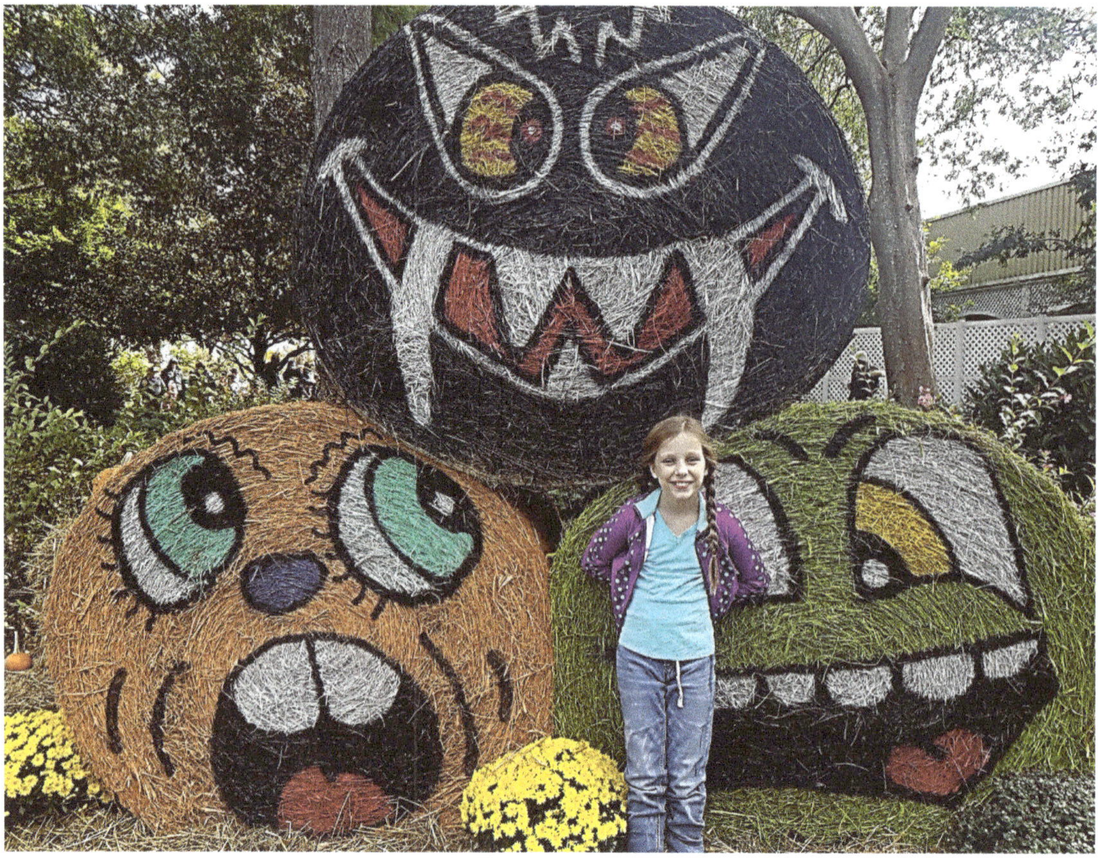

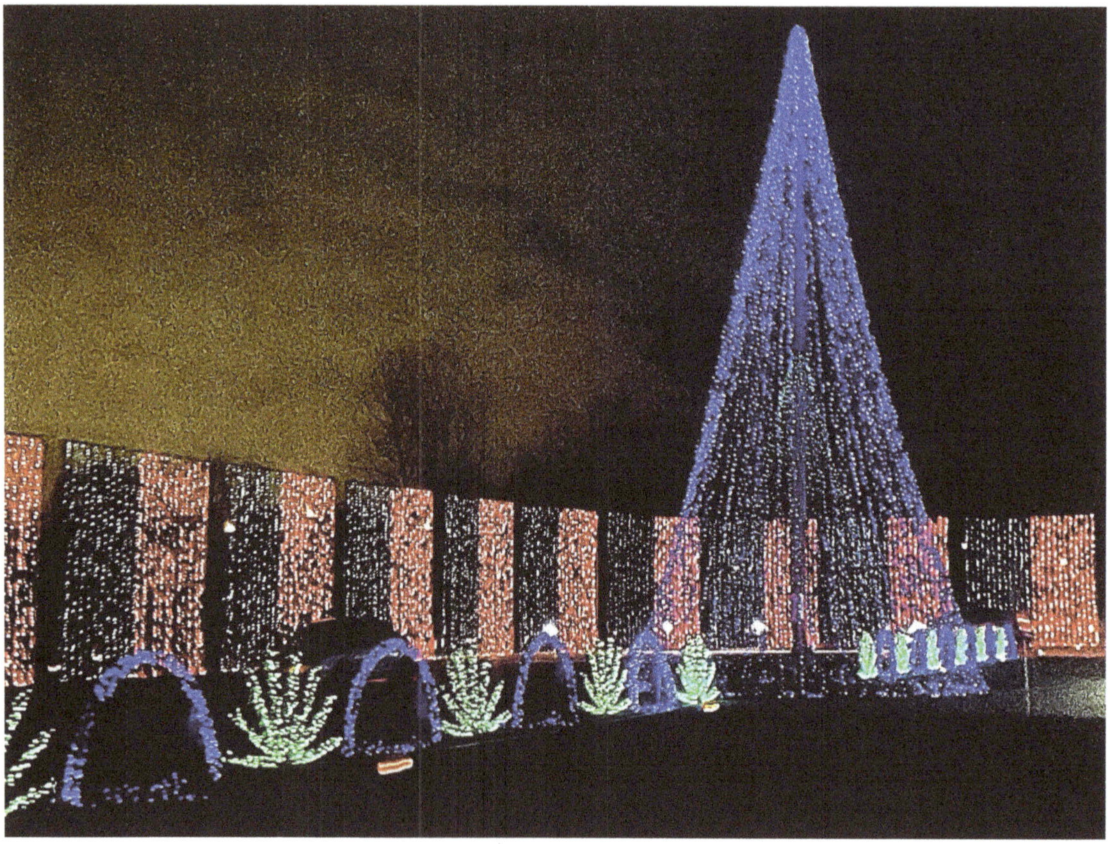

More Memories...

To Coney, with Love, Margie Hueneman

I have a lifetime of wonderful memories of Coney Island. However, my memories followed a different pathway than many Cincinnatians. I grew up on the north side of Cincinnati in the village of Glendale. Many of our celebrations, including end-of-year school outings and my dad's company picnics were scheduled at nearby LeSourdsville Lake and Fantasy Farm, but that doesn't mean we didn't get to experience Coney Island! We just needed to work a little harder!

As I was growing up, there was no I-275. A trip to Coney Island was an all-day event as the drive to Anderson Township and its magical resident named Coney Island could take up to an hour and a half. My mother would pack the picnic basket with homemade fried chicken, baked beans, and potato salad. They hustled my three sisters and myself into our 1962 Chevrolet station wagon and headed northeast. Once we arrived, the goosebumps would rise on my arms! The water fountain, the beautiful flowers, the endless array of rides were a little girl's dream come true! As we grew into our teens, our trips became an opportunity for a day with friends — one parent would drive us to Coney, and another would be in charge of the ride home. My favorite rides were definitely the Lost River and when thrills were in order — the Wild Mouse and the Shooting Star, of course!

As fate would have it, I married a resident of Anderson Township who grew up in Mt. Adams. He and his siblings would catch a bus near Mt. Adams for their trek to Coney Island. By this time, all of the memorable Coney rides had moved to their new location at Kings Island, but we still used the picnic grove and occasionally would see a band at Moonlite Gardens.

Our Coney resurgence began after we had our three children. If you live in Anderson Township and are looking for something fun to occupy your kids during the summer, you need look no further than that amazing establishment at the bottom of Sutton Road! This began many years of family memberships at Coney Island! We loved our summers at Coney Island! Our kids were friends with many other Coney members, including cousins. We packed lunches and spent so many days at Coney. As a special treat, we would order lunch from Sunlite Grill or snack on an ice cream or snow cone. By this time, rides had returned, and I can still close my eyes and see the smiling faces of my children as they rode the Python, the Scrambler, the Flying Bobs and their screaming faces as the floor dropped on the Super Round Up!

It is thanks to Coney that my kids learned to love water and how to swim. Two of my children had their first summer jobs at Coney Island. We had concerts and graduation parties at Moonlite Gardens, birthday parties and after-dark member parties at the pool, and work picnics in Parker's Grove.

So many memories — the water that never seemed to get warm. Watching my kids climb the high steps of the Silver Bullet and praying they didn't fall and then feeling the pride as they flew down the slide with no fear and without a care in the world. Seemingly hours spent at the Island as they jumped into my arms over and over again. What I would do to be able to have that experience again with my grandchildren.

And then there was the Coney rule. It was an unspoken rule that if there was an item on a chair, that chair was taken. Often, I wondered what new guests thought when they saw a large circle of unoccupied chairs with a random float or single flip-flop lying on the chair. But we knew. I remember for fun asking my thirty-five-year-old son who was home from Seattle in 2021, "Do you remember what the Coney rule is?" He replied, "Isn't it as long as you put something on the chair, it is reserved?"

As my children grew and went away to college, my visits to Coney evolved into sitting poolside with family and friends. I didn't even mind going solo with a book in hand because that is when I could appreciate the sounds of Coney: happy voices and giggling children, the splash of water, the sound of someone jumping off the diving board, cheers and clapping as a reluctant swimmer finally let go and slid down the Silver Bullet, the occasional lifeguard's whistle, followed by "No running!", and the background sounds of happy tunes playing on the intercom.

I never dreamed that there would be an end to Coney and how much it would hurt. It has been a part of my entire life and deeply interwoven into my memories. I certainly never expected that it would be treated as if it was nothing — not a historic site, not the largest recirculating pool in North America, not the 12th largest pool in the world, not a center of diversity of generations, cultures, and races, not an opportunity for children to learn to love water and learn to swim, not a center for neighboring children attending day camp to have someplace to have fun. All demolished into a pile of rubble in two days.

As we gathered to celebrate Easter, my daughter reminded me of her final visit to Coney last year when three generations of family rented a cabana and spent the day together. "I just wish I would have known it was the last time." I do too… I *really* do too.

To Coney, with Love, Ashlee Blevins

I held every company summer picnic party and all of my son's birthdays here. I just loved this place and everything it was. It was happiness, joy, history, community. All of it. I will forever miss it AND the years we intended to spend here but never got to. It felt like a rite of passage as a multi-generational Cincinnatian. I appreciate any effort in documenting this and keeping Coney alive.

To Coney, with Love, Cary Stevens

My family and I have been going to Coney Island for a little over 20 years. It all started when my kids were little. My mother-in-law was deathly afraid of water, but she wanted to ensure that my kids grew up knowing how to swim. She sent my 3 daughters to swim lessons when they were little. After my oldest had learned how to swim, she got our family a season pass.

My youngest daughter's first introduction to a pool was Coney Island. She hadn't even taken swim lessons anywhere yet, but at 6 months old we had her in the pool at Coney Island. Ironically, she spent the last 3 summers as a lifeguard there. She had gotten promoted all the way up to Head Guard.

We spent a lot of summers having a membership there. I would take the girls to swim and on "Daddy Days" my husband would take them to ride the rides and see the shows. We saw the famous Nick Wallenda, walk across the pool on a high wire. We were there during a storm once and we were sitting under the canopy by the concession stand and it was the only time in my life I saw lightning hit water. When my daughters got older, we got a membership to a pool closer to home, but we still went to Coney Island one day during the summer for what we called "Family Day".

My daughters are all adults now, but this past summer we had a mandatory "Family Day" at Coney Island. We met my daughter who was lifeguarding there and sadly, it was the very last day the pool would ever be open. The whole situation just makes me very sad! It is such a core memory for my family and my daughters as they were growing up and I can't believe that they will never be able to share it with their future families.

To Coney, with Love, Sandy Durkin

My family has loved Coney for years, and we have many special memories. One of my favorite memories is when we went to a concert at Riverbend. After the show was over, we walked through Coney to get to our car. My brother-in-law, Eric, who lives close by got us lost and we separated from our group. We walked back and forth a few times. We decided to take a shortcut and swing our legs around a fencepost to avoid falling into the lake. It was pretty dark, but we realized we ended up in Moonlite Gardens. We took advantage of the moment and did a quick, little spin on the dance floor. We finally made our way out of the ride area with the help of a few security guards. It was a special moment for us, a good laugh and a wonderful memory.

To Coney, with Love, Irene Murdock

I remember when I went to Coney Island when I was 4. I went with my dad, mom, grandma and my brother. I went on the Frog Jumper and the bumper carts. That was one of the best memories I had at Coney Island. I also went to Coney Island for Cincinnati Children's Walk for my brother. I remember every time we walked a mile or so, the rides would start to move until they turned on all the way. It was so magical. I had a lot of memories at Coney Island.

To Coney, with Love, Kim Coleman

My story of fun times at Coney Island began in the 1960s as a little girl. My dad's company picnic was always held there. My sisters, parents and I would swim in the pool. Then we headed to the park and walked under the giant Land of Oz statue to ride the rides. We looked forward to this day every summer.

In the 1970s, our family purchased Coney passes and we would enjoy the pool all summer long. I spent a lot of time there with my best friend, Nancy, and made new friends as well. My parents, sisters and I went swimming in the evenings after my dad got off work as well as our time there during the day. We met a family who lived in Hyde Park and had passes as well. Our families had such a great time when the pool wasn't so crowded. I remember the building where the lockers and showers were located. We would rent a locker for the summer where we would keep our clothes while we swam. The building was so hot because it wasn't air conditioned but it was a great shelter when it rained. My friends and I had fun in the area next to Kellogg Avenue where we played ping pong and shuffle board. On Labor Day, my family and I would spend the day at the pool for the last swim of the summer. A group of pass holders would dress up in costumes and parade around the pool. Sometimes the life guards would dive into the deep end from the tower high above the 10-foot diving board. We stayed till closing time. It was a bitter/sweet end to the summer.

In 1983, my daughter was born and in the '80s and '90s, we had fun swimming at Coney with family and friends. My cousin, who grew up in Cincinnati and swam with us often when we were younger, would always want to bring her children to Coney when they visited after moving to Chicago. My husband was a Cincinnati firefighter and their company picnic was at Coney for many years. As we did when I was a little girl, we swam with friends then enjoyed a picnic and games with other families in the picnic grove.

In the early 2000s, we still enjoyed going to Coney but not as often since my daughter was busy with college and work. Then Memorial Day weekend in 2008, she had a first date to a wedding at Moonlite Gardens with a man she had met through a friend. She married him in 2011 and they started their family in 2013. By 2015, we were back at Coney regularly in the summer, swimming and riding the rides until they were taken away. My three granddaughters have been taking swim lessons and enjoying the pool, all the slides and diving boards with family and friends. We had such fun summers!

It was a very sad day when we learned that Coney would be closing. I have so many fond memories that I will hold on to as this chapter in my life closes.

*You don't stop playing because you grow old.
You grow old because you stop playing.*
(My favorite sign at Coney)

To Coney, with Love, Karen Adams

I was around 5 years old, and my dad and I were driving to Coney. I loved it there. We were very close, and my dad got pulled over for passing the slow car in front of us. It was a no passing zone. I was SO afraid my dad would not want to still go to Coney. But I remember him saying, "This little ticket is not gonna ruin our day of fun," and it sure didn't.

We had a great time! My favorite ride was the haunted house. We stayed a couple hours riding rides, then before going to our car, we stood at the fence by River Downs (now it's Belterra) and watched the horses run. Great memories of my special time with my dad! Thank you, Coney Island.

To Coney, with Love, Kelly Seelbach

Our family's biggest memory (and annual tradition!) with Coney Island were the Christmas lights. We went every year since my girls were little and in diapers (they are now 9, 11, and 14). We had so much fun! They loved that they could unbuckle and look out the windows at all the lights and would compete to find the most elves! The music was so festive and they would sing and dance as they each popped in and out of the sun roof opening. The Coney lights have always been a Christmas tradition for us and we will forever cherish those memories.

> I loved Coney Island because it was so festive, and we got to go on the sunroof, and we went with our Grandma and Grandpa one year, and it was really fun when we got to look for the elves with them.
>
> From Alyssa Seelbach

> My favorite memeory from Coney Island was how we would go every Christmas and try to find all the elves and we would be jamming with the music and I would stick my head out the sunroof and sing along with music, wave to people, and embarrass myself by dancing crazily but I didn't care. —Ashlynn Seelbach !!

To Coney, with Love, Maureen Slattery Dewing

My parents, Mike and Marge Slattery and my family became annual members of Coney Island Pool when I was around 5 years old, which would have put that at about 1968. The big thrills were jumping off "Monkey Island," going down "the slide" (Silver Bullet) and jumping off the high dive. I still don't know if everyone called "the island" "Monkey Island" or if that was just a term of endearment that my dad bestowed on the island! It was common to spend much of the day there with my three brothers (Mark, Pat, and Mike) and mom, then return in the evening after dinner when Dad was home from work, until the pool closed. The evening visits became a lifelong favorite of mine. NO better way to end a day than to relax in the deep end of the pool as the day fell into night.

My dad was a very upstanding, strict man but never lost his zest for childlike play. He would encourage us 4 kids to swim around the rafts in the shallow region of the pool and find the rafts that were occupied by women. We were given the task of undoing the rubber stopper of the rafts so that the rafts would eventually have the same fate as the Titanic! We would get "extra points" if the women on the rafts appeared to be among the group that "never would get their hair wet" and better yet, if they looked like they just got their hair done. My dad would partially submerge in the water holding up his hands with how many points we kids had just earned as we swam around these rafts. Of course, this took great skill, to not "get caught." Every so often, we would get the "stink eye" by these women, understandably so!

My dad also had the habit of getting in the pool, close to Monkey Island, where all the "monkeys" would hang out, and submerge his head in the water and make a super loud walrus call by blowing air into the pool. It was so loud that my friends on occasion would say, "I knew you were here. I could hear your dad making his walrus call." (Like this was normal!!!)

As we started growing up, my eldest brother Mark (who was born in 1957) would spend hours playing basketball on the basketball court that used to be on "the Kellogg Ave" side of the pool property and often did not even get into the pool. I think maybe he was embarrassed with his fair skin as a teenager I would at times attempt to play "horse" or "pig" with him, which was a thrill, as he was seven years older than me. My twin older brothers Pat and Mike would spend hours tossing a tennis ball in the pool, playing "keep away." They were much better than I! Another game we would play was to attempt to catch a ball that would be thrown to us by one of the other family members, while going down the Silver Bullet slide. Upon catching the ball and being quickly emerged in the pool, it was very satisfying to hold up the ball, keeping it out of the water, as an act of victorious glory!

As a "middle schooler," I graduated to being able to go to the pool with friends, without parents, which was a rite of passage, in this area of town! Half the fun was riding down twisty, bumpy, Four Mile Rd. in Dad's Dodge van. Who needed a roller coaster?

Fast forward to adulthood and bringing my sons, Donovan and Brendan, to Coney with my husband Kendall. My kids took swim lessons at Coney and literally learned to swim, dive at Coney, along with thousands of others. The thrill of watching young kids becoming confident and comfortable in the water is one of the thrills of parenthood. My kids played the same games as we did as children. We also spent hours playing ping pong, going down the Zoom Flume, and playing in the deep end. Of course, we would see who could do a handstand in the water and see who could maintain the straightest legs for the longest period of time.

Every summer each son would get a day in which he could bring 4 or 5 friends for a day and they would enjoy the day going to the rides as well as the pool. Of course, a trip to Skyline and a soft serve ice cream was definitely part of the day!

Once the kids grew up, and moved out of town, my husband and I continued to be members. We loved just walking around the pool, appreciating the flowers, looking at the grand century old trees, and watching the kids have fun in the Typhoon Tower. We would swim laps and watch the clouds float by while listening to the softly played music was "my kind of therapy."

I loved sitting under the grand trees, just relaxing and reading a good book. After my parents died about 20 years ago, I had a memorial brick placed. It was close to the Silver Bullet slide. As I would walk my laps, I would make sure to make eye contact with this brick. I felt this was my way of continuing to share one of my "happy places" with my beloved parents who had first introduced me to this magical place. This property will remain a special sacred place to me for so many different reasons. Thank you, Coney Island. I will always love you and will truly miss you.

To Coney, with Love, Abby Mark

If I had to describe Coney Island in one word, it would be musical. Coney was not only literally musical to everyone, as you could hear music playing over the speakers and kids singing along every summer, but it was also music to anyone's ears who knew they were going to spend a day there. Certain songs that I hear now, instantly bring me back to my time spent at Coney, as I am sure it is the same for many others.

Coney Island created an insane amount of memories for so many people. For some, it was swimming in the pool over the many summers it was open or ordering an ice cream cone dipped in rainbow sprinkles. For me, I'll never forget waiting anxiously for my 15th birthday to be able to apply to work for Coney Island. For years, I thought I would be better off working in concessions or maybe even being a lifeguard, but when I applied, the only positions available were in the Grove working with company picnics and food. However, it never mattered to me where I worked because regardless, I would get to work side by side with my mom.

My mom, Katy Mark, worked in group sales for so many years, and I could never be prouder than to be able to say she's one of the people who is putting this book together. She was always an inspiration to me and everybody else she met.

Katy always had a smile on her face. Working with her is something that will stick with me forever and I would never have that any other way. Being in the Grove my first summer was such an experience. Being able to meet some of the kindest people I've ever met and getting to say I worked at Coney Island for my first job was genuinely a blessing.

Some of my best memories come from Coney Island whether it be having an ice ball fight or eating the most left-over hot dogs — *I'll forever hold that record.*

My second summer at Coney was the best summer of my life. Driving the golf carts around late at night and getting to be a lead in the Grove were some of my favorite moments. I had the time of my life getting to go to the B&B Riverboats tour nearing the end of that summer with my co-workers. I realized that I didn't need anything to be happy other than real friendships and a happy mindset.

I don't know how I ended up lucky enough to claim Coney Island as my first job but I did, and I wouldn't change that for the world. Not only was Coney my first job, but it was my safe space. Taking naps in my mom's office after a long shift and getting discounted ice cream from my friends at the stands made me feel so happy. I always enjoyed eating with my friends in the employee cafeteria, who some remember as the old LaRosa. I will never be able to justify the idea of tearing down Coney, but I am forever grateful of all the memories I was able to make.

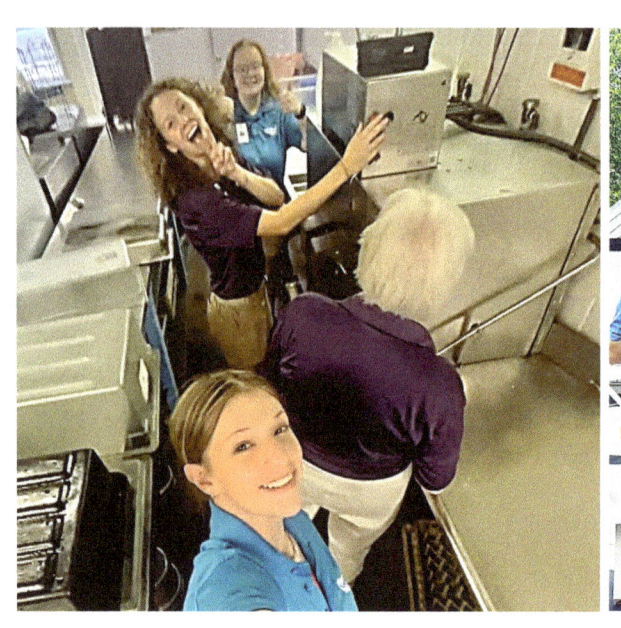

To Coney, with Love, Katy Mark

When walking into the Sunlite Pool at Coney, I remember always taking the time to appreciate the sounds and smells of Coney. Upon entering the pool area, I immediately could smell the coconut sun tan lotion, tasting the Kona Ice (pina colada and dragon blood was my fave), hearing the Sun Burners play their tropical music and feeling the cold water as I inched my way into the pool. I know my family took me to Coney as a toddler when we would come back to Cincinnati to visit family, but my first memories were when my NKU roommate, Theresa, and I would need a study break and go to Coney for a few hours to soak up some sun.

We would bring a raft... *yes, Coney was so cool that they allowed you to have rafts in the pool!* We would go in the middle of the pool, lay in the sun while holding on to the rope, so we didn't float away from each other and just talk for hours. It was so peaceful and relaxing no matter how busy it was and even if footballs were flying over our heads.

Many years later, when I worked for Cincinnati Parent Magazine, I was invited out for a media tour of Moonlite Gardens along with an announcement of the new Typhoon Tower at Sunlite Pool. A few weeks later, I thought of Coney and did a tour to use Moonlite Pavilion for our Cincinnati Parent KidsFest. It was such a huge success with a few thousand in attendance and everyone loved the location. I built a relationship with some awesome Coney employees and it wasn't long after that that I decided I missed working with those people and applied to work at Coney. I got the job in Group Sales and was officially a "full-timer".

There were very few of us that worked full time at Coney so it was pretty hard to get a position. At most, I think we had about 45 full-time employees in the beginning of 2017 and then would hire almost 1000 employees for each summer. In the end, we ended up with about 23 of us in 2023. Most of the full-timers started at the age of 15 or 16, working rides, games, lifeguards and stayed through the years being promoted over and over again. Tom Rhein would have celebrated his 40th work anniversary the season after Coney closed and most of the employees had been there for 20-30 years. I was a newbie with 7 years. Everyone had their job and was very good at it. We all also did many other things over top of our official job to keep the park and pool afloat. It was definitely a passion job for me and the best parts about it were the family of employees, the fun atmosphere, helping build memories for guests and the appreciation of history that we got to enjoy on a day-to-day basis. I'm so thankful that I was even a small speck of history for this incredible venue that started as an apple orchard and turned into a family friendly amusement park and the world's largest recirculating pool.

Even though I worked mostly in the picnic grove with company outings, I made sure to do my laps around the pool to enjoy and witness the moments we were helping create on a daily basis. I think one of my favorite memories was watching an older couple dance together in the shallow end of the pool. Another favorite memory was when there was a concert and I watched a young punk rock kid with a green Mohawk sitting on one end of a bench while an older gentleman with a bow tie and suspenders (waiting for his wife coming from the pool) on the other end just chatting about their day.

My job was to plan company picnics and then help execute them. It was so fun seeing their employees play sand volleyball, have corn hole tournaments, paddleboat races, and picnic on the delicious fried chicken, Montgomery Inn BBQ, burgers and hot dogs. I loved how the shelters gave homage and were named after the old popular rides like Land of OZ, Shooting Star, Wildcat, Cuddle Up, Teddy Bear and Lost River to name a few. My days always started with cleaning the shelters that were needed as well as the private parking lot entrance, getting corn hole bags out, putting the basketballs and volleyballs on the courts, getting company picnic names on the map for each shelter, double checking menus with catering staff, greeting the chairs for the companies coming and getting them any help they needed like banners hung, making sure the table covers got on, confirming face painters/balloon artists or any other extra fun coming in, overseeing the buffet line (we could get 1000 guests through the buffet lines in 16 minutes!) and just checking in with each picnic often to make sure their days were going smooth. We handled multiple company outings per day and they ran from 35 guests up to several thousand. Coney knew how to run the quintessential company picnic for large groups. It wasn't a normal day if I didn't put 20k-30k steps on my pedometer and that was even WITH my golf cart!

As the season winded down, I always hated saying goodbye to all of the seasonal employees, after getting to know them during the summer. It was a nice little break though when things calmed down so we could take a breath and prepare for the next summer. Usually during the off season, we would also deal with flooding. Some years it was just a scare and some years it was a LOT. During the spring after I came on board, we had the 2018 flood, which hit hard. Before it hit, I was told we needed to "bug out". I had no idea what that meant. I learned quickly that it meant I needed to completely empty my office. My job also usually included emptying coworkers' offices while they handled other tasks like moving big things up to the 2nd floor of Moonlite Gardens. Coney Island had handling floods down to a science. They knew when it hit every foot above flood stage where it would be flooding in the park. In 2018, the flood in my office was above my hips. As soon as the water crested and went back down, it was time for the full timers to be boated in (it literally was an Island) and we spent the next several days soaking up the water, using fire hoses to get mud off of walls/rides, disinfecting, and putting things back. I remember the President of Coney asking me if I've had my Tetanus shot and what size boots I wore. That was eye opening. It was these days that helped us all bond together even more seeing everyone work so hard to get the park and pool glistening again and open up in time, which we always did.

Working at Coney was special because it felt like a family. Probably because half of us WERE family. So many of us had kids, parents, siblings, spouses working there as well. If your family wanted to see you in the summer they had to visit or work at Coney. My kids basically grew up at Coney. In the off season, if they had a day off from school you could see them riding their bikes around the park or sleeping on a raft in my office. I taught my girls how to drive in the parking lot after hours on my golf cart. During the busy season, I would pay a friend $10 an hour to just be at the pool so my girls could hang out and have fun or sometimes I would walk by and see them "working" the games line.

My favorite time of year as an employee though was the time just leading up to opening, and then all of the summer. It just felt like a fresh breath of air as the "seasonals" came back. There was excitement in the air when I drove by the entrance seeing the regulars at the gates before we opened each day outside of their cars talking with each other. Coney Island is and will always be a special place. Thank you, Coney Island, for the memories you gave my family. We will never forget all that you gave us and so many others.

To Coney, with Love, Matt Suddendorf

Back in the summer of 1993, I had the opportunity to earn my Open Water SCUBA Certification as a young teenager. The course included several classroom sessions at the shop on Beechmont Avenue, but it also required 5 in-water sessions for practical skills training. The venue for these lessons was none other than Sunlite Pool! Having been a patron of Coney Island and Sunlite Pool for years (even across generations of my Cincinnati-based family), I felt an extreme amount of excitement during these SCUBA lessons. The lifeguards would close off the entire deep end of the pool for us, and the rowboat guard would slowly circle overhead while we were 10 feet underwater, making sure no one disturbed our lessons. A fascinating part of the experience was finding the myriad "treasures" that would settle to the bottom of the pool: money, toys, and other personal items were commonplace. It was a thrill to have this magnificent place all to ourselves, and a unique way to experience my beloved Sunlite Pool! I enjoyed the experience so much that I began working at the SCUBA shop during my high school summers (I'm a graduate of McNicholas HS). Part of my responsibilities was managing all of the gear for each student class, which included several more trips down to Sunlite during those dusky summer evenings. I will always cherish these memories and feel privileged to have had such a unique view of Coney that few other Cincinnati residents can claim to have had!

To Coney, with Love, Mary Beth Ganote

I started working at Coney in 1988 as a swim instructor under Sally Mills, teaching Water Aerobics and Intermediate lessons. Over the years, I also taught Red Cross Lifeguarding classes and did a Safety presentation for all the lessons which we held under the Skyline snack area. In 1999, I became the Swim Lesson director, taking over from Pam Fischer who continued to assist. Our biggest enrollment was in 2001 when we had 1,320 students and 102 instructors. Our last year of lessons in 2023 we had 434 students. We participated in the World's Largest Swim lesson for several years, which helps bring awareness to drowning prevention.

We had many instructors who taught for 25 years or longer and I put up a plaque in the office with their names. We set up our registration table in multiple locations around the pool before finally having a permanent pad of concrete poured close to the pool office. My office also had many locations throughout the years before finally taking up residence in an old ticket booth outside of the pool entrance. We were even able to have lessons the year of the pandemic, which was something many pools were afraid of doing!

Sunlite Pool was one of the best pools to teach, especially for beginning swimmers who could learn to float on their back or front but yet still have their hands close to the bottom. It could also be challenging because lessons took place while the pool was open so you had to deal with almost getting jumped on, and patrons making off with supplies. Our instructors suffered through many cold and rainy days but students showed up despite the weather. Over and over, I heard comments from parents that their kids learned more and made more progress than anywhere else they had gone. There was nothing like having a student who was afraid to get their feet off the bottom or to put their face in the water, and then, eventually, take off and swim on their own!

Both of my kids learned to swim here and were in the pool or on the rides constantly. Both of them got their first job here, one as a lifeguard and one working in the Season Pass department, and eventually, the Pool Office.

I was so fortunate to work with hundreds of dedicated instructors and support people who made our lessons program one of the best in the tri-state area. I would especially like to thank Sally Mills, Pam Fischer, Chris Haynes, Tina Weiss, Amanda Bonnell, Cathy McMahon, Cathy Kirstein, Nancy Wetterer, Coleen Vogelgesang, Steve Gerth, Dot Becker, Cindy Leen, Char Bledsoe, Cathy McDonough, Barb Miller, Terry Miller, Becky Monahan, Cindy Kohrs, Kathy Frazer, Laura Hatfield, Jodi Plessinger, Alison Gray, Jeanne Rasfeld, Paula Anstaett, Deb Price, Caryl Miller... plus countless others! Thanks to all the kids and swim teamers who volunteered as helpers. Coney = summer and now our summers will never be the same.

To Coney, with Love, Michelle Schultz

I loved how simple Coney Island was. It was affordable family fun that spanned many generations! I always loved going to my father's company picnics at Coney and years later, my own! The Christmas Nights of Lights were also a family favorite! It was such a wholesome, simple park that was affordable and just as fun as the big-name parks!

To Coney, with Love, Tim McMahon

I've been a member or a worker with you since 1972. I was 11 years old when my family joined Coney Island/Sunlite Pool and the memories are too abundant to put into words. We joined the swim team immediately and that put my life on a path that I believe, determined who I ultimately am. The long days and early mornings of swim team, jumping in your cold water and practicing for hours freezing as a 11-year-old. When practice was over, laying on your warm sun, drench deck to warm up again. The noise, the sounds and sights of swim meets both day and night. The thrills of the screams and the races and the friendships that were built have lasted a lifetime and still endure. As soon as Coney started a diving team, I joined it and never looked back. It gave me a new sport to fall in love with that took me from a summer diving league into high school and ultimately to Ohio University and diving in college. Learning new dives those first summers and feeling the sting of not getting them right are vivid.

Through my summers of swimming and diving at your wonderful pool, I met and befriended many of the lifeguards and at 18 started my guarding career with you. I got the job because of the Captain of the Guards, Bob Lowe, was a big fan of my diving. I learned from the older guards that were there for many years taught me what to look and listen for, and how to be a good guard. I got to be in one of the most iconic pictures of the guards as a 19-year-old lifeguard there and that picture lives in many people's homes and hearts. You gave me many friends in the four years of guarding there, who are still big parts of my life today, thank you. I met many wonderful old patrons and became good friends with them as well. Sadly, losing them over the 53 years of being a member with you. I met 2 old German gentlemen who played chess every day and taught several patrons to play the game, Carl and Paul. I remember coming home from college and working out on your boards and showing all of my friends the new dives that I had learned. I hope that I gave the crowds watching a small part of the thrill that I got from being able to live my summers in your pool.

That picture not only has a few my best friends who are still in my life, but it also has the girl that ultimately became my wife. We spent summers together in the rowboat, climbing up in each other's chairs to visit, during the day Nights at Coney parties were some of the best times of my life. We went on to have five children and all of them grew up swimming in the water and warming in the sun at your beautiful facility. Our oldest we took to you when he was just two years old so it's very easy to say that Coney Island and Sunlite Pool is in our blood. Two of our boys went on to lifeguard with you meeting some of their very good friends as well.

The memories of you are all around my home and life. I cherish them and visit them often and will never forget the gift that was Coney Island's Sunlite Pool.

Thank you, I will always miss you. Tim McMahon Lifeguard/Diving Coach 1979-1983

To Coney, with Love, Brandon W. Flickner

Growing up at Coney had some many wonderful memories for me. My most cherished were of my time on the swim team, the Coney Island Aquanauts. Early morning practices were made even better when we got to enjoy some of the pool's amenities without the crowds.

One special practice event was the "Greenie Meenie." From the deep end you do a 50 butterfly to the island, a 50-back stroke to the Silver Bullet, up and down we went, then a 50-breaststroke back to the island and finally a 50 freestyle to the deep end. The only problem with the Greenie Meenie was the slide. Often times, the bravest would go down headfirst. The craziest went down headfirst on their back. And a few adventuring souls would go grab a tray from the cafeteria (when Coney had one) and see how far they could skip across the water while sitting on the tray (10 yards was the max).

Also, many times after practice we would get Zoom Flume time. We broke every rule that was ever written. We blocked the water to go faster, we stopped and made massively long trains, and some of even surfed down the slide. The longest I remember was maybe 20 kids. And whoever was the last kid in the train always got some sort of concussion or bloody nose. But it was the 80s, we were tough.

Kids waiting in line outside the pool were staring at us like we the coolest kids ever — and we were. The swim team kids ruled the pool, why not rule the park. Around 1987 or so, several of us decided to skip practice and roam around Coney. We ended up down by the river. Some rowers had just put in for their morning practice. The rowers had left their shoes just sitting there on the shores of the Ohio river, just daring us to do something. So, we did. We tied all their shoes together. Twenty pairs of shoes tied together in various knots of all shapes and sizes. It was funny — so funny in fact that I still remember the day quite well.

Being on the Coney Island Swim Team meant far more to each of us than just being on a swim team. I had swum on many teams in my younger days, but none more memorable than Coney. From the frigid early morning practices to the Tuesday night swim meets, lifelong friendships got formed in that pool. Coney as we know it might be gone but nothing will erase the memories I have of our favorite pool.

To Coney, with Love, Amy Calo

Every year growing up, we spent our 4th of Julys at Coney Island with our big extended family. Had a big potluck in the picnic area, then went to the shows and rode the rides. My cousins and I loved the bumper boats and pedaling out to the middle of the lake. We would watch the fireworks from our cars before heading home. Such sweet memories! We loved hearing how our grandparents loved that place growing up too!

To Coney, with Love, Sarah Rogers

I was a lifeguard from 2006 to 2009 (just saying that makes me feel so old). On shift one day, a storm was coming so I tapped off to put my umbrella down. Just as I was doing that, the wind picked up and the umbrella and I went into the deep end Mary Poppins style. Safe to say Coney had some high durability umbrellas.

To Coney, with Love, Mindy Ellis

Coney holds a special place in our hearts for not only providing fun summer memories but it is where my husband and I got married 11 years ago. The night was magical! We took photos on the Ferris wheel, the merry-go-round and in front of Moonlite Gardens. Every time we pass by Coney, I have nothing but great feelings. Several years after our marriage we went back with our photographer and took photos with our children!

To Coney, with Love, Caleb Ebert

    This morning, at 2:59 am, I woke up. That happens sometimes, where my dumb brain decides I need to be awake for maybe half an hour in the middle of the night. But this time was different. Out of nowhere, I felt the tears come to my eyes, I felt the tightening of my throat, and I felt the long overdue rush of grief. I realized that, nearly five months after I heard the news, it had finally hit me. I would never go to Coney Island again.

My name is Caleb Ebert, and I'm sixteen years old. Sixteen summers spent with a season pass to Sunlite Water Adventures. Coney has never not been a part of my life, and maybe the reason it took so long to sink in was because of just that. The demolition started two weeks ago, and this weekend we drove by, and I saw the bulldozers and the big trucks and so much ugly grayness that the clouds decided to follow suit. Maybe that was what did it for me. I remember driving by and seeing the typhoon tower, standing strong and proud as always.

This morning, I thought of the typhoon tower. I thought of him crashing to the ground, snarling defiantly as he helplessly fell, and how great it would be if he could have his last hurrah. How I would love for him to spew water on his assailants, sending them scurrying backwards, crying in alarm. Maybe he would smile for once. But the bulldozers would come, the wrecking balls would rain, the cement trucks would pour, and the backhoes would do whatever backhoes do. These poor vehicles. They were designed to crush steel and cement, not dreams and memories. The blood of my childhood and many others is on their hands. But they were just doing their job.

I thought of the park in ruins. I thought of the blue walls on the side of the pool, whose hue and touch I know like the feel of my own hands. But I wouldn't climb up them anymore. I thought of the trees I would sit under, laughing with my family and watching my younger brother sink a jalapeno Cheeto into my dad's mouth from like fifteen feet. I wouldn't sit under them anymore. I thought of jumping up and touching the blue umbrellas, or just sitting under them and reading Percy Jackson and the Titan's Curse. Those umbrellas would no longer shade my pages or feel my hands anymore.

I thought of these and many other things. And above all, I thought of giant, broken slabs of cement upon the once smooth pool floor, the carnage of stone and steel, as if a bomb had gone off there. I know that is probably not what it looks like, but it doesn't matter what it looks like. I just want it to look like it did last summer.

I eventually fell back asleep, and woke up with my mood hardly improved. I felt like someone had died. I went downstairs, and I told my mom what had happened. She stood up from her red recliner chair and gave me a big hug, and she told me that it was natural to feel sad and that it was hard to lose Coney, she was special. And that's when I realized the extent of our loss. Coney was not a place. She was much, much more than that. A place doesn't make you wake up at three in the morning and cry. A place doesn't... doesn't... I can't find the words. A place doesn't leave you speechless, wondering how you can possibly put into words what it has meant to you. Hopefully, the tears will be enough.

So that is why I am writing this letter, not to the CFO of the music concert thingy, not to my fellow pool goers, but to Coney herself. My closest childhood friend. Because I realized that someone really had died.

I drove past you this weekend. You're not looking so good. I would tell you to stay strong, but I know there is not anything to be done. I wish I could hold your hand through this. How could they do this to you? How could they do this to us? I had no way of knowing that the last time I left your gates would truly be the last. I probably didn't even think about you twice. This morning, I woke up and cried, and I almost cried throughout the day as well. It finally hit me today that I would never see you again, and I thought I would write to you. I don't know what I'm going to say, but I'll figure it out. I don't feel very sad right now, but please don't be offended. I know that the grief will come in waves. Maybe another will hit me in the writing of this letter. I'll let you know at the end. I know it took a while for me to come around, but I'm here now, Coney.

I told some people at school about what happened this morning. About the loss. They were nice, but none of them really understood. How could they not cry, too? It is because they don't know you like I do, Coney. They don't love you like I do. But they got me through the day. I hold no grudges. How could they understand? One of my friends is gonna work at Kings Island this summer. If it'd make you feel better, I can get her fired. You've taken too much Kings Island slander over the years. Your roller coasters weren't as high, who needs a high roller coaster anyway? That's not what makes a place special.

Coney, I have so much to say. I can't imagine this is the only letter I will write to you. The memories will flow, the grief will come. Perhaps even the anger will come. The gratitude will come, of that, I am sure. I'll get there when I get there.

You are beautiful, Coney. Did you know that? Prettier than the prettiest person, with your sparkly blue water, as it rippled during the day, it was so shiny, but still and clear as the most beautiful piece of glass past eight pm. I wish I could do that. But your beauty is not intimidating, it is charming, inviting, and I wish I had appreciated it sooner. I wish other people would appreciate it too. If that CFO saw you full of laughing, smiling people, gleaming on a cloudless summer day, he would have moved to Antarctica once he thought about buying the property that you live on, so great would his shame be. This CFO character. I'm not mad at him. I don't care about him. Not at all. Perhaps the anger will come. But I don't hate him as might be expected. What a useless thing it would be, to hate someone while something so sad is happening. But we're people. We do useless things all the time.

We sang this stupid song "Count on me like one two three" or something for our sixth-grade graduation. I can't remember who it's by. Taylor Swift or Justin Beber. One of the two. I never liked that song, but for some reason, it's made me think of you today. It's made me emotional. Maybe Taylor or Justin knew that the song would take on a new meaning for us at some point in our lives. Maybe not. Speaking of music. I'm sorry Coney, but your taste in music is *terrible*. One time you played the same song like three times in one day. It wasn't even a good song. It's not that hard to put on some good music. But I'll probably miss that music someday. I'm beginning to already.

How can I put into words the feeling of the water rushing past me as I dive into the pool in the deep end? Coney, I have no idea how to express what you have meant to me. I hope that other people can love someone like I have loved you. I feel like every tear is a tribute. I could fill up your pool with tears and it wouldn't be enough. I can't tell you how I feel. Maybe in time. But for now, I hope you understand. You have meant more to me and more to many others than you can know. And I can't believe that I will never see you again. I have a vision of me, coming back to you after ten years. Feeling the rush of memories, feeling like a little boy again. Smelling the wonderful pool smell, feeling the burning cement on my feet, and feeling the smile creep onto my face that always creeps onto my face on opening day. And then diving into the pool. Splashing through the shallow end, running up the stairs of the twister, launching myself off the topmost diving board, shooting down the silver slide, cannon balling off this island, and screaming with joy as the Typhoon Tower spews his water on me. That will never happen. My kids, if I have them, will never know Coney Island.

But let me tell you a secret, Coney, dearest of friends. I am afraid. I am afraid that I can't do it. People say that something never really dies if it lives on through you, but what if you die in me, too? What if I forget? What if I forget? What if I can't do it? I can't honor you? What if I forget the feeling? The feeling? That Coney feeling, the one that words can't describe. How can anyone else know that there is no sun like Coney sun, no water like Coney water, no joy like Coney joy? Without you there to nourish me, to remind me every summer, will I forget? Will you fade? Will the memories, so bountiful and raw right now, become distant, faded, and bland? What would I do then, Coney? Help me. I can't let that happen. But it might. It might, because I will never see you again. And that scares me. I don't want to lose you Coney. Please don't let me. Please don't. I will do my best. But I am picturing myself sitting in some sad, square little pool with annoying lifeguards and annoying people. Is the magic of Coney gone forever? Gone forever. Gone.

But my family and I will do our best. My wonderful, beautiful family. Don't worry Coney, they are worthy. They love you just as much as I do. But of course, you know this. You know this better than anyone. We love you so much. Our family owes so, so much to you, and we will never forget that, even if the magic slips away. We love you so much. We have so many memories with you, it is unspeakable. Someday in the future, one of us will be like "remember when…" and then we will reminisce. We will grieve. We will love. That is how we will keep you alive. And if we fail, I hope you know right now that I love you.

This letter has turned out longer than I thought, I hope you don't mind. I am very proud of it, and I hear that they are making a book of letters to you, written by people who love you just like me. I hope mine makes the cut. I would dearly love to have contributed to a book with such a noble cause. I'll send mine in. Would you like that? I'll show it to some other people too. Maybe it will help them understand. But I have more to say. I have memories to share. I am going to share them so that in five, ten, fifty years, I can read them, and maybe, for a brief moment, experience the magic again. But I'll put them on another document. If I show this letter to people, and they see that it's like twenty frickin' pages, it might be a little daunting. These memories can be between me and you. Special. *Special*. Yes, I'll do that.

Goodbye, Coney. Goodbye forever, but I will talk to you soon. This is not the last you will hear from me. I hope that with this letter, this raw and unfiltered and unedited letter, that it will help me repay you, just a tiny bit. But then, you were never one for debts. You were never greedy. Just happy. And because of that, we were happy too. You demanded nothing of us. Sure, the pass cost money, but the money was nothing. Maybe because my grandma paid for it and not me. But I would pay any sum for another summer with you. Because now I understand, I understand what I didn't understand before. I love you Coney, with all my heart. And I wish there was a world where it wasn't too late.

Love,
Caleb Ebert and the Ebert clan. A Coney family if there ever was one, through and through.

To Coney, with Love, Sherry A. Andrews

Four generations of my family have been going to Coney Island. My parents rode the Island Queen up the river to dance at Moonlite Gardens. I spent my summers there as a teenager swimming and riding the rides. For the past 18 plus years, I've taken my niece there with her kids. Her youngest was still in diapers! We've had season passes every year since then. Now the kids are in college. We also went to the balloon glows, fall festivals, fireworks over Lake Como, hayrides, and company picnics. We would even go on cloudy days just to ride the rides. I'm so glad to have shared all these fun times with them, memories that will last a lifetime. Coney will always hold a special place near and dear to my heart.

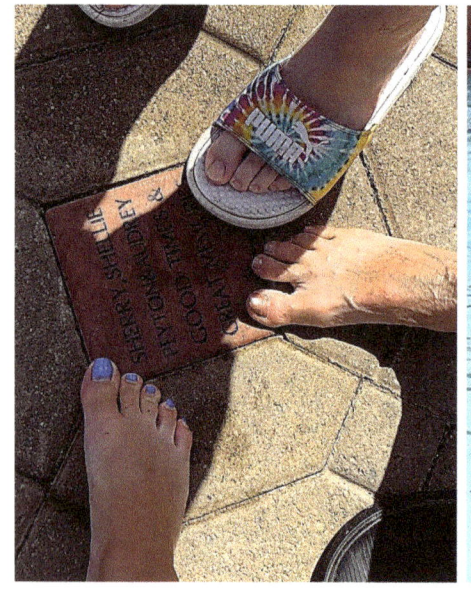

To Coney, with Love, Jennifer Barnhart

I started going to Coney Island before I was in the first grade. It was absolutely love at first sight for me. I remember pulling through the front gate and seeing that amazing, huge shade tree. My family would sit on the same bench in the deep end for years. My all-time favorite lifeguard was Ruthie Moon. She was also my swim team coach at Coney, and again when I got to high school. She wasn't the only lifeguard working at Anderson HS when I was there. Greg Schrand (also a former Coney lifeguard) was my freshman year English teacher. Ruthie even showed me the ropes when I became a lifeguard at Coney.

When I was a guard, I met a family of 3 little boys, Christopher, Roger and Mattie, and their mom, Sandy — *the Schaefer family*. I babysat the boys, and now those little boys are grown up with their own kids, and we are still in each other's lives. I remember the splinters from the Zoom Flume, the wedgies from the Zip, the smell of the Race Track in the mornings for swim team.

I'll forever be grateful for Coney Island. I learned more than I'll ever be able to express from all the years there. I've made lifelong friends that I would never have if I hadn't had Coney. I can honestly say, Coney Island will live in my heart for as long as I'm around. So much gratitude and thanks to every person and every experience that I've taken away from a lifetime spent at the world's largest recirculating pool.

To Coney, with Love, Shannon Platen

My mom raised us a single mom. We never had money for vacations but every summer she made sure we got to go to Coney Island at least once. It's one if my favorite childhood memories. I'm now 33 years old, and when I had my daughter 4 years ago Coney was the first place we ever took her swimming.

To Coney, with Love, Kelly Sharkey Biesenbender

My brother, Jerry Sharkey, and I grew up at Coney Island. We went every day with our babysitter, Mrs. Casey, along with her kids, and a few other strays. We loved the Silver Bullet and the Island. I can remember my dad throwing us up in the air as high as he could. When I got older, my mom and I would lay on our rafts and listen to the classical music on Sunday mornings. All of our kids and our grandkids enjoyed Coney Island as well. We have so many great memories at Coney. It will be deeply missed!

To Coney, with Love, Stephanie Downs

In the 1950s, my dad was in his late teens growing up in Cincinnati, and took a date to Coney Island, Sunlite Pool. He had enough money to pay for them both to get in and only a little bit left over money for his date. When they got in the water, she saw people floating on rafts and thought that looked very relaxing and fun. My dad wanted to impress her. He took what money he had left went in the Island gift shop and had exactly enough money left to purchase her a raft. They went to the air pumps on the wall to fill it up and "the big man on campus" got overly air zealous and filled it too full and the opposite end burst open and blew out. He was so embarrassed, and he had no more money to buy another one. A couple years later he met my mom, they married and had me. I learned to swim at Coney at the age of two. I grew up to be a competitive swimmer, a synchronized swimmer, lifeguard and pool manager. My dad ended up going into the savings and loan business. He didn't want to be without ever again! He always would say, "Be careful, bring plenty of cash, and watch out for those air pumps!"

To Coney, with Love, Lisa Turner Deavy

I grew up swimming at Coney! We had a family pass in the '70s. When my daughter needed to learn to swim, we got passes again in 2005 and she learned to swim from the classes. My favorite memories will always be of the children! Generations of us jumping off the island, sliding down the Silver Bullet, diving off the side and off the board in the deep end! Generations climbed up the ladder of the Silver Bullet, me as a kid, my daughter, and now my great nieces and great nephews! As the sign on the wall says, we grow old because we stop playing! Summer meant swimming at Coney Sunlite Pool.

To Coney, with Love, Marisa Deavy

I enjoyed so many fun summers and memories swimming with family and friends!

To Coney, with Love, Karin Dietz Smith

Coney will always have a dear place in my heart. Aside from the many stories from my grandmother and mother and their joyous times there as kids, I personally have so many memories. I remember as a small child riding the Zoom Flume and Zip! The Zip was pretty intense for a little kiddo! When I got to my pre-teen years, I was allowed to go to Coney alone with my friends and we had a blast! I remember diving off the diving board, riding the rides and eating Skyline like we were on top of the world.

In 1998, I got my first job in the picnic grove. Man, was it hot and those uniforms did not help! I advanced in my employment and somehow got the job handing out the tennis rackets in the air-conditioned sports shed. That was very ideal in summer! As I became an adult and started my own family, I tried to get a yearly pass each year and take my children. They loved it so much. It was the main event of our summers! I also got my husband hooked on swimming in the deep end. Coney was truly part of my life since birth and will be forever missed.

To Coney, with Love, Terri Knabb

My mother Evelyn Navaro Knabb told me she went there with her friends to swim when she was younger and had a great time. My dad, Robert Knabb, told me his dad William Knabb was an Anderson Township Solar Hills Ranger and worked at Coney one summer directing for parking. My mom and dad took my siblings and me there for a day, for picnics, swimming, once we rode the boat down to Coney. When I had my daughter, I started bringing her there for swimming, the rides, picnics, the Appalachian fest, Summerfair, balloon glow, fireworks, and Christmas lights. I went to a class reunion there, and a couple of dances. My daughter and I loved Coney and all our memories that were made there. Thank you, Coney. We will always love you.

To Coney, with Love, Nancy Hilton Flaherty Denman

There are so many memories I cherish of Coney, as our family had a membership for several years in the 1960s and early '70s when I was a kid. One of my favorites was a day when we observed another family walking alongside the shallow end of the pool where several floats were lined up with beautiful women laying on them; the Playboy Bunnies would come and sun, much to the pleasure of the dads. The dad of the family walking by was focused on the line-up of floats rather than where he was going, so consequently he stumbled over the edge of the pool fell in!

To Coney, with Love, Ella Vance

Growing up, my aunt had a pool and we would spend all summer at her house. When she had to move, we lost our pool. We decided to try Coney as a family. Every Wednesday from the week Coney opened till the week it closed, we would go from open to close. There would be at least 15 of us every week. My cousins and I made friends at Coney that we talk to regularly now. Coney brought us closer together than ever. We enjoyed our tradition of going to the pool!

To Coney, with Love, Frannie Arlinghaus

Coney was the entirety of my childhood, and that starts before I can even remember. Summer 2004, Memorial Day Weekend, was the first time I ever went to Coney. Memorial Day Weekend 2004, I happened to only be about 1-month-old, my mom has shown me pictures of me as a baby, sitting under the first blue umbrella by the Island Shop laying on towels in the shade and dipping my feet into the water. Ever since that weekend, my summers consisted of being at Coney 4-5 days a week and as a young child, I felt like I owned the place. Coney felt like the only place I could go off with my little sister and our friends for hours at a time and they didn't have to worry about us. We would beg our parents and grandma to let us stay late in the evening to help with swim lessons or watch the swim meets, which we then joined as well. I had a Coney pass from 2006 to 2020. However, in 2020, I became a lifeguard for Coney, my first real job and it only felt right that it was at Coney. I hold the memories that Coney gave me near and dear to my heart. Coney thank you for a wonderful childhood and the best first job I could've had. With all my love, Frannie

To Coney, with Love, Janette Yauch

As a full-time working mom, I don't get to spend as much time with my children as I'd like. Thankfully, I am blessed with a mom who loves children, and who decided to dedicate her retirement years to loving and caring for my children. And, the reason she was willing to give up her relaxing life in northern Ohio for us? Coney Island. My mom, Rita, LOVED Coney Island. She loved the pool, she loved the diving boards, she loved the rides, she loved Moonlite Gardens, she loved it all. And who did that benefit? My girls. My girls, Mackenzie and Natalie, grew up at Coney Island. They rode the rides, they took swimming lesson — both sessions, even on those cold June days. Since they were babies, they dove off the diving board, my 5-year-old LOVED the high dive. They putt-putted, they ate shaved ice and even got stung a few times, they did it all, and they loved it all. They bonded with their grandmother in a way that couldn't have been achieved anywhere else in the world. And we owe that bond to Coney Island. Life really won't be the same without it and we have a Sunlite Pool sized hole in our hearts because of it.

To Coney, with Love, Lynn Herman

We didn't have much money growing up so it was once a year that we were able to go to Coney. I think that made it extra special. My uncle worked at the gas and electric company and they had their yearly picnic at Coney. We would meet at the picnic ground where they would have "picnic" type games for the kids with prizes. It was such fun and we would be there with our cousins, which doubled the fun. Each child would receive a strip of ride tickets. Now comes the best part, the 4 older cousins, which I was one of, were allowed to go ride the big rides on our own. I was probably 9. I'm pretty sure we ran from ride to ride. I remember waiting several turns just to ride in the first seat of the Shooting Star. We were having so much fun. We didn't even want to stop to eat. We didn't want to any carry prizes, so we would wait until the end of the day before having someone guess our weight and ages. I was small for my age and was always able to pick a prize. One of the 4 older boys was good at basketball and would win stuffed animals for us. I wish I'd saved those memorabilia. It never occurred to me that such a magical place would ever not exist. I'm sad it's gone but my memories still bring me joy.

To Coney, with Love, Susy Walltets Hisch

I lifeguarded with the legendary Bob Lowe during the summers of 1979 through 1986. He even gave me dating advice. He was a precious, precious human being. Being the Captain of the Guards, he never let his guard down when he was in his chair. If a patron in his assigned swimming area was struggling, he didn't hold back! He blew that long whistle and dove right in and made his own saves!

He wasn't just there sitting in that chair to look like a stud. He WAS a stud! He was and still is a legend. I am so blessed to have been at the pool during a portion of his long (50 years) tenure there.

I have so many great memories but it would require my own book if I tried to share it all. The VERY best years of my life were spent as a lifeguard, swim team coach and swimming instructor at Coney Island Sunlite Pool. I'm pretty sure I was on the inaugural CIA — Coney Island Aquanauts swim team! I may have started in year #2 of that amazingness. I still have my red and white striped swim team suit with the zipper! The crazy tan lines we got from those swim suits! Best days EVERRRRRRR.

So many great friendships made with the different lifeguards. Everyone really loved going to work. My first real job was on the Zoom Flume water slide when I turned 15. This was the first major step to getting moved over to the "Big Pool" because you could not be part of that greatness until you turned 16.

I remember hide and seek in the old locker rooms, way over crowded Pepsi Days, finding lots of money on the bottom of the deep end of the pool on Mondays at early morning swim team practice after a crowded weekend, swimming 50 yards underwater from the deep end to the island, parachutists landing on the island, tower divers doing amazing dives, mucking out tons of mud after multiple big floods, swim meets after dark, rainy days sitting in the guard chair fully dressed, pool employee after-hours parties, Jim Mahan, Vic Nolting and John Ellison as pool managers and the memories just flow and flow. So do my tears. I am heartbroken that it's gone.

To Coney, with Love, Diana Carey

I am 76 years old and still have fond memories of old Coney. Every summer my parents took our family and friends to the park. These visits were our vacations. Mother rode the Shooting Star with me. Dad's job was to take me on the Lost River ride. I loved the ride until I heard the clinking of the chain pulling the boat up the ramp. Then I wanted to get off... but down we went. At the end of our visit, us kids always bought a helium balloon and an all-day lollipop. I now collect souvenirs from Coney. I would love to find something like a sign from the demolishing of the park.

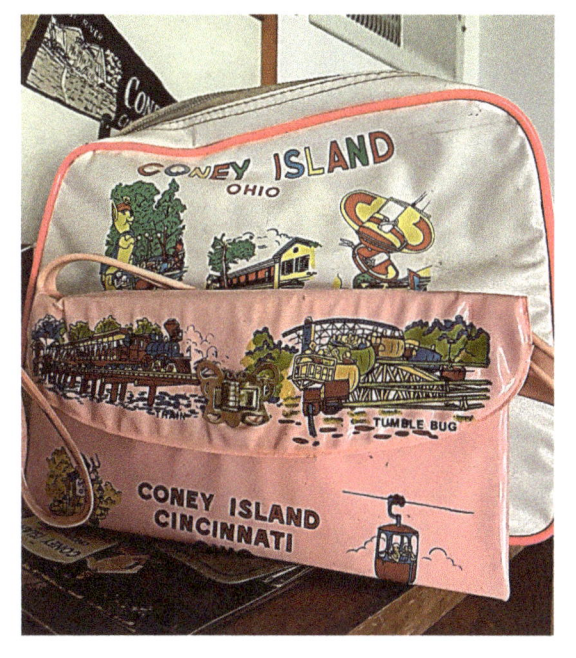

To Coney, with Love, Monica Lippmeier

During the summer months, my brother and I would be dropped off for swim lessons every morning during the week. We would spend the entire day there at the pool. The awesome lifeguards were always a treat especially being able to ride in the small boat in the deep end from side to side, enjoying our time at Coney pool daily. Pictures included from Old Coney Amusement park August 1968 and August 1969.

To Coney, with Love, Katie Lewis

I grew up going to Coney Island in the '90s. I have memories of being in the backseat of the car in my swimsuit, listening to "Crush" by Jennifer Paige, while eating out of my Orange Crush bubblegum jug and seeing the entrance to Coney. I have memories of going to the park for my grandma's work event and winning a cheerleader Kewpie doll that was glued to my side for two years until I lost it one fateful day. I remember being terrified to go down the Silver Bullet and having a lifeguard talk me through it while a line of people behind me cheered me on (and were probably tired of waiting, too).

When I got older, I wanted my son Damon to have those kinds of memories. We made it a tradition to go to Sunlite Pool every summer. We would sit by the shallow end, and I would get sunburned while I watched him play. I created new memories as an adult. Sitting with him in the shade while we ate Montgomery Inn pulled pork sandwiches.

I also remember almost losing my swim top because I misjudged the water pressure at Typhoon Tower (whoops). I loved walking down the ramp to the pool with my son and feeling the ice-cold water on a 97° day and riding with him on the Python for his first (and last) coaster.

I can still see him exhausted in the backseat, after a summer day well-spent, that he could tell his teachers about on his first day back to school. Our tradition may have gone away, but the photos and memories will last forever. Coney definitely had it, and I'm grateful we got to come out and play for so many years.

To Coney, with Love, Scot Howell

One summer my family was attending Coney Island with another long-time family of friends. It was a perfect June day; summer had just begun. My friend Pat and I were playing on the diving boards at the deep end. These boards were great. You could make some fun leaps into the pool, turn and swim back to the ladder near the board you just jumped from. After a few fun jumps, my friend Pat decided he was going to make a nice long dive out into the center of the deep side then paddle over to the concrete island that began the area leading to shallower water. I didn't plan on that. In fact, I was a little hesitant. I'm an average swimmer, nothing great, and I don't tend to push boundaries.

With Pat's vocal encouragement, I made a decent head-first dive. I didn't go far, but my form was good. I began paddling out towards him and the island. While taking a breath, I also took in a mouthful of water. That was NOT planned or expected. A huge gulp of water surprised me enough that I stopped paddling, instead pausing to tread water while I caught my breath. When that didn't happen as quickly as I wanted, my treading became more animated and my breathing became more labored. It was quickly obvious I had become panicked. At that time a lifeguard was stationed in a small paddle boat for just such occasions. He quickly was at my side along with a lifeguard who made a dive off their guard's chair. I was quickly pulled to the side with a float. They made me lay down and calm my breathing. Of course, ALL of Coney Island had to stop and get a view of the situation. I was offered some advice to stay in the shallower water, perhaps practice my swim strokes over there. Pat and I laughed it off.

I never truly thought I was drowning, but my actions were quite dramatic. I have since told my friends and family of the time I was saved at Sunlite Pool. I add some flair to the story to keep people thinking, *is he saying he was baptized?!?* Starting a story by saying "I went to Sunlite Pool and got SAVED!" always gets a raised eyebrow and makes me laugh about the time I should've just turned to head back to the ladder instead of going the distance.

To Coney, with Love, Vicky Brock

As a young girl, we went once a year, and my favorite "ride" was the trip through the haunted house. I can still see the skeletons that were all sitting around a dining room table covered in cobwebs. Loved it! And who didn't love The Scrambler, throwing you all the way to the corner of the seat. Once an adult, I worked for the same Cincinnati company for 37 years. Many of our company picnics were held at Coney. I missed one in 2003 due to our first of nine grandchildren being born. Twelve years later, my husband and I took all six of our granddaughters to the picnic. That is the photo you see below. Three of those granddaughters have now graduated from high school.

To Coney, with Love, Frank Prudent

My grandfather, George N. Prudent, was a union carpenter at Coney. He only had four fingers on one hand as one was lost in an accident at work. He always said it was buried behind the Shooting Star.

My father eventually became a licensed chief engineer on steamboats including the Delta Queen and the Belle of Louisville. Before he got out of high school, he started working on the second Island Queen (IQ) as a striker in the engine room. A striker, sometimes called a cub engineer kept the engines clean, well oiled. He would climb into the cooled down boilers to clean out the week's accumulated caked on river sediments and would grease the paddlewheel bearings. Strikers also would handle the engines under the careful eye of the licensed engineers. The IQ had two paddle wheels with one on each side located in the wheelhouses. A striker's job would take them with a can of grease out into the wheelhouses to climb the steel a-frame up to the bearing where the paddlewheel's shaft rested about 25 feet above the water. Dad went out into the wheelhouse to grease the bearing and while out there someone in the engine room opened the engine's throttle and the wheel began to roll giving my father a river water shower he didn't ask for. Below is my Chief Engineer father and mom at Tall Stacks.

To Coney, with Love, Diane Roesener Pursinger

I went to Coney Island Amusement Park as a child. Being from a family of 6 kids, the trips to Coney were a special treat. On really special occasions, our parents would buy us a string bracelet to be able to ride as many rides as we wanted. Oh, the joy!

I began working at Coney Island at age 15. The first year I worked the front gate and collected parking money or waved members through. The "regulars" would get a little peeved if you didn't remember them and wave them through quickly enough!

After that first year, I worked in the Administration Building, first handling memberships then I moved into the cash room. The years before Riverbend was built were tame and I'd get off work by 9pm. Once Riverbend came into play, quitting time was usually midnight to 2 am, depending on the concert and beer consumption! I loved working there and looked forward to each of my 10 seasons. So many friendships were made and my boss, Linda Layton, was just about the nicest person I ever met.

My favorite memories of working at Coney were the employee parties — planned or spontaneous! Every so often, a group of employees would meet around the pool after closing and a tapped, but not empty, keg from the picnic grove would make its way to the gathering. Trains of 10-20 or more people would go down the Zoom Flume. Somehow, no one was hurt, at least not badly enough to stop the fun! Swimming in Sunlite Pool at night with just a handful of others was a treat!

I met my husband at Coney, and we took our children there many times when they were little.

Strolling the grounds during Summerfair, Appalachian Festival, when my employer hosted company picnics, and before Riverbend concerts always brought back so many memories. I never thought there would be a time when Coney Island didn't exist. It's heartbreaking.

To Coney, with Love, Diane Leah Burns-Levitt

My cousin was diagnosed with terminal lung cancer. Knowing each month was her bringing her closer to the end of her life, she was looking forward to celebrating her final Christmas with her family and friends. In early December, we decided to take her to Coney Island's Nights of Lights. I had been there many times in the past, but my cousin hadn't. The lines could be incredibly long, zigzagging through the parking lot and all the way out onto Kellogg Avenue — sometimes an hour or more to get into the show.

It didn't matter to her because we were all so happy just being together, the night was perfect, we even opened the car windows, and my cousin relished every moment. We had so much fun laughing and reminiscing and when we finally got into the start of the light show we were all so excited we couldn't imagine it getting any better! Of course it got better. This was Coney's Christmas Night of Lights! Every year it changed up a bit, but the old standards stayed, like the singing Christmas trees and the light tunnel and the music was always fantastic. I'll never forget singing along to the songs and my cousin's joy as we all soaked in the lights and counted the elves together. There were eight. That night was hands down the BEST time I'd ever spent at Coney. I'm so grateful to Coney for hosting their amazing light shows every year in the 'off season' and to be able to bring my cousin for her first and last time.

With a terminal diagnosis, although painful and heartbreaking, you are blessed to be able to say goodbye to your loved ones. I think what hurt many of us when Coney Island closed is that there really wasn't any closure. We didn't get a chance to say goodbye before we lost it. We didn't know that the last time we went to Coney would be the last time we went to Coney.

To Coney, with Love, Julianne Ritter

Our family of 12 enjoyed the summers at Coney. Much fun always! And my parents also, as teenagers, with sand under their feet!

To Coney, with Love, Lori Fulton Brookbank

It is hard to pick a favorite memory but the feeling of excitement I'd get every time driving to Coney, even as an adult, took me right back to my younger years. Coney Island was like a living person to me. I loved her dearly and always will. I knew how special she was and never had one doubt in my mind that everyone felt the same as me. Her beauty and uniqueness kept her in a class of her own. That is where Coney Island will always remain. My family will never forget our special days spent with her.

To Coney, with Love, Connie Hadley

When I was in 5th grade, my teacher gave a few of us an opportunity to go to Coney Island. I had never been there before, and I was so excited to go. When we got there, I wanted to ride the Scrambler but the only other person that wanted to ride it was a boy named Teddy, who I was not a fan of. We got on the ride, and little did I know that the inside person (me) would slide into the outside person (Teddy) every time it spun! I was mortified that I had to sit that close to him and couldn't wait to get off the ride.

To Coney, with Love, Malina Hensley

Ah, Coney Island! From the moment we got off the highway exit, it was happiness. Every summer we would go for the wave pool and the Pepsi Python. That coaster was the first one I ever rode as a child, and it instilled my love for the adrenaline rush that comes from rollercoasters. My dad used to make us wait a little longer so we could ride in the very front row. He said, "You get to see everything as it was meant to be experienced with no distractions. It's the best seat in the house."

Now that I have my own kids who have a hunger for the adrenaline rush like I did, will also 'wait a little longer' to experience the 'best seat in the house.' I'm just sad that it won't be on the ride that made me the enthusiast that I am today.

To Coney, with Love, Teresa (Terri) Lynn Diebel

"Memories and Milestones"
"The Diebel and Noble Families"

Thus read the caption on our memorial brick. Those two words, "memories" and "milestones", sum it all up. From first swim lessons to first jobs to first performances, it all happened at Coney Island.

Growing up in Anderson Township, Coney Island was right in our own backyard, so to speak. We went there as kids and often frequented Sunlite Pool. We witnessed the changes through the years and were even in attendance on Coney Island's last day before moving to Kings Island. Incidentally, my first summer job was at Kings Island during its inaugural season, the Summer of 1972. So, it goes without saying that, like so many others, our own children grew up with Sunlite Pool and Old Coney being a huge part of their childhood.

As adults, my sister, Missy Noble, and I started going regularly to Sunlite Pool in the summer of 1991 after our youngest sons, Nick and Scott, were born. We rented a locker in which we kept a port-a-crib. We'd arrive early each morning, choose our favorite spot under an umbrella and set up for the day, with babies in tow. Our older children enjoyed the vastness of the pool, the thrill of the slides, and faced their fears on the high diving boards! All of our children, seven in total between my sister and I, took swim lessons at Sunlite Pool each summer, and for four of them, Coney even provided their first summer job experience. Bobby Noble worked the games line from 2003 to 2005 and even did a stint in the pool gift shop. Nick Noble, Keri Noble, and Scott Diebel all followed suit in 2004, working the games line for a number of years, nine in fact for Scott. Nick and Scott both even moved into management roles. Keri went on to perform in the live shows during the summers of 2006 and 2007. She remembers a music through the decades show, a kids' magic forest show, and an Americana themed show. Keri was a dancer and singer in those shows, which provided her first paid performances! Her picture was even included in many of the promotional materials, including the infamous refillable souvenir cup! Keri actually went on to perform on Holland America cruise line and has since gone on to become cruise director with MSC Cruises. But it was Coney that provided her first gig as a paid performer.

In more recent years, my sister and I enjoyed taking our grandchildren to Sunlite Pool. We were saddened when the rides and games were removed, and like so many others, devastated by the news of Sunlite Pool's closing. But we have many "memories" to cherish, and we are thankful for the "milestones" achieved. Goodbye Coney, we'll remember you fondly!

To Coney, with Love, Melinda Holt

In the summer of 1996, I was thankfully able to have that summer off work and spend it with my two kids. They were 14 and 11. Sunlite Pool was so affordable that the kids and I spent almost every day there just soaking up the sun and enjoying the water. I, of course, got the worst sunburn ever but still would not trade my memories for the world. Sunlite Pool had so many things and areas for everyone to enjoy. My kids loved it and still mention it to this day. It was a great time for the three of us.

To Coney, with Love, Carolyn Hudson

Our family joined in 1976 and were members until 1980. Our three 3 children learned to swim there. My husband was US Marine. We moved away in 1980 but when we returned for a summer on leave in 1982, we got a family pass and came almost every day for our 30-day leave! We loved the fireworks in the summer and the balloon glow was always a favorite, as well as miniature golf and gaining the courage to jump off that 10-foot diving board. Our youngest child tried to imitate Olympic divers and scared us half to death! During those early years, the best memories were staying late enough for our husbands to come after work. We'd stay, have dinner, and close the pool.

To Coney, with Love, Catherine Ampfer

My memories of Coney Island and Sunlite Pool are from the modern era. I have two sons and when they were 8 and 10, we wanted to join our local swim club but found there was a 10 year wait list for new members. A friend knew that I was a swimmer and recommended that I teach swim lessons at Sunlite Pool. At that time the swim instructors could either receive monetary payment or a family pass. I contacted Mary Beth Ganote at Coney and joined the team of Coney swim instructors. This was one of the best decisions I could have made for my family.

I did not grow up in Cincinnati, so I was not familiar with Sunlite Pool. I was amazed at the sheer size of the place. There could be a thousand people there and the pool did not feel crowded. I soon settled into teaching the Gold swim lessons, which is for kids who were comfortable going under water and were ready to learn the basic arm and leg movements of freestyle swimming. I taught swim lessons from 2011 until 2019 and loved every minute of it. My favorite part of swim lessons was seeing the thrill in a child's eyes when he or she learns to move through the water in the basic freestyle or jumping off the diving board for the first time. Coney's swim lessons were unique in that they were progressive with 4 consecutive days of instruction for 4 weeks. This allowed the swim instructor to build on each skill a little every day. They say repetition is the best way to learn a new skill and I saw this in action with the Coney swim lessons. Coney taught thousands of kids how to swim and was an invaluable resource to our community. My own children graduated from the Coney swim lesson program, and both are certified lifeguards, with my oldest working two years as a Coney guard.

My best memories of Coney were the regular summer days. We would get up early, grab all of our pool gear and head to Sunlite, arriving before the official opening to get set up for the day's swim lessons. I remember there would always be a line of people at the entrance waiting to get in, then when the gates opened the clear blue water would beckon with "Coney Has It!" playing through the speakers. After lessons we would gather on the pool deck for a quick picnic lunch and then I would retire to my float, holding on to the rope near the guard chair to keep from drifting away while the boys would spend their afternoon swimming, going on the slides, playing ping pong or riding the rides in the park. These days were magical in their simplicity. I feel so blessed that my kids grew up spending their summers at Sunlite Pool and Coney Island.

Sunlite Pool was always clear, cool, and refreshing. I would joke that Sunlite Pool water was cold, colder or coldest. I believe this is because the water was drawn from an artesian well which maintained a steady cool temperature. On hot July and August days nothing felt better.

In later years, my husband and I enjoyed relaxing afternoons at Sunlite after a long day at work. The beautiful sunsets over the pool — the "Golden Hour" between 7:00 and 8:00 — was the perfect way to end the day.

"Sunday Fundays with the Sunburners" was the highlight of the week. Sunlite Pool was my happy summer place. I never for a minute thought that it would be taken away. I figured that almost 100 years of existence guaranteed its importance in the community and protected it from destruction. I was wrong. I worked with the Save Coney Islanders group to save the pool but to no avail. We needed a hero, a person with clout and money to swoop in and save this Cincinnati treasure. Unfortunately, no one came to our rescue. Our beautiful blue oasis on Kellogg Avenue is now a pile of dust. My heart will forever be broken over the loss of this place that held so many wonderful memories for me and my family.

One of my favorite things to do after a stressful week would be to float in the deep end, staring at the blue sky and letting all of the anxieties of the world slip away. I never want to forget that feeling, so I wrote a poem about it:

Floating in the Deep End

The anchor of anxiety
drags heavy behind me.
I take a breath and jump
into the deep.
The cool water rushes around me
the solid ground is gone.
My feet lightly lift,
the water is alive,
flowing, moving, holding me.
The sun kisses my face,
I float, my worries drift away.
I am free.
I shut my eyes and dream,
This must be
what heaven feels like.

To Coney, with Love, Barbara Thornton

I spent most of my time on the diving boards (my favorite being the 5 ft board by the Captain of the Guards chair, Bob Lowe!) I was approached by a young man (approximately my age) who was doing back flips, and he asked me to show him how to do an inward. I said yes, if he would teach me how to do the backflip. I had been too afraid to do flips!

I had been able to get do a flip without smacking the board, then he did one and went straight up, flipped and came straight down and hit the edge of the board with his chin. The lifeguard helped him out and I walked with them both to the first aid station. He lost a tooth and while the aid person turned their back he grabbed my hand, put his tooth in my hand and grabbed a pen and paper and asked for my number. I gave it to him, and we dated for over six months.

Ironically, Bob Lowe used to tell me that if I had gotten any closer to the board, I would have lost my suit!

To Coney, with Love, Missy Rappoport and Family

Paul:

A group of us met on a Friday evening in August of 1962 playing miniature golf. We planned on getting together the following evening at Coney Island because there was a lot to do there. Early in the evening, we decided to have a group photo taken with the western tavern setting background.

Part way through the evening, we changed dates, feeling we were more compatible, but also knowing that we would never see each other again. As pairs we went riding in the pedal boats on Lake Como. We thought we were going to be spending time on Lake Como, and somehow, we tipped and ended up IN Lake Como. This has been a great comical family memory throughout the years. I would like to claim that I was a hero and saved her from drowning, but in reality, the water wasn't even waist deep. We have had a lot of laughs with this throughout the years. August 18, 1962, was our official first date.

We couldn't foresee the future at that time, and here we are getting ready to celebrate our 60th wedding anniversary on June 27, 2024.

Coney Island has been a magnet for generations of our family throughout the years. I remember stories of my parents spending a lot of time at Moonlite Gardens with their friends.

Fran:

I have fond memories of my parents taking me and my friends to Moonlite Gardens. Such nice memories!

I worked for Gibson Greeting Cards, and we had our softball games at Coney Island ball fields.

My dad would have his annual company picnic at Coney Island. After we were married, we would take our 3 children (Missy, Kristine and Doug) through the years as they were growing up. It was an event that we all looked forward to every year. We had 3 generations all spending the day together having a great time!

As my children grew up and eventually had children of their own, we all would go to Coney Island together.

Missy (oldest child):

I remember taking my son, Josh, when he was a year old to Coney. The best times were when my parents, my sister, and my brother would all go together. When Josh was about 5 years old, he and I moved to Anderson. We got season passes to Coney every year. It was so nice being 10 minutes away!

Josh's first job was at Coney Island. He would work there every summer and met some great people while working there. He eventually worked his way up to a manager position.

Coney Island has been an extremely strong part of our family for generations. We are sad to see it go, but we are left with endless great memories.

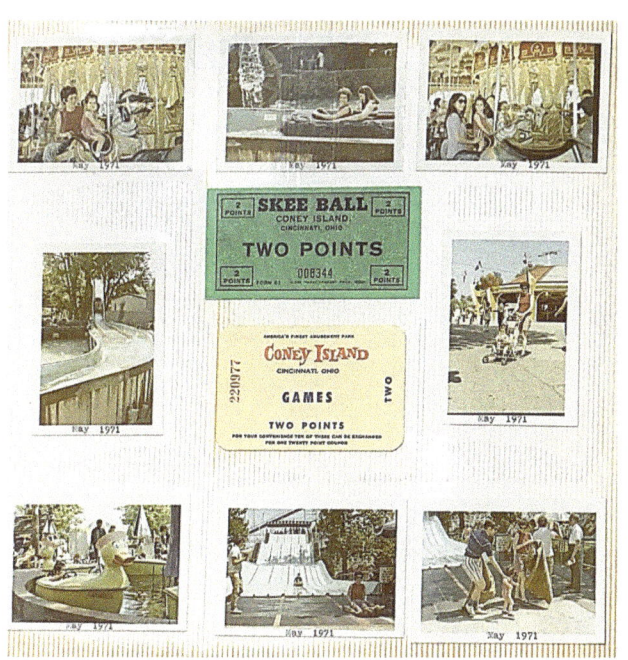

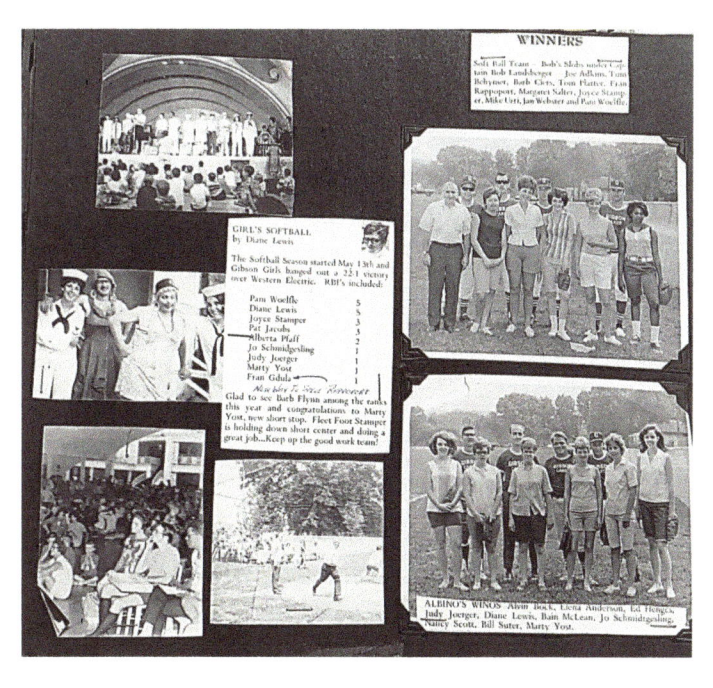

To Coney, with Love, Tom Hughes

When someone asks me what was the best job I ever had, there is no hesitancy when I tell them it was driving the Litter Gitter at Coney Island during the summer of 1970. I did have other jobs within the refreshment division at Coney — selling slices of watermelon, drawing beer — but the Litter Gitter was the best. This was basically a dump truck on the back of gasoline-fueled golf cart. It also had a manual transmission, which was how I learned to drive a stick shift and use a clutch. My responsibility was to drive around the park, emptying all of the trash cans into the back of the cart and then dumping the load into a full-sized garbage truck.

While not the most glamorous of jobs, as long as I kept the trash cans emptied, management was satisfied. It also allowed me to take my breaks along the riverside. Sitting there, in the Litter Gitter, watching the barges go by was the highlight of my day. For someone who grew up in Cincinnati and heard the stories of my parents and their friends going to Coney on the Island Queen, it provided quiet time to reflect on what they might have witnessed.

Payday was a great day, especially for a teenager who looked forward to getting paid. We really weren't paid with a check — Coney paid us with a voucher. On the outside of the Administration Building was a line of windows, probably 12 in all, behind which were cashiers. We presented our vouchers and received cash. How great it was to go home with the bills and change jingling in our pockets.

I worked for many local and international corporations since those summers in the early 70s, even at one point owning my own company, but no job compared to the time I spent driving the Litter Gitter at Coney Island.

To Coney, with Love, Joyce Prince

Coming from the west side of town, we knew we were close to Coney Island (paradise) when we rode over the 'singing' bridge on Kellogg Avenue. Extended family members made the trip; the women packed all kinds of delicious food for our dinner and put it in the shelter area; most of the adults went to the races at River Downs; and the rest of us had a mini vacation at the Sunlite Pool. There was a large building with big lockers which could be used as dressing rooms; and we quickly got ready for our swimming adventure.

Originally, there was sand in the large grassy area near the entrance, and you had to go through sprinklers from the 'beach' to the pool. We loved the huge slide in the shallow end of the pool; and many lifeguards, including one in a rowboat, protected swimmers in the deep end. There were 3-foot and 5-foot diving boards, plus a 10-foot board that extended way higher for special diving exhibitions. On Sunday afternoons, Bob Braun televised a 'pool party' which featured divers showing off their skills from the 10-foot board.

After swimming, the women pinned up their hair until it dried, and then we got dressed and headed for Lake Como to meet the others for our picnic feast. Afterward, all of us kids took off to ride everything we could for the rest of the night. The Shooting Star and Wildcat roller coasters were breathtaking; and we liked the Lost River boat ride which went through a dark tunnel before zooming down a steep hill at the end of the ride. We rode the Cuddle Up, the Dodge 'ems, the Whip and the Tumble Bug; and some went on the airplanes, but I liked the Roter, which spun so fast that you stuck to the wall when the floor dropped out.

The gigantic Ferris wheel was very popular; and you could see the over entire park, all lit up, when you were at the top. The huge, ornate Merry-Go-Round was fantastic — cheerful music played as the beautiful horses went up and down, and round and round. People enjoyed paddling canoes out onto Lake Como; and others rode live horses around a track located down by the Ohio river. The Land of Oz featured kiddie rides such as the Teddy Bear roller coaster, and little hand-wheeled carts that zipped along a track.

There was a great big Fun House that had moving and slanted floors and funny mirrors. One upstairs area of the house was out in the open, sort of like a bridge with a railing on the side; and those nearby in the park could watch people walk through that section. Gusts of air periodically shot up from the floor of the bridge as they crossed over. Most of the women wore skirts or dresses in those days; and they'd scream when the blasts of air "poofed" their skirts, as in a Marilyn Monroe picture.

There were all kinds of games of skill where you could win prizes, and guys who would guess your weight or age. The Penny Arcade offered movie star cards and a mechanical fortune teller lady in a glass box.

Many more rides and games were located throughout the park; and the grounds were immaculate, and decorated with sculptured bushes, a large flower clock, and lovely, brightly colored flower arrangements everywhere.

On Friday and Saturday nights, big bands and popular performers appeared at the Moonlite Gardens dance pavilion. Couples, all dressed up for a romantic evening, enjoyed the music and glided under the stars on a smooth-as-silk dance floor. When the band took breaks, those fancy guys and gals headed for a fling on Coney's rides, too. We dreamed of joining their ranks in the years to come; and my husband and I went there on our first date.

Coney Island was kind of a magical place for us; it had just about everything you could ever wish for in an amusement park.

To Coney, with Love, William Kemner

I am 83 but I have fond memories of Coney Island. When I was 7, my Aunt Clara would take me on the riverboat from downtown to the park. It was a great anticipation walking up the hill from the river into the park. There were so many rides including two roller coasters, the boat ride through the tunnel, the bumper cars, the Ferris wheel, flying gliders, and all the games along the arcade. Of course, the pool was fantastic and very busy. After dark we would watch the fireworks across the lake not to mention the rowboats on the lake during the day.

When I was older in high school the big thing was to see the concerts in Moonlite Gardens. My first concert was the Champs with their big hit Tequila. Coney was everything you could want in those days completely on par with the Kings Island of today. Many years later, I visited the park when my company held its annual picnic there. All the rides and games were gone, but it was very nice to relive the memories there.

I also had become a musician in a band and we once had a gig for a wedding held at Moonlite Gardens. That was an unbelievable experience playing on the same stage where I had watched the biggest stars of the day some 30 years earlier.

To Coney, with Love, Annette Harrison

I started working at Coney Island the summer of 1993 as a seasonal in the housekeeping department. I worked 3 summers there as a seasonal then joined the full-time staff January of 1996. This place became a loving coworker family with wonderful friends. My husband, Ron was the electrician at Coney Island too. He worked there for 30 years putting in a lot of electric for many different things in the park and the pool. Our daughter Lisa was only 4 years old when she would come to work with us and spend all day interacting with everyone. Later on, she worked at Coney Island in several departments. Our son Bryan worked a couple summer seasons in the maintenance department.

Through the years working at Coney Island, I have learned a lot from being an employee working under a manager to moving up the ladder to managing the housekeeping department. I loved Coney Island.

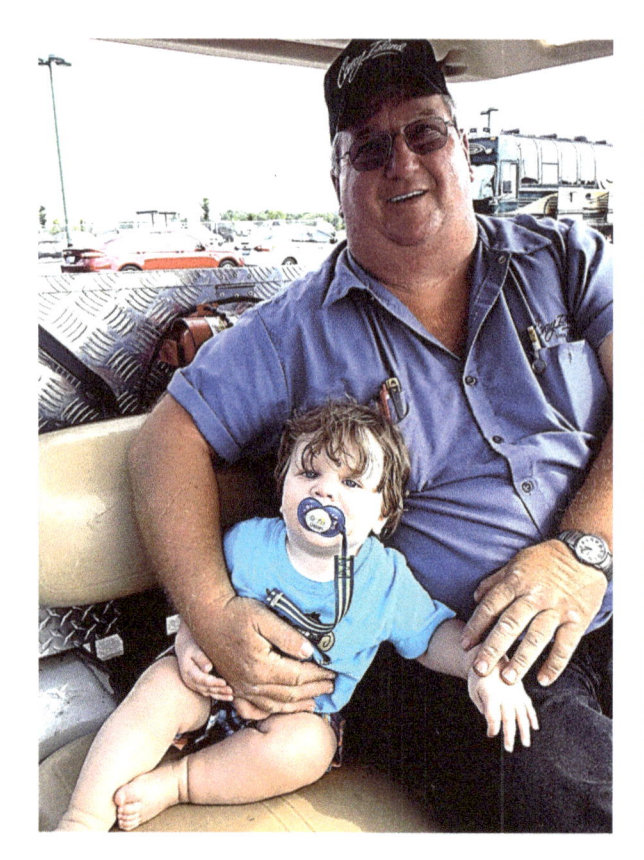

To Coney, with Love, Eleanor Miles (as told to Linda Mason)

PART ONE: Eleanor's Story

Sometime back, one of our Coney Island members (Donna K) mentioned that her good friend, Eleanor had worked at Coney during the 1940s and had some good stories to share. I wanted to hear these stories so Donna along with Eleanor's daughter helped me arrange an interview with Eleanor who will be 93 in August. The day of the interview I arrived at the assisted living facility where Eleanor is living and the first thing I saw upon entering the lobby was a large painted wall mural of Cincinnati's Island Queen and the river entrance to Coney Island. Eleanor's daughter met me in the lobby and escorted me to her mother's room. Eleanor is delightful and she was as anxious and happy to share her stories as I was to hear them.

Eleanor grew up in Anderson Township living at the corner of Sutton and Four Mile with her parents and 7 siblings. She attended school at Anderson. It was school work that led her to get a job at Coney Island. She needed 25cents to purchase paper to do her school work and upon asking her father for the money, his reply was "Go get a job".

So, that's just what she did! At age 15 she got a job at Coney Island; the year was 1944. Many a time she would walk to work and if it was late at night her mother would drive down and pick her up in the family car. She worked as a ticket taker on the Lost River and The Shooting Star.

She worked 12 hours a day, 6 days a week, a total of 72 hours and at the end of the week she got $23 for her week's worth of work, roughly 32 cents an hour.

Each payday when she got home, she would take a little money out for herself, but the rest she gave to her mother so her mother could pay bills and buy food for the family. For 72 hours a week she worked in the wooden ticket boxes, it was hot and the hours long. There were no bathroom breaks for employees, you just had to wait till the next person came to take your place in the ticket box. On days that rain would temporarily close the rides, employees were allowed to wait in the cafeteria where they were given free water and ice tea to drink.

Eleanor met her husband, Truman Miles at Coney. One day Truman insisted she come ride with him on the Lost River Ride and that's where he stole his first kiss.

Truman worked at Coney too, as did Eleanor's cousin, Bill Corcoran, who helped build The Shooting Star.

In May of 1947, Mrs. Lucille Clemons fell off the Shooting Star and later died of her injuries. Eleanor was working that day. They shut down the ride immediately and employees searched for Lucille.

It was Eleanor's husband, Truman who found Lucille. Visible blood seen on one of the ride's posts led him to the body lying on the ground. Eleanor said, the sight of Lucille's condition made Truman sick to his stomach. Lucille Clemons would later pass from her injuries. *Eleanor believed Lucille's husband had pushed her out of the roller coaster on purpose to possibly sue the park for her death.

They did check the ride and found it to be safe (of course we all know now seat belts would have kept passengers in their seats).

Eleanor shared some more joyful memories of her and her girlfriends enjoying dancing at Moonlite Gardens on their nights off. No matter how late it was that they decided to leave, she'd call her mother to come get her and her friends. They would pile into the car, some having to sit on the floor so they would all fit. Up Sutton they drove and once home, her friends lived close enough to walk to their houses.

Eleanor worked at Coney Island from 1944 to 1948, leaving as she was about to have her first child.

At the time of this interview, the interviewer, Linda Mason, couldn't find any newspaper stories that confirmed the park's rumors of this particular death.

PART TWO: Eleanor's Story

While visiting with Eleanor and her daughter, her daughter said, "Oh, you have to talk with my uncle, Chuck." She pulled out her phone and soon we had Chuck on speaker phone to join in on the conversation.

You see, Eleanor wasn't the only one in her family working at Coney Island. In 1944, at the age of 9 (yes, NINE), her younger brother, Chuck, also worked at Coney.

He worked in the games section of the park or as he referred to it, Suckers Alley! He was a "Hawker." The word Hawker, referred to a "vendor of merchandise", or in this case, a Hawker of prizes.

Chuck worked the fishing pond, where customers (suckers as he called them) spent their hard-earned money at a chance to pull a fish out of the pond, which may have had a big prize number on it. The prizes he said were cheap little prizes. Chuck also worked the milk bottle game. Like his sister, Chuck shares an August birthday with Eleanor and he will turn 87 this year.

While we didn't talk about how much money he made or how many hours he worked, he shared with me that he was working towards buying a horse/pony.

As luck would have it, it was getting too expensive to keep the live pony rides at Coney, and the park decided to sell them off. At the age of 14 or 15 Chuck purchased one of the horses. He didn't recall what he had paid for it, but once purchased he rode that horse all the way out to Bethel, Ohio to keep it at a friend's house. I didn't ask him how he got home or how long he kept the horse. But none the less he worked hard and purchased that horse.

Back at home, Eleanor and Chuck's brother, Leo had returned home from service. He had been shot in the leg and honorably discharged. If you recall from part one of this story, Eleanor would give her mother almost all of her weekly pay check to help pay the family bills. Leo now that he was home, he needed drinking money for when he went out with his buddies.

Eleanor's mother handed to Leo the week's pay that Eleanor had given her. Eleanor was not happy about that one bit and said it was the last time she shared her weekly earnings with her mother.

PART THREE: Eleanor's Story
The death of Lucille Clemons, May 1947

As you learned in part one of Eleanor's story, Eleanor shared being at the park the day Lucille Clemons fell off the Shooting Star and it was Eleanor's husband, Truman who found Lucille's body. The sight made him sick to his stomach. Lucille was alive with multiple skull fractures and broken fingers. She was taken by private ambulance to General Hospital, where she would die the following morning.

Eleanor told me that on the day that Lucille fell out of the Shooting Star, two park patrons had overheard a very disturbing conversation between two men. The men were plotting to push a woman out of the roller coaster for the purpose of making some money by suing Coney Island. The park patrons went to the park office, and a written report was taken, although they didn't see the faces of men they had overheard talking.

In the late 1960s, the story of a woman grabbing for her hat and falling out of the Shooting Star, was still being circulated. According to Lucille Clemons husband, Arthur, his wife was not wearing a hat on the ride the day she fell out. **Yet some 20 years later, the "hat story" was still being told.

**After another attempt to find articles or court documents to the effect that Arthur had pushed his wife out or that he tried to sue the park, none could be found.

In June of 1945, Arthur was charged with grand larceny for stealing $300.00 from a women's apartment and in August of that same year, he was caught up in a Speak Easy raid.

In 1951, Arthur got into an altercation with three men and died from his injuries in the same General Hospital as Lucille had died, back in 1947. The three men were charged in his murder.

Be it a push or a fall, the story of Lucille's death is one that was kept alive by park employees and patrons for years to come. Her death was tragic and may have led to seatbelts, lap bars, and safer amusement rides of today.

Skee Ball cost 5 cents and offered prizes. (Coney Island Inc.)

To Coney, with Love, Linda Ferrell-Brooksbank

Coney was my "home away from home." I felt safe, happy, and relaxed there. Over many summer days that spanned several years, I raised my two youngest kids at Sunlite Pool and Coney Island. They both took swim lessons there as well. My oldest daughter's first job was as a ride's operator for Coney Island Amusement Park. The following summer, she became a lifeguard for Sunlite Pool.

I have great memories of our family time at Coney Island (both rides and pool). I wanted to keep making more memories there for many years to come. I am so sad that my favorite place is gone.

I miss the sounds: popular music playing over the speakers; water splashing while kids are playing; adults socializing; lifeguards blowing an occasional whistle to remind someone to "walk." I miss the smells: chlorinated water, sunscreen, the green grass, LaRosa's pizza, and burgers from the grill all filling the hot, summer air. I miss the sights: friendly faces of strangers and bodies of all types;

familiar faces of people I knew because I always ran into friends or acquaintances; the sign by the deep end that read, "You don't stop playing because you grow old. You grow old because you stop playing."

To Coney, with Love, Becky Murphy

I remember going to Coney as a young child on Kroger Day. My grandparents would buy the Kroger tickets at 5 cents each. My grandma would buy 20 for each of the six grandchildren. I remember at age 6 trying to calculate my tickets to the number each ride cost versus was it really worth it to give up my coveted tickets. I knew once they were gone there would be no more.

I so wanted to drive the Turnpike like my older brothers, but I wasn't tall enough. I recall it was 7 tickets. I had to decide if it was worth it to be a passenger with my youngest brother, he was 2 years older than me. I gave in to my excitement and parted with 7 of my tickets. And I loved every minute of driving out around the lake.

Then I was off to the Lost River. I liked the idea of the boat sliding down at the end. I decided that if I did this ride, I'd have just enough left to ride the Whip. So that's what I did. I didn't think about the ride being a ride for others to kiss in the dark. And I was surprised by my neighbors in the boat with me. Back then you could ride the rides unaccompanied if you met any of the park's requirements for the ride.

Wee..., down the boat slide, onto the Whip. I waited in line and when turned loose I ran to an empty car and climbed inside. I had to scoot over for another lady and child. Oh my, I was thrown into my car mates and giggled every time it whipped me around and it happened many times to the other child, too.

I remember the funny mirrors outside the Whip. They made you look distorted. One made you look short and stout and the other tall and thin. Another giggly memory.

We had eaten dinner before we went so most of us met up with grandparents and we shared some cotton candy. First time for me and it was so good. The texture of it disintegrating in my mouth leaving only the sweetness it was such an exciting sensation, that I couldn't wait for the next bite. But I only took my share, unlike my older brothers. Grandma had to scold them.

That was my first trip to Coney and I'll never forget it as I approach age 70. I am so happy to have saved some old souvenirs!

To Coney, with Love, Jesse T. Wilson (AKA "J.T.")

What did Coney Island mean to me?

As I sit down for the third or fourth or fifteenth time to write this, I still struggle with that question. Not because I have trouble finding the words, but more because I have trouble expressing the enormity of Coney's meaning to me.

Coney was the job that I got when I turned sixteen. I was painfully shy. Through eleven summer seasons I slowly and painfully became less introverted. I was recognized for my talents and gradually got promoted, eventually to Pool Office Manager. At that point, I could hire for my department, something that I very much enjoyed doing.

When a new computer system was put in at the pool gates, I was tasked with its implementation. I was just out of college, armed with a history degree and no real interest in computers, but here I was, in charge of my own little network. I had to look up the meaning of 'network.' I felt that there was no way that I could do what had been asked of me. After some sleepless nights, I decided that because my bosses believed in me, I might as well start believing in myself. The point-of-sale system eventually lasted for over twenty years, and was in use until the end of Coney's existence.

When I was finally hired full-time in June of 2003, I was extremely excited. I had grown to love the people that I worked with and the public that I served. The sense of community and the sense of belonging during the summer months especially were things that I craved. I cherish the relationships that I formed at Coney. Relationships with peers, relationships with staff, relationships with all the many people that visited Sunlite Pool throughout the decades.

One of the very last members of my staff called the people of Coney Island a "displaced community." I have pondered that thought over the months since December 2023 when the closing was announced, and every time I think of it, the phrase seems more apt. Perhaps it would be best to think of the community as being sent out into the world to share bits and pieces of the joy that Coney Island brought to us.

As long as the stories persist, Coney will never truly be gone. As long as people are around who remember it, Sunlite Pool will live on.

The memories are all that's left now. At least they are happy ones.

"Smile! It's Coney and you love(d) it!"

To Coney, with Love, Rachel Collins

My mom took me to Coney and told me about how much going to Coney meant to her as a kid. She was the oldest of 6 and it was a treat. Then I took my daughter there and told her about her grandma going there. We always enjoyed the laid-back nostalgic feeling of the rides and the pool. It was a lot of fun for our family over the years!

To Coney, with Love, Chuck Fitzpatrick

I had the pleasure of being a lifeguard with Bob Lowe, Captain of the Guards, at Coney Sunlite Pool. Let me start by saying that I enjoyed working with Bob and learned a lot from him as a lifeguard at the Pool in the mid-60s. He was the icon of Sunlite Pool. He was a great teacher and always knew even when the pool was packed, when someone was getting into trouble and would alert us.

He was a serious lifeguard, but he also had his humorous side, especially with the new guys. As part of our training, the new guys had to learn how to clean the bottom of the pool in the deep end by the diving boards. The equipment consisted of a heavy diving helmet with an air hose that was fed air by a compressor up top. After you had been down there for a while, Bob would place some real smelly stuff in a bucket and place it by the air intake for the compressor for you to get air under the water. It took your breath away and you had to remove the heavy helmet and race to the top for air. Everyone would be waiting for you to surface and would laugh themselves silly. You couldn't help but start laughing, too. The bad part was you had to go back down, with the bucket removed, and finish the job.

Another training event was getting confidence with the rowboat that patrolled the deep end. On a day when the pool was practically empty, he would wait until you were out in the middle of the deep end with the boat and get the other guys to distract your attention as he swam to the back of the boat and would push the boat plug out of the boat. Eventually, the boat would get harder to row and start sinking. You would have to row the boat to the shallow end as fast as you could empty the boat, find the plug, and get back to your duty. Again, the laughter could be heard around the pool.

He was also a lot fun to be with at the lifeguard parties, but when he noticed something at the pool that needed attention or correction, he never hesitated to inform you and correct you but always positively and respectfully. I remember his speed boat, the small car that could go on water and land, and that gorgeous Porsche 904 and the magnificent sound it made going down Kellogg Ave past the pool as his mechanic would tune it up, wind it up, and blow it out — *what a pleasing sound!* To summarize, Bob was a character, great to be with, and never a dull moment with a smile always on his face. That was my first job and I cherish the great memories and people I had the pleasure to meet and work with.

To Coney, with Love, Laura Woodruff

We love Coney Island! I grew up spending my summers at Coney. Those were the best days! When I became a mom, I started taking my kids there. I loved continuing the summer tradition. My kids are 10, 9, 6 and 2. They love Coney as much as I do!! We spent our summers at Coney. We could be found under the first umbrella by the tiki bar from Monday to Thursday and lots of Fridays, too. We have made some of the best of friends over the years. Friends that became family and some friends that we would only see over the summer at Coney.

Coney was the best for summer fun. My kids learned how to swim at Coney. They learned how to live, love, make friends, and have a fun time in the sun during their summers at Coney. This was our happy place. It was what we waited all year long for. My daughters, Emma and Mia, swam their first laps there. Mia even swam her first mile at Coney! She was hoping to join the swim team. My son, Knox, loved the Twister, bounce pad and making new friends. During our last couple days at Coney, he finally got up the courage to go down the Silver Bullet and dive boards. We couldn't keep him off them once he started. He was so looking forward to spending his summer days on the dive boards. My youngest, June, also loved Coney. She enjoyed making friends, practicing her kicking, and taking naps with Grandma. She was going to learn to swim at Coney. We have the best memories. We would have loved to make more memories. We love Coney Island!! I included pics of us and our Coney friends. Coney friends are the best!! We love our summer friends!! This is our last family pic at Coney. August 4, 2023.

To Coney, with Love, Michael Morris

Oh, how to start? Coney is and was so much to so many people. For many of us, and myself, it was our first jobs, where we made our best friends, where we met our significant others, and raised our families. All of that was true for me. Starting in 1998, I was 16 and worked in security. My first official shift was a post at the Appalachian Festival.

A couple of years later, I became a full-timer running security. After that, I moved to maintenance and became the maintenance manager and followed up by becoming the director of facilities and operations manager. To describe a typical day is hard because you never really had the same day twice. There were a few of the same duties but every experience was different, from getting ready for picnics to working special events and concerts. Let's not forget about the busy pool days and ride days. Each group that came in was different. Which added so many different experiences, too many to put into words. There are a few standouts like the Jimmy Buffett crowds and the AFL/CIO groups along with our fireworks shows.

Coney was so much more than a job. It was family. In the off-season, everyone thought we were taking it easy. But the staff that I worked with along with myself, would tell you otherwise. The off-season was planning and repairing. Not to mention cleaning up from some pretty bad floods. I am glad I got to meet my family and friends there. That place will always bring smiles to faces. So, I say To Coney, with Love, thank you for everything and God bless. I wouldn't be who I became without you.

To Coney, with Love, Scott Kristof

I was raised in Liberty Township in Butler County, so every summer was spent going to Kings Island since it was nearby. However, my mother and father visited Coney Island during their youth. About once or twice per year, my parents would take us to Coney Island to experience the park that they called home several years before. Although smaller than its spiritual successor in my backyard, it was always a treat visiting Coney whenever we did.

My maternal grandmother (we all called her Nonnie) once recalled a story about my late Uncle Nicky, who passed away a year before I was born. Nonnie remembered that one day during a visit to Coney Island, Uncle Nicky had wandered off into the crowd. He had disappeared for a while. I don't remember how long she said he was gone, but eventually, they were reunited, with Nicky coming up carrying a teddy bear. Nonnie asked him where he got the bear from. He responded, enthusiastically, "I got to be on Bob Braun's show!" Bob Braun was a lifeguard at Sunlite Pool before rising to stardom on the radio and television scene in Cincinnati. During his days at WLW, he hosted a poolside radio show at Sunlite Pool called "Splatter Party," and my Uncle Nicky was one of his guests. For those of us who knew Nicky or Nonnie, this story will always bring a smile to our faces.

To Coney, with Love, Sharon Fitzpatrick Fitzwater

I grew up in Mt. Washington and Coney Island was the main attraction! I never worked there, although my brother, Chuck Fitzpatrick, and my sister, Denise Fitzpatrick Long, had that pleasure. I remember going to Coney with my parents, but it seemed like it was only on nights with some gentle rain since my dad did not like crowds.

In high school I went to Sunlite Pool sometimes and rode the rides with friends. I remember the pool water being very, very cold, and so deep at one end. They had a very high platform that certain people. Lifeguards like my brother, would jump from occasionally. I remember how proud we would be to finally swim all the way out to the "raft" from the side of the pool.

In the winter, we would go ice skating on Lake Como, but we had to climb over the turnstile to get in! During college, a group from the University of Cincinnati Newman Center would gather for the dances at Moonlite Gardens.

My husband, Michael, was in the Air Force, and whenever we would visit Cincinnati in the summer the same group from the UC Newman Center would gather at Moonlite Gardens so we could re-connect with them. As our family grew, we would visit and take our daughters to Sunlite Pool. A few years ago, we rented a house and our daughters and their families came to enjoy the pool and ride some rides. We even had our infant grandson under one of the big umbrellas! Both our daughters were sad to hear it was closing.

To Coney, with Love, Jane Barrows

Like many others, I grew up swimming at Coney almost every weekend. Great memories of jumping off the high board. My mom continued her love of swimming by having a season pass until she was 97, driving herself there multiple times a week. Mom passed away last year at 103 years old. Swimming played a major part in her exceptionally long life.

To Coney, with Love, Alfred Freeman

Here are some photos I took of the Shooting Star. The picture below shows Burt operating the Shooting Star. The Shooting Star was designed by Herbert Schmeck who took the lift hill of the Clipper coaster and its final enclosed curved tunnel and built the Shooting Star from it.

To Coney, with Love, Teresa Knabb

One of my memories is of my grandpa on my father's side, dad telling me about his summer job working at Coney as an Anderson Township Solar Ranger. Another memory is of my parents, my siblings, and I taking a boat down to Coney to spend the day. We had a lot of fun times there swimming, riding rides, having picnics. When I had my daughter, she and I made our own memories there; swimming, picnics, riding the rides, and playing on the playground. We took walks there and enjoyed the Appalachian Festival, summer fairs, and balloon glows.

I went to dances there, and I had my 5-year class reunion there. My mom always said she and some of her friends often went to Coney when they were younger to swim. We have always enjoyed the sights, sounds, laughter, and the river there at Coney.

To Coney, with Love, Mitzi Goebel

Coney Island was where my grandparents took me when I was little. The first bumper boat ride was a blast. My grandmother and I would get on the paddle boats and pedal for hours, I loved how sparkly the water and the boat were. We rode the Ferris wheel, the Viking ship, the racer, and so many more. The frog hopper was amazing bouncing fun. The games were a blast. Coney Island Christmas lights were amazing. Coney Island will truly be missed, like a lost friend. Just like my late grandparents, forever loved in my memories.

To Coney, with Love, Vickie Bowman

I have many years of wonderful memories at Coney and Sunlite Pool. I want to share the story of my Sweet Mom, Virginia Ritter, she always glowed when talking about Coney. She would pay one dime to ride the Island Queen from downtown Cincinnati to Coney…dancing on the boat…then dancing at Moonlite Gardens all night…then embarking on the Island Queen and dancing all the way back to downtown. She took me to Coney, via 2 buses, every summer. We would ride rides all day and then run to catch the last bus of the night. I will always cherish how fun she made our time together there.

To Coney, with Love, Chuck Cullen

Skee Ball and Snoopy
A Coney Island Love Story

Skee Ball is not a difficult game to learn but getting a high score takes a little skill and practice. The ball has a diameter of just over three inches, and it must be rolled up the playing ramp and onto the scoring area, which has a series of holes below a vertical silo or barrier. Each hole is assigned points, based upon the degree of difficulty of rolling a ball into that hole. Points range from 10 to 100, with 20, 30, 40, and 50 points also available. For each game, players receive nine balls after placing a token into the Skee Ball machine. The tokens are issued from a vending machine that magically converts cash into game tokens. The goal is to accumulate as many points as possible with the nine balls. As each ball enters a hole, points would be displayed at the top of the machine. A minimum number of points must be earned before getting any game reward tickets. As the total points increase, so do the number of game reward tickets dispensed. One could tear off the game reward tickets after each game or let the tickets spread onto the floor to demonstrate to the world one's Skee Ball accomplishment.

I recall playing a few times as a child when visiting Coney Island with my parents, but the game did not fascinate me at that youthful age. It wasn't until I could go to Coney by myself that my love story had its roots. My first solo trip was in 1968 at the age of 16. I had a summer job and a 1957 Ford that I purchased for $60. That allowed me to visit Coney Island at my leisure. That summer, the Skee Ball Arcade at Coney was the destination for me. I became fascinated with a row of machines dispensing little reward tickets upon the completion of each game.

I began observing the rolling techniques used by others. Some used a run-up-to-the-machine and release approach. Others mastered a fast roll while still others employed a precise banking release to reach that coveted 100-point silo. I became skilled at hitting the 40 or 50-point hole in the center of the scoring area. I was satisfied with three or four 50-point rolls each game. Too often I tried for the

100-point silo only to have gravity lead the ball down to the 10-point hole. When it came to Skee Ball, I learned to just accept what produced the most points for me.

I suddenly began to accumulate reward tickets. These tickets could be redeemed for prizes, but plastic rings, small bouncing balls, candy, or pliable bugs did not interest me. I focused my eyes on a battery-operated AM-FM radio that was on the shelf behind the counter where the trinkets were located. The shelf was where the true prizes were kept. Besides the radio, there were large stuffed animals and even some small kitchen appliances. Items on the shelves, however, required more game reward tickets, a lot more. I projected I would earn enough reward tickets by early next summer (1969) to get that radio. So, I would regularly exchange my individual reward tickets for multi-point coupons. The coupons made it easier to store my earned rewards. So, over the winter, the coupons remained at home just waiting for the next Coney season.

I earned more reward tickets early the next summer and by the end of June, I was ready to proudly point to that radio on the shelf and demand my dream reward. But the radio never became a reality. I exchanged my coupons for a stuffed Snoopy dog, complete with eye goggles. I had to make do with the AM radio in my car. But I didn't mind.

For on June 28, 1969, I met a girl, and our first date was at Coney Island. I brought my arcade coupons and wore a new pair of "Chucky's" shoes. We had an enchanting time riding the Lost River, Cuddle Up, Sky Ride, and more. That girl, Rita, was not very interested in the coasters like the Shooting Star or the Wild Mouse but there was plenty of other attractions to keep us occupied. But she really enjoyed the boat ride on Lake Como. I think we ventured out onto the lake several times that evening. Towards the end of the evening, we visited the arcade and tried our hands at Skee Ball. We then went to the prize counter to redeem our reward tickets from the night. We agreed that if we combined our resources, we could share a larger prize — maybe two pieces of candy. I could then get my radio and play it for her on the way home. Suddenly, however, I heard a voice in my head telling me to share all my reward coupons with Rita. The voice got louder as we approached the prize counter. "Forget the radio," it said repeatedly. It wasn't until later that I discovered the source of that voice.

Once at the counter, Rita laid down the tickets and, as the attendant began to count them, I reached into my pocket and presented my coupons from the previous trips to Coney. I told her to pick anything she wanted using all the tickets and coupons. At first, she was hesitant, but she finally meekly pointed toward the large stuffed Snoopy dog. It became hers to keep and keep it she did. I believe it was Snoopy that placed that voice in my head minutes ago. And I believe that same stuffed dog also silently whispered to Rita to choose Snoopy after foretelling to her of the wonderful future the three of us would have together. Outside the arcade, Rita removed the purple decorative scarf from her neck and tied our wrists together in a romantic gesture. And so, we strolled the rest of the evening through Coney Island joined by that scarf and accompanied by Snoopy. Exactly five years later, on June 28, 1974, Rita and I replaced that scarf with two wedding rings. On our honeymoon, we remarked how that first date at Coney changed our lives for the better with the encouragement of Snoopy.

Maybe Snoopy could really predict the future. It was glad to find a loving home before Coney Island, as we knew it, began a gradual transformation into history. As the years went on, Rita and I would take our kids to Sunlite Pool for swimming lessons and attend some summer events (Summerfair, Appalachian Festival, etc.). The kids also got to enjoy a few rides during the years they were available. Our older son even worked at Coney one summer in the warehouse. Rita would recall the "wonderful future" prediction that Snoopy made to her when she selected it from the shelf. I don't believe Snoopy ever stopped talking to Rita. Rita placed her trust in the Almighty, but always had an ear open for Snoopy.

As the years went by, our children moved out leaving us and Snoopy alone once again. Yet, anytime we drove by Coney Island, we glanced at the Main Gate and remembered Snoopy, all the great memories that we had behind that entrance, and the beautiful life we had outside of that gate. We would then remark on how much we missed the arcade, the Lost River, and other rides. If it was daylight, we would also fondly recall our trips on Lake Como. And we always remembered how Skee Ball and Snoopy somehow became part of our life together.

On June 28, 2019, exactly fifty years after our first date at Coney, Rita and I went to church that Friday morning, repeated our wedding vows, and returned to Coney for a swim at Sunlite Pool and a boat ride on Lake Como. The lake ride was once again memorable even though it took us a little extra time to get into and out of the boat.

On December 14, 2023, the Cincinnati Enquirer reported that Coney had been sold and would be transformed into a music venue. The next day, Rita died. Was it cancer or the loss of Coney that caused her death? I'll never be certain and Snoopy, now yellowed from age, no longer whispers any advice.

Written on Snoopy's paw.

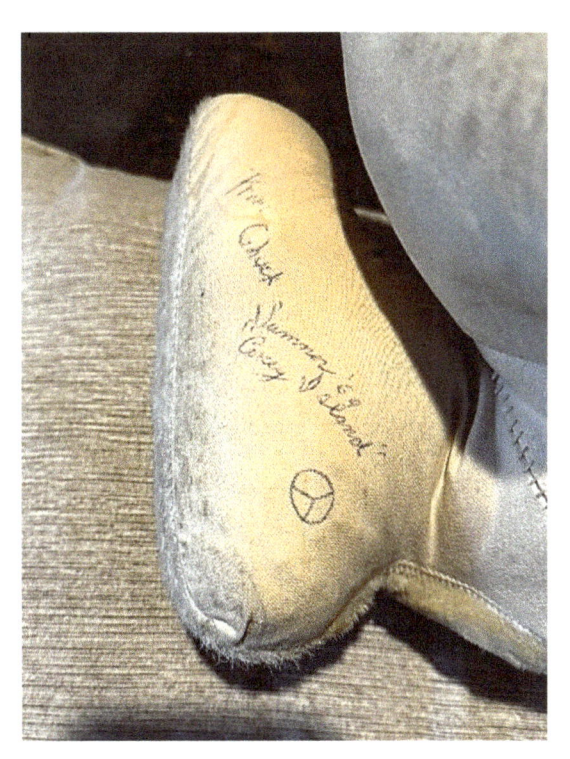

To Coney, with Love, Jackie McGraw

Coney was our summer oasis. We will always remember the anticipation of completing our season pass registration and shopping for that perfect pool float every May. If you were a regular you knew the orange and lime green seat floats always ripped after the first month. We were the ones floating on the line. Over the years, we were smacked by soaring tossed balls and had endless water spots on our sunglasses from kids kicking as hard as they could to dive under the line. Everyone knew where we would be, soaking the rays up floating, and listening to the Coney Island radio on the speakers. We could even predict the next song. We often heard that loud POP at the air compressor stations from all the amateurs overfilling their floats. We were the pool watchers; we had a view of the silver bullet and the island. Over the years, we watched many scared kids build up the courage to take their first slide as proud parents and bystanders applauded. Such happy times floating on the line. Our daughter is almost an adult now and she spent her last season floating on the line with us after 17 years of doing all the busy kid's activities. We will never forget all our memories of Coney spent floating on the line together.

To Coney, with Love, Chris Evans

Coney Island has been fading away piece by piece just as it evolved from Parker's Grove to the amusement park in its heyday as Coney Island. My grandparents operated the salt water and cotton candy concession beginning in the mid-thirties. My grandmother retired from the business earlier but my grandfather maintained the concession until Kings Island opened. At one point, my mother worked in the business. This is how my memories began to take shape.

A day at Coney Island with mom meant swimming at Sunlite Pool. I was only a toddler on my first visit but I absolutely loved to splash in the water. Mom wanted me to learn how to swim early on so spending time at the pool was a must. Afterwards we would have lunch in the cafeteria. Mom always had the bread pudding for dessert!

Finally, we went on the rides. I patiently waited all day for this. A few of my favorites were the Teddy Bear roller coaster, the Cuddle Up, and the Whip. If we had extra time before heading home, we would head over to the games area. They had a rather heavy-metal car that you would push on a track. It would bounce off stoppers at each end of the small track. Lined up along the back of the track were souvenir gifts. When the car stopped, the item behind it was your special prize. Oh, what a great day at Coney!

As time passed, I placed more emphasis on Sunlite Pool. I can still visualize in my mind walking out of the changing area and seeing that enormous, beautiful pool. I just couldn't believe it! When I think about it, I can still close my eyes and detect the scent of chlorine. Wonderful memories! Forever in my mind and heart.

To Coney, with Love, Holly Knabb

Trying to write down some of my memories of Coney Island is like trying to sum up a lifetime of my childhood into a short story.

My earliest memories were walking down from our house on Sutton Rd., four houses up from Coney, and visiting with my grandparents. My grandma, Irma Lanter, worked at the front gates. We would then we would hang out with grandpa (Clinton A. Lanter) and my dad (Clint E. Lanter), who both worked on Lake Como on the docks, taking tickets for the canoes.

I remember Grandpa always playing his harmonica, smoking his pipe, and yelling out to people that their time was up and to head back to the docks.

My brothers had their first jobs there and most of my aunts, uncles, cousins, and neighbors worked there, or at River Downs.

I remember fishing with my family on the Lake in the summer after Coney was closed at night for night fishing and we would go ice skating on the lake when it froze in the winter.

The little forts and Indian teepees that were around the tracks of the train ride that went around Lake Como were our "playhouses" when we were kids.

My mom and dad were good friends with the Captain of the Lifeguards, Bob Lowe and my dad was friends with Rosemary Clooney. He said that he hung out with her when she came to Moonlite Gardens to sing.

Coney closed its rides when I was a teenager and to me, it died back then. My family lost their jobs and then the company that bought Coney, bought the properties on Sutton Rd. where I lived and down Kellogg to across from Coney's west gate, my Grandparents' house.

They were going to build a big hotel on the hill across from Coney and then re-build Coney with rides that they were buying from Texas... this never happened.

They tore down my Grandparents' house on Kellogg Ave and everything in between, all the way to the front gate (to Coney). The house that my dad built on Sutton Rd. is still there.

I spent my whole childhood at Coney, every day of the summer, and took swim lessons at Sunlite, then I took my kids to Sunlite Pool. We would pick up Bob Lowe on the way, and we would walk around the pool with him while holding hands.

Last Year, my son Nick and granddaughter Hailey came to Cincinnati from Hawaii. We all went to Coney for a Family Day. It was Hailey's first time there and she was amazed by it.

My daughter, who had terminal brain cancer was with us and she got to see Coney's pool for her last time, but we didn't realize it would be our last time there as well. My daughter Amber passed away on April 10, 2024. I am so happy that all of us got to spend one last day there together, for what would be all of our last days at Coney's Sunlite Pool.

Clint Lanter's Coney Scrapbooks

To Coney, with Love, Michelle Wray

It's hard to begin to pick out a favorite memory at Coney Island as there are many memories! The one that stands out is the one with my parents.

I was about 6 or 7 years old. My parents and I would take the bus downtown to catch the bus to Coney Island. After picking up our locker key and our Coney Island towels, we'd head to our lockers into a tiny little space to change your clothes that only one person could fit into at a time. We'd put our key around our ankle, jump in, and begin enjoying the pool. At noon, my dad would walk over to River Downs to try his luck on what I would call the GeeGee's. Mom and I would spend the rest of the time in the pool and having lunch. We'd walk up to the cafeteria-style building and get lunch. We'd stand in line, and order hamburgers, fresh off the grill, and fries, right out of the fryer. Then we would pick up soda and ice cream.

We'd enjoy the rest of the afternoon until about 3:00 when we'd watch for my dad. He would walk up to the fence and put his hands up on the fence. That was how we knew it was time to go home. We'd change, and drop off our towels and key. We went through the turnstile and headed home. I'd fall asleep on the bus after a long, fun day at Coney Island.

To Coney, with Love, Bettina Ramundo

Here's the group with the Sun Burners that always danced by the Sun Burners, we will truly miss this!!

To Coney, with Love, Mary Fender

My family belonged to Coney during the 1980s and much of the 1990s. My childhood summers were spent shivering at early morning swim lessons and later when the water warmed, watching my grandmother glide through the water as she gracefully took her quick daily dip in the pool. My mother would rub down her fair skin with sunscreen, while my aunt bathed herself in baby oil. I remember repeatedly racing down the slick silver slide with my cousin, and giggling down the Zoom Flume with my brothers, squealing with excitement the whole time. I remember some evenings we would meet my dad after work for dinner at LaRosas and even get to play a few games or ride the paddle boats across Lake Como.

I remember once driving from our home in Northern Kentucky and arriving at Coney, only to realize my little sister was still wearing her pajamas and not her swimsuit. My memories are full of laughter, peanut butter crackers for lunch, the cicada invasion of 1987, and jumping off the island at least 100 times a day. So, Coney, I thank you for the most simple, wonderful, magical, loving family moments any kid could wish for. They will be forever etched in my memory, with so much love.

To Coney, with Love, Mary Ann Hofmann

My entire extended family and I would not be here on earth if it wasn't for Coney Island.

On a hot summer day in 1930, a young Italian girl by the name of Lucia Paolucci was at the Coney Island pool with friends. Despite being unable to swim she jumped into the deep end of the pool on a dare. A young Irish-German boy named Thomas Purcell was also there with friends and noticed a dark-haired girl struggling in the water. He jumped in and rescued her and from then on, she was the center of his life.

They married in 1936, had four children, and twenty-seven grandchildren and I have lost count of the number of great and great-great grandchildren.

I am devastated that Coney Island has been destroyed. In addition to the story of my grandparents, I too enjoyed the rides and pool as a child. My mother, their daughter, danced at Moonlite Gardens. As a teenager, I rode the ferry from Kentucky to Coney Island with my boyfriend to enjoy a day at the pool. Then as a parent and now a grandparent I shared the joy of Coney with my children and grandchildren. Losing Coney fills me with sadness, but the wonderful memories I have will endure.

To Coney, with Love, Holly Knoechel Changet

This is my mom, Tanya Dee Vincent Knoechel, in 1948, the year she met my dad at Coney Island. They married in 1949, and had 6 kids; 3 boys, and 3 girls (in order, Sandy, Jeff, Scott, Chip, Holly and Julie). My dad, Carl Knoechel, passed in November 1982, and my mom passed in 2018. They have many grandchildren and many great-grandchildren, the newest one born in April 2024, Claire.

It all began at Coney when my mom was 17 and they married the next year. That's my mom, Tanya Knoechel, by the bathrooms.

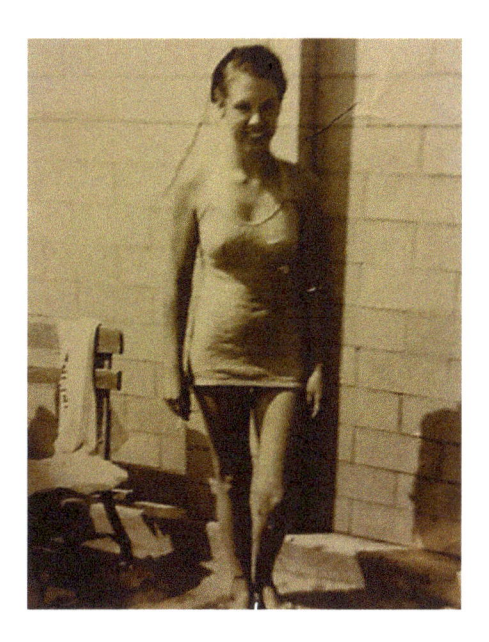

To Coney, with Love, Dennis Flemming

Here are a few pictures we have to share. These were given to me by Ed Brogan before his passing. Ed and our dad Tom Fleming, both from Ludlow KY, stayed great friends throughout their lives. As the story goes Coney was paying a team of Italian divers to do exhibition dives from the tower above the diving boards, a little above 70 feet. As Ed's version of the story goes my dad stopped the man in charge as they were relaxing around the pool. Asking the gentleman how much they were paying the divers, my dad replied I know someone who will do it for free. Ed was surprised, to say the least, that my dad had volunteered him for the job. Dad eased his nerves when he told Ed he would be joining him. I'm not sure how long they did the dives but as we entered the pool area there were many pictures of Dad and Eddie doing their dives. The photographer would lay on the 10-foot board while taking pictures of them coming off of the tower.

First photo on steps: Pre-War Coney Island group of Friends *Top Row*: Foots Delaney, Shorty Fleming, Bud Crowley *Middle*: Ed Brogan *Bottom*: Jim Hutson, WW II Ace Pilot, Tom Fleming, Tee Harding

Second photo 1960 cousins: Three families of cousins out for their annual vacation day. *Left to Right*: Arin McDonald, Tom Fleming, Becky Hughes, Dan Corbett, Dennis Fleming, Don Hughes, Colleen McDonald, Mike McDonald

To Coney, with Love, Linda Schmidt Hanson

Every year in August, Proctor and Gamble (P & G) took over Coney Island for their families. We arrived early in the morning and saved a table with our basket of food and cooler of drinks for the day. Then we headed out to the large field in the back of the shelter for games and contests for the children of the P & G employees. Each event was offered to a certain age group. The very young toddlers ran around the field scattered with P & G products and picked up as many items as they could hold. My mom tied an apron backwards around my baby sister, so she could fill it up. It was so cute to watch! There were relay races and 3 legged races for the older ones. I won once and my prize was a gift certificate to a store in downtown Cincinnati. When the contests were over, we ate lunch with the family; fried chicken and all the fixin's. The rest of the day we were free to go on any rides we wanted to, play the games Coney offered, and just ride and run and have the best day of our lives at Coney Island.

To Coney, with Love, Jamie Smith

My family went to Coney for many years to celebrate Grandma Bonnie's birthday until she passed. Dearwester and Smith family with Grandma Bonnie.

To Coney, with Love, Janet L Schroeder

Here is a copy of a black-and-white photo of Betty and Clete Schroeder with their toddler son Ricky and baby daughter Connie in a buggy the couple rented as they entered Coney Island Amusement Park. I framed 5x7s for each of Rick's 6 siblings who spent their summers at Sunlite Pool

As a kid growing up in East Cleveland, I graduated from the University of Cincinnati and was treated to this tradition as soon as I married Rick in 1977. We took our 3 kids to Coney often as well. What a thrill it was a magical but so down-to-earth entertainment venue. I'm 74 and didn't grow up on the east side like the 7 Schroeders did, and still, I can hardly believe Coney is no longer there!

To Coney, with Love, Sharon Stern

This photo is from my mother, Helen Gundling, taken probably in the 40s based on the swimsuit styles. She would take the streetcar downtown to board the Island Queen to Coney at least once a week. She loved it there. When I hear the word Coney Island, I think of her.

To Coney, with Love, Kathy Rossell

Coney Island! Just those two words bring a cherished memory. Coney Island was one of my favorite places. I remember going there with my grandmother and cousins to Sunlite Pool, then to ride the rides, the Cuddle Up, The Whip, and The Tumble Bug. Oh, how we giggled. Then The Lost River, that one always scared me. I remember Price Hill Day, packing a lunch, riding the bus. What a long ride across town for a child of 8 or 9 filled with excitement. At age 15 was my first ride on the Shooting Star. I was so frightened going up that first hill, but oh what a thrill those hills that followed. I would end up riding it 4 or 5 times in a row! To this day it is my favorite roller coaster ever.

I was there in the summer of 1971 when Coney had its last day of operation as an amusement park. I cried my heart out.

When I had two sons of my own, I shared Coney with them. We had passes every year, enjoying summer days, water fun with friends, and the best swim lessons! Balloon Glow and Fireworks add to my fond memories!

Closing our beautiful Coney is heartbreaking. It should have been preserved as a historical landmark for all to enjoy for generations to come.

Thank you for allowing me to share my memories. They will forever be in my heart!

To Coney, with Love, William L. Woods

What made Coney Island special for my wife and I is that it is where we met. First, I would like to give a little backstory. My wife, Nancy A. Burkhardt, and I had exchanged glances on two separate occasions. You know, when you look at someone and you're not sure if the other person was looking at you or not, but you feel that you did lock eyes. We both confirmed it later on. The first time was at Highlands High School, at the Friday night canteen. The second time was at Campbell County High

School during school bus loading. But we never actually met. Months later, at the end of the school year, a friend and I decided to skip school and hop on the Ohio River ferry and go to Coney Island. It was Catholic School Day at the park. Another act of fate, my friend recognized a girl at the park and she was with this same girl that I had seen before and desperately wanted to meet.

Well, that was it, the year was 1966, and we finally met in that magical kingdom called Coney Island. Can you believe that was 58 years ago? Our first kiss was in Coney Island's Lost River ride that same day. From that day forward we have been inseparable.

Over the years, we have attended so many functions at Coney Island: concerts and dances at Moonlite Gardens; Sunlite Pool; Balloon Glows; Halloween Farm Fest; Appalachian Fest and many others.

The photo below appears to be on the back of a boat and has a sign that reads, "Coney Island 1956." Hard to believe that just 10 years after this photo was taken, I would meet my life partner, 1966, at Coney Island, it was just meant to be!

To Coney, with Love, Laura Hackett Case

For years, Coney Island's Sunlite Pool was my favorite part of summer. As a child, we were lucky to go once a summer, but as a teenager, I would spend most of my days there. My mom and I would always sit in the same spot, behind the Silver Bullet to the right. Laying out, floating on a raft, reading, and good Coney food. Friends and family knew where to find us.

As I got older, my boyfriend-turned-husband, would join us on the weekends. We always would be there as the gates opened at 10 am or 9:30 am once they introduced the platinum pass. Once I had kids, I was thrilled to introduce them to Sunlite Pool. We would always go with my mom, their Gram. To this day, they call it "Gram's Pool Coney." We enjoyed our days there, even as they changed from sunbathing to following kids around and sitting on the edge in the shallow. My son Henry had his first swim lessons there as a toddler. It was a perfect pool for little ones as they began exploring the water. We will always hold our special memories of Coney Island and Sunlite Pool dear to us. I wish we had one more adventure at Gram's Pool Coney.

To Coney, with Love, JC Callebs and Jim Robinson

Jim Robinson and JC Callebs (40 years and 39 years, respectively) have been parking cars at Coney Island since the mid-80s. We've seen the park reinvent itself into a wonderful family entertainment venue to now being sold and no longer existing. The park flourished until Covid in 2020. The rides were sold off shortly before that.

Many memories come to mind during our time there. Here we'll mention a few.

1) Rowing Races – rowing races were being held at East Fork and Coney management invited the participants to Coney for a celebratory dinner. After the dinner, several of the rowers (male & female) decided to go skinny dipping in Lake Como. Security was called and at least one officer kept his flashlight on the embarrassed swimmers.

2) The Swamp Thing – We were leaving after a concert and heard a groaning sound from the corner of Lake Como. We walked over and found a guy covered with moss and weeds with his upper body on the bank and his lower body still in the lake. We grabbed his arms and pulled him up onto the bank,

he was hypothermic, shivering, and in a mild state of shock. We wrapped him in a raincoat and called for medical assistance!

3) Grateful Dead – these concerts are always eventful and since they were an all-day event, many things happened. The fans start showing up 2 or 3 days ahead of the concert. Many of them would go down to the boat ramp on the Ohio River, take a bath, and put the same clothes back on. In 1985, in the old bathhouse, Coney staff caught some Deadheads tie-dying t-shirts in the toilets to sell!

4) In the early 90s, we had a young man named Jonathon Zimmerman working for us. Coney had cleared a lot called the Clover Lot near the end of Penn Avenue. Jonathon was often assigned to park that lot for several years. We started calling the parking area the Z Lot after Z-Man. That's how that lot got its name!!

5) The Drain Man – One night after parking a concert, we heard someone moaning and calling for help. After tracing the sounds, we found that they were coming from a storm drain in Lot 4. When we arrived, we found a human in the drain. It took about 4 people to lift the drain lid up and out came the man covered in mud and slime. He was a hideous sight. That drain goes all the way to the river, at least a quarter mile away. We figured he came up from the river. When he crawled out, he started running through the lot and over cars and into the night.

We have made many memories and appreciate our time at Beautiful Coney Island. Our wives, children, and grandchildren have all worked with us. It has been a true blessing to us and our families!!!!!

To Coney, with Love, Annie Dischar aka Little Orphan Annie

Some of my fondest memories of Coney Island happened in the early to mid '80s. My friends and I would pile into my mom's car, and she would drop us off at the back entrance. We would quickly make our way to our favorite spot by the deep end in the grass. Like most young teens back then, we layered on the baby oil, sat back, and enjoyed getting the darkest tan. The wooden lounge chairs weren't made for comfort when trying to get your back tan, so we would walk around the pool and capture the rays that way. On one of these walks, an older gentleman stopped me and asked if he could tell me a joke. I said sure and he proceeded to tell me his joke. I totally didn't get it but laughed hysterically anyway. He smiled and I went on to catch up with my friends. On our 4th or 5th trek around the pool, the gentleman stopped me again and said, "You didn't get it, did you?" Not wanting to hurt his feelings, I said, yes, I did, and he smiled at me again, then I said no, I didn't get it, but it sounded funny. He just laughed and introduced himself, as Bob (Lowe). I told him my name was Annie and he immediately started calling me Little Orphan Annie.

Over the years, Bob and I formed a remarkable friendship. He was like the grandfather I never had and always wanted. Every day I'd stop by his chair before making my way to the spot my friends secured. He always had a joke for me, and by this time I was beginning to "get them". There were days when Bob wasn't in his lifeguard chair, he was in the rowboat in the middle of the deep end. I'd swim up to the boat and try to surprise him, but he always saw me coming. We'd talk a bit, and then he'd take me to the side of the pool and drop me off. I always thought it was so cool being in the rowboat.

Years passed, but Bob and I remained friends. I'd invite him to my parent's Christmas dinners, which was also Bob's birthday. My entire family loved Bob, but seriously who didn't? Even after getting married and having a child, Bob and I stayed very close. We'd still pick him up for family Christmas/Birthday dinner and always looked forward to our time spent together.

In 1992, I got a phone call from Bob's son Rob, aka Robbie per Bob, telling me his father passed the night before. The news was devastating, and I was beside myself, but those precious memories that started from Coney, will be forever in my heart. I only wish Coney would have stayed, so others could have experienced all the magic it held.

Love always,
Little Orphan Annie

To Coney, with Love, Laura Schweikert-Wilson

Our family moved to Anderson Township in 1969. I was 4 years old and that was my first year as a Coney pass holder.

My Coney memories are:

Mom took us all to the pool, I was the youngest of 5, and finding her spot under the trees near the parking lot side next to a brick shelter with a roof that predated the Island Shop. We knew where to find her for lunch and when to check-in. We also knew she was leaving at 4:30 to beat River Downs traffic and get home to start supper. When we got a little older, Mom dropped us off when Coney opened and would be back in the parking lot to get us again to beat the race track traffic! We'd find our friends from school and neighborhood kids and we SWAM. We only stopped for lunch. You'd wander to the picnic grove to find your Playmate cooler and eat your peanut butter and jelly sandwiches, chips, and whatever cookies Thriftway had 3 for $1 that week. There would be a thermos filled with Kool-Aid or lemonade. When Mom arrived to take us home, we were waterlogged. Your lungs hurt from swimming so much — usually trying to keep up with the older kids jumping off a diving board, swimming across the deep end, running across the island, walk, please! And jump in and continue onto the Silver Bullet and do it all over again in reverse after going down the slide. The ride home took us up Sutton past the "pair of dice" house (or the crazy house) as we called it, with all the windows down making a mess of your chlorine-soaked hair. You got a sunburn? Oh well, Mom would say just wear a T-shirt tomorrow as in, you weren't staying home!

On the rare day when Mom had appointments or it stormed, we'd go down late afternoon and dad would join us for a picnic supper and swim. Standing on his shoulders and jumping off or being thrown literally feeling as if you were flying. The day crowd had gone home and you felt like you had the pool to yourself.

When we got older, we'd wander over to play putt-putt and sometimes the balls from miniature golf came back to the pool with you. Pretty sure we were the reason only softballs were allowed in the pool at some point. After a hot round of golf, it was back to the pool!

My Coney memories continued when my high school held their Prom at Moonlite Pavilion and later on, our wedding reception was at Moonlite! We were married over the 4th of July weekend and my relatives all thought the fireworks from the symphony were just for us!

I began taking my children down when they were little. Many nights they got their showers there. Put them in jammies and they were asleep on the road home, often by the time we were out of the parking lot.

I loved that the swim instructors that my firstborn had were the same as my 3rd child. My children went through the entire swim lesson levels. Such an amazing program and a loss to the community to lose the swim lesson program at Coney.

The summers where I became the mom in the chair, home base, for the kids to check in with and got to visit with my friends who also brought their kids down. We were under a tree on the roadside behind the Curley Cue slide. We would pull our chairs in a circle and chat the day away, getting up to wander into the pool to cool down from time to time. Leave by 2:30 or 3 because you had to leave them wanting more for the next day!

Oh, and the midnight swims. So much FUN. Riding the Zoom Flume in the dark was terrifying and amazing at the same time as a child and as an adult.

Kids running amok and coming down after sports practices. The boys would go in the bathroom, cover their backs with soap, and then run to the curly cue slide, still don't know its proper name. They claimed they went faster with the soap. They spent endless hours tossing balls, playing tag, and racing down the slides. Anything we could do to reduce the kids' "screen time" as moms, and Coney did this. I had hoped to continue the memories with my grandson.

Coney Island, Old Coney, Sunlite Pool… you had it all, and are going to be missed.

To Coney, with Love, Elise Strasser

My mom, who passed away with a stroke in September 2019, along with my daughter, would come every September or October to Coney Island's Fall-O-Ween. They had a love for Halloween and amusement parks. We were so sad when they no longer decided to have that festival.

To Coney, with Love, Shelle Meyers

My family made the annual trip to Coney just about every June, before it got too hot or humid and hopefully, the Ohio River hadn't flooded, or it rained. I anxiously anticipated the thrill of riding as many of the rides as possible, but especially the roller coasters, namely the Shooting Star. We worked our way from one end of Coney Mall to the other and I wanted to stop and ride every ride, including the Haunted House.

My most memorable visit was in June 1970. My family worked our way around Coney Mall as usual, but at the far end of the mall was a building with a sign Circus 70 above. My mom was eager for my sister, age 5, and me, age 9 to come inside with her and dad. The building was air-conditioned, which was wonderful since the sun was beating down on us. The first surprise inside was black lighting, which caused anything white to glow. My matching flower-patterned sleeveless top and shorts as well as my white socks and shoestrings lit up. Cool. The next surprise was a puppet show created by Sid and Marty Krofft, which included hand puppets as well as human-sized puppets, one being H.R. Pufnstuf! I was completely taken by the show. I was already a fan of Larry Smith's puppets on WXIX and I had the opportunity to meet Mr. Pufnstuf after the show just outside the doors of Circus 70. I shook his hand and told him I thought he put on a very good show, and he nodded his head at me...*Wow!*

My mom turned on the T.V. one Saturday morning in September of that year. Imagine my delight seeing H.R. Pufnstuf looking back I didn't know this program was already showing and the shows were in reruns. I will always hold Coney Island near and dear for allowing me to meet a T.V. star, but most importantly for making my all "kid" summers so wonderful to remember.

To Coney, with Love, Charlene Brown

Honeymoon at Coney Island

This submission is on behalf of Robert and Leetha Tomlinson. My mom is Leetha Tomlinson, as soon as she saw this opportunity to share about Coney Island, she wanted me to make sure that I told her and my father's story. My mom and my dad were married in 1958, November 7, they never had a honeymoon because they could not afford one. They went to Coney Island to celebrate their honeymoon. They danced at Moonlite Gardens many times throughout the years and they enjoyed it so much. It is a memory that she will never forget. My father has passed on now, it's been three years. This was a sentimental time for her seeing Coney being taken down her memories are still vivid. When I was a little girl, we went there many times, I remember it like it was yesterday. My first two daughters got to go there when they were little. I have a special needs daughter who got to participate in one of the shows because they thought she was so cute dancing with them. Our family has many memories. Coney Island will always be a part of our family. My mom wanted me to share this photo of her and my father at Coney Island, many years ago since they had their honeymoon there and had this picture taken one year later.

To Coney, with Love, Holly Jones

It must have been 1965 after we moved to Cincinnati. I was 5 years old. I remember my brothers and I couldn't wait to go to Coney Island once a year. It was a huge treat for us. I vaguely remember riding the Wild Mouse with my dad. I would sit in front of him. No one else would go with him but me. I remember that ride whipping us around the turns up high on the track.

Also, once I got lost from my family at Coney Island. I won a little plastic spinning top game on string. I was so busy playing with it that, my family must have turned and I kept walking. We were in a large group with our neighbors that year. I remember I just started crying when I realized my family and group weren't to be seen. A nice man helped me. He took me to the white building and they gave me a lollipop. Soon after my parents came and got me. We had talked about if anyone got lost that evening to go to the white building. Those were the good old days! Lots of good memories.

To Coney, with Love, Jeffrey Maxwell

The best day at Coney Island (amusements) was the last lay, Sept 4, 1971. We had been there a few times, but the older I got, the clearer the memory. Most of these photos are all from that date. It's easy to determine because the flowers on the date by the sign confirm the date. Kings Island started that same tradition when they opened, but it's fallen by the wayside.

We enjoyed the train, the little cars you could drive as a kid, the Sky Ride above the park, and the big black thing I think called the Octopus. I was also able to be at the very first opening day at Kings Island because our Indian Hill High School band performed on the preview day while WLWT personalities filmed at the park. The Sky Ride and Octopus both made the trip to Kings Island, and although the Sky Ride is gone the renamed Monster brings back the joy of Coney Island.

Coney's Sunlite Pool was among the very first pools I was ever in.

To Coney, with Love, Karen (Lipp) Fischer

I recall the Lost River ride as a young child, and I was terrified. It's funny how the Log Flume ride at Kings Island was so much fun when I was older.

I do have a bad memory at Coney. I was going down the slide and my brother was behind me. He came down too close behind me and that pushed me into the deeper end of the pool or at least deeper into the water. I about panicked when I found someone's legs and found my way to the surface thank the good Lord. I thought I was going to drown.

I had many more great days at Coney including our prom in 1976. I also took my kids there a few times. That is the saddest part of losing Coney. The generations of memories.

To Coney, with Love, Carla Dishon

Coney Island was a place of joy for so many people for so many years that the memories need to be preserved. Thank you for caring so deeply and seeing that this happens. My photos are from our old family albums of my sister and parents before I was even born.

To Coney, with Love, Lauren Marcagi Heis

As a 15-year-old, I applied for my first real job at Coney Island in the summer of 1971. I was hired, issued a blue and white uniform, and placed in training with Mr. Gorido. I was assigned to be a weight and age guesser at a booth, and without any instruction about how to do that, began working the next day. When I asked Mr. Gorido about losing to the customer each time, thus awarding them a prize, he replied, "That's ok kid, you'll get the hang of it!" Indeed, I did and in a few weeks was very skilled at guesstimating age and weight, usually "winning" for Coney. I worked there the entire summer, 8-hour shifts with two fifteen-minute breaks, making $1.25 an hour. I believe I still have some pay stubs!

My friend Pam and I made other friendships there and were often asked out by the Wackenhut security guys, but were never allowed to go out with any of them. It was a summer to remember.

To Coney, with Love, Karen Claybaugh

My earliest memory is as a young child riding on the Island Queen to get to Coney Island walking up the ramp, from there it was quite a walk to get to the rides. I was the youngest of three and was never tall enough to ride the regular roller coaster rides. We each were given a strip of tickets, which did not last long. It was a yearly trip as my dad would get passes for Dividend Day for P & G. It was always very hot, and I didn't know why we couldn't go swimming in the pool. I can still remember participating in a company kids' relay race in the picnic area. The company products were in a laundry basket, and we had a certain amount of time to grab as many as possible and carry them to another basket. Whatever was in the basket at the end you got to take home. I remember hearing that it flooded a lot and that is why Kings Island opened, they reassembled some of the rides there. When I was older, I remember going once to the pool at Coney and another time for Summerfair. We were on the west side of town and not really close so mainly it was a once-a-year visit. I heard stories of Moonlite Gardens dances and would imagine a dance floor full of people dancing.

To Coney, with Love, Robyn Kueper

In the 1970s, Coney Island was introduced to my family and me via volleyball of all things. My father, Tom Braunm, was an avid volleyball player at the M. E. Lyons YMCA. The group of volleyball players at the YMCA told my dad that they play every Sunday at Coney. Every Sunday morning, my dad would fry up chicken and make a cooler of lemonade to spend the entire day down at Coney. My mom, Mary Jo, and my dad would play volleyball behind the old locker house. My brother, Dan, and I would dive from the boards, slide on the Silver Bullet, and play in the arcade room.

Dan and I eventually joined the Coney Island Aquanaut swim team, and we had an instant summer family. We would arrive at Coney every weekday at 7:45 to meet up with 50 plus swimmers to dive into that cold water and practice for 2 hours. The rest of the day was hanging out with the other swimmers, eating our packed lunch, making friends with the lifeguards and porters, helping teach swim lessons, joining the tennis team, and finally being picked up at 2 pm. That was a typical day for all the swimmers on the team and no parents! Our swim team family grew into a lifeguard family at Coney. The fun continued, swim practice, teaching swim lessons, lifeguarding and then going out with the lifeguard staff just to wake up and do it all over again the next day. Coney summers were great summers!

When I was 15, I started as an assistant Coney Island Aquanaut with Suzie Walters. The day I started with her was the day I was hooked on coaching. I continued to grow within the program and became the head coach at age 19. I continued to coach for the next 30 years. The blessings I have had as a Coney Island Aquanaut swim coach are numerous! I had the honor and joy to coach hundreds of swimmers. They all are special to my heart, but the last group will forever be the group that I will never forget. Twenty-five 15 to 18-year-olds, and fifteen of them were girls. They were so fun and worked so hard!

I also loved creating bonds with moms and dads, grandmas, and grandpas, some of which I am still connected to today. I have worked with the kindest and most loving staff over all the years, some who were past swimmers! Not only that, but I had the privilege of working with some of my best friends, who I still see today, Krista and Debbie. It was such a joy to share my life with this summer swim team family from high school graduation, and college graduation, to my wedding receptions at Moonlite Gardens, my biggest supporter, Brent, to being pregnant with my three boys. So many swim team moms walked my babies around the pool during practice so I could coach. I loved sharing the love of Coney with my immediate family.

I got to fulfill my dream of raising my family at Coney. They swam on the swim team and had their swim team crew every day to hang out with. Their swim team crew was a special group of sweet and supportive kids. Tears are in my eyes remembering those families, and the bond we will forever have.

The biggest blessing was having the Howard family right by the side of the Kueper family. Mike and Krista Howard were such an advocate for the swim team and the swim team families.

My boys and their swim team crew helped with swim lessons, they rode the rides, dove off the boards, and went down all the water slides. My mom and dad would still make fried chicken and a cooler of lemonade, and the entire family would spend Sundays at the pool. Cole and Ethan became lifeguards and got to experience the practice, working all day and hanging out with their lifeguard friends. What a wonderful summer tradition!

To Coney, with Love, Katherine Leurck

As it turns out, the Coney Island Flower Show and the mother/daughter tea have provided lovely memories for my daughters, grandmothers, and myself over the years.

Walking into the flower show at Coney Island was like stepping into a floral fairytale. Coney Island was transformed and as you strolled through the floral displays the scent and scenery were a feast for the senses. It was difficult to know where to look as so many flowers and colors begged for your attention.

My little girls bustled around like butterflies running with excitement from one display to the next, resisting the urge to touch. The floral arrangements made a beautiful backdrop for their spring dresses, patent leather shoes, and ribboned hair, and the breathtaking creations offered inspiration and delight.

These moments were not lost on me as their mother, and I knew that spending this time with my mother, mother-in-law, and daughters was a time-honored tradition to be cherished for years to come.

The children squealed with excitement as they pointed out the Coney Island Ferris wheel and Swan Ride, which all looked like a storybook picture. I gratefully held their tiny little hands in mine and was thankful for the precious gift of our mother/daughter flower show tea dates.

As it turns out, the flower show at Coney Island was about much more than flowers, it was about building memories that will last a lifetime. It created the opportunity to slow down, connect, cherish beauty, and cherish one another.

Thank you, Coney Island, for all the memories.

Love,

Katherine, Alexandra, and Audrey Leurck

To Coney, with Love, Mary McGing Duckworth

I am sharing on behalf of my family. My parents, Delia Kilcoyne McGing and Philip McGing, both were from Ireland. My mom was born in Louisburgh, County Mayo, and my dad was born in Tourmakeady, County Mayo. Born in small villages about 30 miles apart from one another, both of them came to America in the 1940s and both settled in Cincinnati, Ohio.

A few years later, they met at the Irish Day Picnic held at Coney Island. The rest is history, as they eventually were married and had 4 kids. I am proud to carry on their legacy through my Irish Dancing school, which has performed countless times at Coney Island in our 45+ year history. I think this story depicts the culture of Cincinnati so well as it tells the story of two young immigrants who grew up miles apart in Ireland but met here in Cincinnati at Coney Island.

To Coney, with Love, Ron Higgins

Coney Island has been an incredibly special place for my twin brother Don and me. We first attended the amusement park in 1971 with our mother and grandmother. Then, in 1989, we started working there and have continued to work there as seasonal employees up through the final 2023 season. Most years we were bartenders at Riverbend. However, through the years, we've worked at Moonlite Gardens, Moonlite Pavilion, Sunlite Pool, Moonlite Grille, and in the picnic grove. Four of our children have worked there too. Our parents told us stories about dancing at Moonlite Gardens in the '50s and in 2004 we took them back there to see an Elvis impersonator for their 50th wedding anniversary. My brother and I have fond memories and have made many lifelong friends from working at Coney Island.

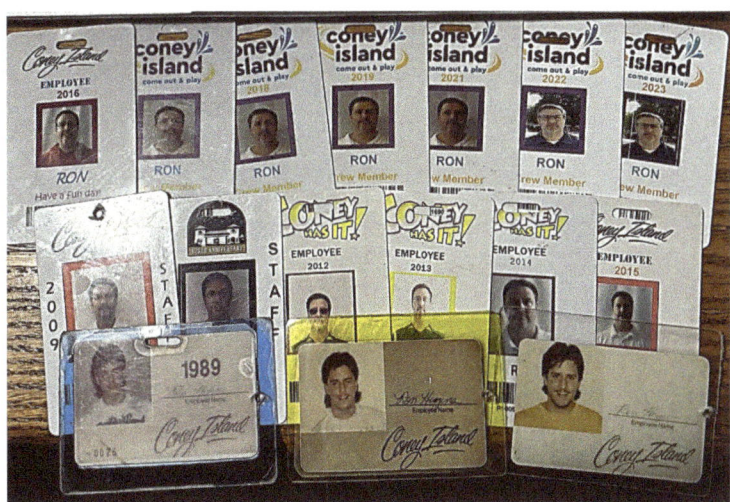

To Coney, with Love, Lori Humphress

The first time I remember going to Coney Island was when I was about 5 or 6 years old. In the 1960s, we rode the ferry from Silver Grove, KY across the Ohio River to the landing at Coney Island. The fun began even before we got to the park as riding the ferry was part of the fun. We met my aunt, who was already at the park and spent the rest of the day riding the rides. It was always one of my favorite places to spend a nice summer day.

To Coney, with Love, Emily Strubbe

I have always loved to swim, and my family joined Coney Island before I was born.

I took swim lessons at Coney, completing the highest level, which included swimming for 10 minutes with your clothes on. I learned to navigate the deep end, avoiding divers going off the diving board, the lifeguard rowing his boat, and kids jumping off the side, trying to touch the bottom of the 10-foot-deep pool.

I remember the day an outgoing staff member, Tim Timmons, came up to a group of my friends and me, telling us about the joys of being on a swim team. Coney was going to start a swim team, and he was recruiting swimmers I wish I could say he had hand-picked me after seeing me splash around the pool, but I think he just needed participants who could swim 50 yards without having to stop. We decided to give it a try, and it was one of the best decisions I have ever made. My friends and I did have a moment of hesitation when we realized how cold the water was at 7 am, and that we were expected to swim approximately a mile every morning. Tim had glossed over these points when talking about the joys of a swim team.

However, we quickly learned the fun, friendships, and sense of accomplishment outweighed the cold water and early hours. We also thought the red and white vertical striped bathing suits were flattering. Meets truly were wonderful, as all your teammates stood at the end of your lane, urging you on. Everyone was a winner. It was celebrated if you improved your time by 2 seconds. I learned little improvements mattered, and friends were proud and supportive even if you ended last. Times in between events were spent eating powdered Jello for "energy", playing cards, and cheering on teammates. Meets would end with the entire team going to the newly built McDonald's on Beechmont, where $1 would get you a cheeseburger, small fries, and a small Coke. The swim team broadened my world; I made friends with kids from all different schools and different parts of the city. It is where I learned that people basically want the same things and are more alike than different… all while having a heck of a good time.

To Coney, with Love, Krista Howard

I spent most of my childhood and adult life at Coney Island, over 40 years. Summer after summer. I took swim lessons, swam on the swim team, and then started my first job at age 16 as a lifeguard. I loved everything about the pool including all of the people. The love I had for Coney Island infiltrated my soul, and I knew I could never leave. It is hard to put into words how much I truly enjoyed that place. I wanted to help other kids enjoy what I loved too, so I decided to teach swim lessons, coach the swim team, and help lead the lifeguard staff. Although I loved teaching swim lessons and coaching the swim team, my true love was being a part of the lifeguard staff. I started as a slide guard at Sunlite Pool in 1986. I loved it so much, that I moved into teaching and instructing the lifeguards. I stayed with the lifeguard staff until 2017. I ventured away to another area water park for one summer but quickly realized that no other water park, no other group of members, and no other staff could rival what I had at Coney, so I came back.

Thirty-one summers I worked at Sunlite Pool, which meant thirty-one lifeguard staffs. I loved every single one of the lifeguards I worked with. We were like family. Speaking of family — I met my husband, Mike, at Coney Island. He started in 1985 as a parking attendant and then ventured into landscaping. Eventually, he made it to the pool area — where we met. At Sunlite Pool, he started as a manager and then navigated his way to park operations. At the young age of 19, he became a full-time employee. Due to his love for people, his admiration for the entire park, and his incredible work ethic, he ended up as the Sr. Vice President and General Manager. We loved the park. We loved our jobs. Most importantly, we loved the people. The members and the employees brought us joy every single day. Fortunately, our three daughters, Kaitlyn, Kylie, and Kenna, were able to experience the love we had for Coney Island. All 3 girls started swim lessons at age 4 and began the swim team at age 6. Our oldest daughter, Kaitlyn, taught swim lessons and helped coach the swim team. She also lifeguarded for me and was promoted to head lifeguard. Although Kylie and Kenna never got the opportunity to lifeguard at Sunlite Pool, they definitely share a love for aquatics and the park.

Although there were so many good times I had as an employee at Sunlite Pool, my favorite memories were training and managing the lifeguard staff and walking laps around the pool deck each day talking to the members. Coney Island was a special place for sure and I will always cherish the times I had. The experiences as well as the people helped mold me into who I am today. Thank you, Coney Island, you will forever hold a special place in my heart.

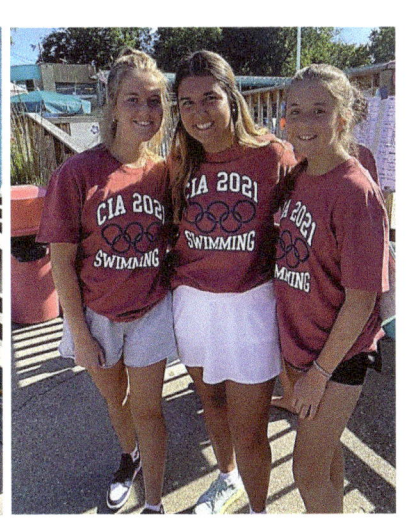

To Coney, with Love, Lisa Miller

My two sisters and I would not exist if it weren't for Coney Island's Sunlite Pool. That's where our parents met. Fate had it that Mom and her sisters had traveled up from Independence, Kentucky on the same day that my dad and his school buddies went swimming there. My mom had never learned how to swim but enjoyed walking around in the water. When my dad saw another guy trying to dunk my mom under the water and saw how panicked she was, he went over and told the guy to stop. The guy asked my dad what he was going to do about it. So, my dad promptly "made" the guy stop! My mom and dad started talking and hung out together the rest of the day. That evening my dad commented, "I met the girl I'm going to marry at Sunlite Pool today!" The rest is history.

Coney Island became a yearly pilgrimage for our family since my dad's union, CWA (Communications Workers of America), had their annual picnic there on Labor Day for many years. We loved spending the whole day there, riding all the rides, eating in the picnic grove, and going home exhausted, but happy!

Later, when my husband and I were dating, he took me to Sunlite Pool one day to swim. He wasn't much for swimming, but I think he took me there because he knew it had such a special meaning for me!

Both my mom and dad have now gone to heaven. Mom died from Alzheimer's in October 2010, and dad died from the same disease in October 2022. I'm glad they weren't alive to see Coney Island and Sunlite Pool close. It would have been devastating for them.

To Coney, with Love, Nicole Galbreath

My best Coney Island memories are taking my children there and watching them have the times of their lives. I am 33 now and have been going to Coney since I was a little girl. It was a family thing for us. Because I was young riding the rides back then, my favorites were the ones that would go forward and backward. My daughter loved the kid area and my son loved the diving boards. I remember letting him finally go to the deep end when he was old enough. We are truly saddened about the closing of Coney but will always have the great memories of swimming, fireworks, and just spending time with family.

To Coney, with Love, Richard Atkinson

I worked at Sunlite Pool as a lifeguard for several years during the mid-1970s. The 1975 picture is below. From left to right: Dave Raye, Greg Farrell, ?, Bob Lowe (Captain), Bob Farrell, Greg Schrand, Nick Deiters, Tom Maguire, Bob Anderson, Mark Sterbling, Dick (Rich) Atkinson. I have a lot of great memories from working with this group of guys. It was a hard pool to guard due to its size but we also had a lot of fun, with each other and the folks in the pool. The kids were the best part. Part of our initiation was to jump off the top of the 90 ft (if I remember correctly) diving tower. Bob Lowe was so great to work with. He would pull so many pranks on both the guards and the customers. He was so much fun.

After lifeguarding, I worked as a bartender when they did the dances at Moonlite Pavilion on the weekends and as a bartender when the ATP was still at Coney.

I worked with a lot of great people during those years and made a lot of friends. I have memories of all the other folks who worked there from the porters to the ladies in the cafeteria. It was a great place to work as a college kid. I also swam on the Coney Island Aquanauts from 1968 to 1973. Also pictured below. Tim Timmons was the coach.

We had family memberships there when I was growing up and after I got married and had kids, we had membership until we moved to Kentucky in the 1990s

I am truly going to miss Sunlite Pool. It is such a shame that they couldn't find a way to keep the pool. There are so many memories from there.

To Coney, with Love, Sarah Brulport

Coney Island was a part of my life from the time my memories began. Imagining scenes as my grandmother told me stories about making her dresses to attend romantic dances and listening to popular bands at Moonlite Gardens. Thinking my mother and father were so brave as they describe movements and speed while riding a ride of the past, called the Wild Mouse! Then, making my own memories, being so proud of wanting my picture for my season pass even though a photo wasn't needed at the age of 3, morning swim lessons and finally making it to the island to jump off all by myself. There was night swimming at member nights with my friends, winning tickets from water balloon tosses. I attended the Lion King movie premier from Q102 (radio) days, played mini golf, rode paddle boats around what seemed at the time a hidden jungle island in the middle of the lake, to finally having it be my very first job at 15 years old. Coney Island defined my childhood, and what a lucky child I was!!

To Coney, with Love, Denis Larrick

As a 10-year-old, we traveled once from Dayton to Cincinnati so Dad could see my eyes the first time I rode a coaster. The Shooting Star's sudden left curve at the top of the lift hill was cool since you were facing the river and the tunnel at the end was over before I knew we were in one. The Wildcat was just rough. What scared me most was a slow, peaceful ride through the tunnel of Lost River. The musty concrete block tunnel was spooky dark with all kinds of hokey light leaks and unused boats clanking together off to the side, it stunk of river water, and I was certain a giant snake would jump into the boat at any time. The lift hill and splashdown were an anticlimactic relief to this somewhat claustrophobic kid. I still will take a coaster over a dark ride.

Have you ever wondered what happened to the Coney Island and Lake Como Railroad trains? You can ride behind both of them today. #34 Mad Anthony Wayne is at Oil Ranch in Hockley, Texas, while #35 George Rogers Clark is operating at Lake Winnipesaukee amusement park in Rossville, Georgia.

To Coney, with Love, Jill Marie Holdeman – Lee

For ten summers of my life, I spent my days at Coney Island with my mom and dad, Marcella and Robert Holdeman. My father taught me to swim at Sunlite Pool, as he did with my sisters, Beth and Gloria, and my brothers, Daryl and Greg. We had season passes for as long as I can remember. For the next thirty-seven years of my life, I spent my summers at Coney Island swimming in Sunlite Pool with my mom, usually on Sundays.

Last year, I spent my one and only summer at Coney Island swimming at Sunlite Pool without my mom or dad, since they have both now passed away. It was hard to be in the deep end without my mom. This year would have been my 50th Summer at Coney Island but I will not get to dip a toe in that beautiful blue water.

My best memories of Coney Island are of Sunlite Pool and conquering the fear of jumping off the pier, swimming all the way across the deep end, sliding down the slide, and going home exhausted with the sweet smell of chlorine in my matted hair. My first concert was Whitney Houston, who performed at Riverbend. My brother's brilliant blue Camaro caught on fire under the overpass on Kellogg and I had to go to the bathroom so bad, that my sister walked with me back to Coney Island and we were allowed to use the restroom. I recall member's swims on Friday nights with the DJs, the music, and the unique experience of the pool at night. One September, my husband Jake and I went to the pool for the fireworks show. It was quite different to sit in lawn chairs at the bottom of the empty pool. The majority of my memories from Sunlite Pool involve family and friends. The first swim of the season, going to Summerfair, Balloon Glow, September car shows, the Fall-O-Ween, and Nights of Lights. Truly, Coney was the place to be. Sunlite Pool was built in 1925 and it is terribly sad that it will not make 100 years in 2025.

I will miss and love Coney Island always. I am beyond grateful to my parents, for introducing me to a place where time sort of stood still and where I learned the famous motto: *You don't stop playing because you grow old. You grow old because you stop playing*

To Coney, with Love, Stella Darlene Waits

Dad always had his company picnic, American Standard, at Coney Island every year. I vividly remember that at nighttime the Shooting Star rollercoaster was lit up and there was a sign that said: "do not stand up". Lots of the grown-up men would stand up and try to touch that sign! Thanks for all the great memories.

I think this photo was taken at Moonlite Gardens in 1959 with my father, mother, and sister.

To Coney, with Love, Kate Farlow

As a child, I came to Coney Island with my family on the Island Queen. As a teenager, I came with my friends and my boyfriend for a great day riding rides and swimming at Sunlite Pool. My fiancé and I danced at Moonlite before we got married, and when we were married, we danced under that beautiful blue ceiling. Moonlite was so breathtaking and then we would go out onto the lake and enjoy the paddle boats.

I remember seeing Brenda Lee, and Kenny Rogers and the First Edition, and I attended the hot wax dances later on. Moonlite Gardens was always filled with people enjoying themselves on a hot summer's evening with friends during special concerts.

My daughter and I swam at Sunlite Pool and we brought my granddaughters from the time. We would sit under the umbrellas when they were teenagers. Hanging on the rope on my raft, provided me with such a relaxing day after a hard week at work. I have a brick at Sunlite Pool that was given to me by my children and grandchildren for my birthday. I bought a brick at Moonlite Gardens that says my husband and I danced under the stars at Moonlite from 1963, when we first met, to 2009 when he passed. I also was an event coordinator at TriHealth and worked with Jim Chrisman to hold several of our employee picnics at Coney. Employees thoroughly enjoyed the day, the food, dancing and games, and the many rides and Sunlite Pool. We had wonderful feedback from them about that special day. I can't say that I have one specific memory but the ones I have from my childhood to my adulthood to my career I never will forget, and they are special to me. Thank you for the memories.

To Coney, with Love, Colleen Phillips

My mom and dad loved going to Coney Island. Even before they met, my mom and her siblings would ride the Island Queen to Coney Island to spend the day. My folks loved to play Fascination at the games pavilion. They set their sights on a set of flowered dishes and by the end of one summer they had enough points for a lovely eight-piece setting. I called them their Coney Island dishes and my mom proudly displayed them in every home she lived in. They are mine now.

When Coney Island had live horses and pony rides in The Land of Oz, I would head there to give my favorite pony a treat. I don't remember how old I was when they got rid of the live rides but it was a sad day when I went there and the horses were gone. My favorite memory was meeting Moe Howard when the Three Stooges made an appearance there. I was maybe five years old and short so my dad picked me up and put me on the table so I could see Moe. I was so excited to meet him and I remember he was very nice. I was at Coney Island (Amusement) the last night it was open in 1971. I watched the fireworks at Lake Como. It was bittersweet.

To Coney, with Love, Lisa Wormald

I was born in September 1967 and was fortunate to visit Coney Island, with my family, aunt, uncle, and cousins in the summer of 1971 just before the amusement section closed. I wasn't quite 4 years old, but remember that visit fairly well and the fun we had riding rides, eating sweet treats, and enjoying a packed picnic fried chicken dinner that my mom and aunt prepared.

I grew up hearing stories and looking at many photos of Coney Island from my parents, including stories of trips on the ferry boat and the Island Queen to get there, rides on the Shooting Star, log flume, whip, and many others, dancing at Moonlite Gardens and of course, swimming at Sunlite Pool.

I always knew Coney Island was a special place, but only came to truly appreciate it as I grew up. I enjoyed countless great times at Sunlite Pool with friends and family. One of my first dates with my husband 34 years ago was at Sunlite Pool. Coney Island and Sunlite Pool were one of our favorite places to spend time together. I felt like I took a trip back in time when we danced at Moonlite Gardens as my parents and grandparents had done.

Once our children were born, Coney Island and Sunlite Pool were special parts of each of our summers. From their first amusement park rides as young children to enjoying the thrill rides with their friends as they grew — so many happy memories were made. The rides and pool were perfect for kids of all ages. They loved jumping off the "island" into their dad's arms, riding the water slides, and swimming and splashing the day away.

One of my happiest memories is when we took my mom to Coney Island to watch our children ride the rides. As we walked around the beautiful park, she shared stories with our children of the "former" Coney Island and how it looked. Our oldest son's first job was at LaRosa's at Coney Island. My company picnic was held each year at Coney Island. The food was delicious, and the atmosphere was the best!

There will never be another place like Coney Island and Sunlite Pool — the nostalgia of a park along the river with such a rich history, the beautiful flowers, the sound of laughter, and the smiles on the faces of young and old. I will cherish the memories forever.

To Coney, with Love, Jaclyn Ard

Some of my favorite memories from the last 13 summers have been at Coney Island! My daughter was just 1 when we started with mommy and me swim lessons. She learned so many great skills in swim lessons through age 6 and it was a place where she and I could recoup from the hectic school year routine. We loved floating, jumping off the diving boards, and going to the island for jumps.

Another favorite memory is having a day with my soul sister at the pool, then getting ready in the bathhouse and walking over to Riverbend for a country concert. My soul sister died of cancer in 2022 but we had so many precious memories at Coney together.

We love Coney so much and will miss it tremendously.

To Coney, with Love, Sandy Cox

Back in the 1950s my dad, Bob Sharp, was in his early teens and he lived in Mt. Adams. He grew up on the poor side, like most of his friends from the hill. His buddies, Skin Cochran, Jim Miley, and Billy Freeze would hitchhike to Coney Island and spend the day at the pool. Sometimes they would take a break and go to Bill Barlage's on Penn Ave. for lunch. Bill was from the hill as well, and Penn Ave. butted up to Coney Island, which was convenient. My dad said they didn't require a pass for the ride back to Mt. Adams; he and his friends would catch a ride back home on the Island Queen.

To Coney, with Love, Cindy Theuring

This is a picture from 1964 when I was 7. I marched with the Judy Link Drum and Baton Core and we performed at Coney Island several times in the summer. This was the first time my dad could watch us march. He had his own business and worked 7 days a week. This picture means so much to me. It was the best way for a little girl to show off her dad.

My dad saved my life that day. We rode the Lost River and as we headed to the top of the hill to go down the ride broke down. We were stuck for over 1 hour when Coney decided to walk the people down the ramp. It was our turn, and my dad got out first. The ride started to move forward. My dad jumped back into the cart and held on to me and we went over. WE DID NOT HAVE THE safety belt on. If it wasn't for my dad I would have fallen out. I LOVE YOU DAD. I miss you so much.

As you can tell he was worn out but made it through for his little girl. THANK YOU!

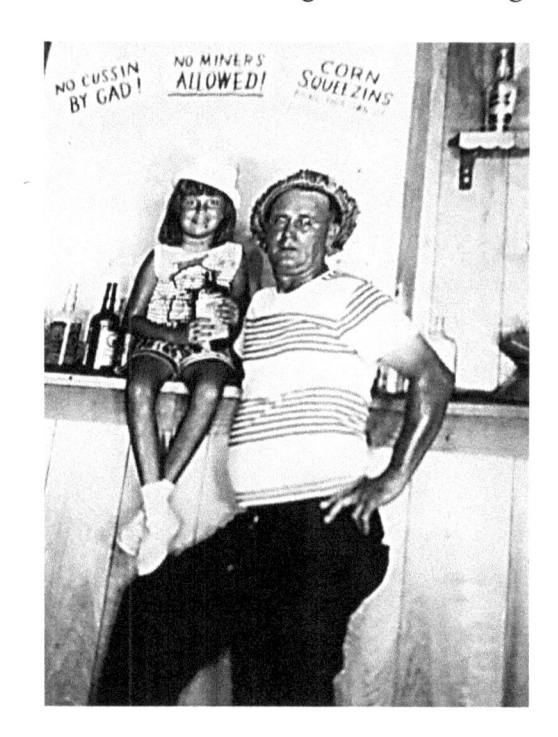

To Coney, with Love, Eileen Krauss

As a family, we would go at least 2 times a year. There were eventually seven kids in our family. Mom and Dad paid for the tickets/armband for rides. We had to save our allowance to spend on other things we wanted to do, like Skee Ball, the penny arcade, etc. We also would eat in the restaurant. Mom would ride with the kids who wanted to ride the roller coasters and dad would ride with the kids who wanted to ride the rides. We would stay for the fireworks.

I remember 2 things about my love of Coney Island. Our parents took us to New York City one time. Mom asked the three oldest kids if we wanted to go to Coney Island in NY. I remember my brother, sister and I all said there could never be a better Coney Island than the one in Cincinnati. So, we chose to go to a small park up there.

I also remember my mom told me when I was little, I'll say maybe 7 or 8 years old that I wanted to go down the slide in the pool, but when I got to the top, I refused to come down. My mom was waiting for me at the bottom. I guess someone finally gave me a gentle push and I loved it ever since.

I was devastated when they took out most of the rides when they opened Kings Island. It just wasn't the same for me.

To Coney, with Love, Andrea J. Ware

The best times at Coney for my family were getting together at Coney Island for Italian Day every summer. My father came from Italy to the U.S. with his family when he was 9 years old. He had several family members in this area. Every year on Italian Day at Coney all the families would pack up their most delicious homemade Italian dishes and go to Coney to picnic, get together to catch up on family news, and of course to ride the rides. It was so much fun and most memorable! My Italian grandmother made the best homemade spaghetti and meatballs! She even made her own spaghetti!

To Coney, with Love, Lisa Mauch

Besides having tons of childhood memories, I also recently found out that's where my grandparents met. I always wondered how a West-side girl met an East-side boy! And I recently found some photos of my grandma at Coney. I'm attaching two pictures of my grandma from 1928.

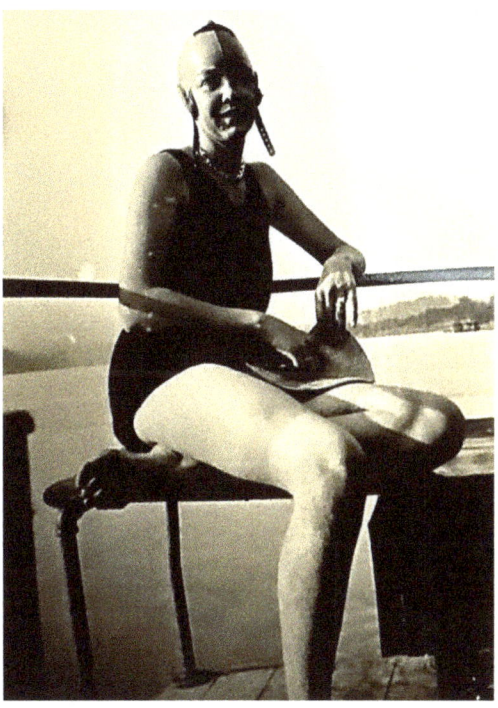

To Coney, with Love, Stephen Amann

I was only two years old, but my dad has told this story many times. Coney had two of my favorite roller coasters, the Shooting Star and the Wildcat. According to my dad, we were in line for the Wildcat when we heard a couple of young ladies trying to talk their male friend into riding the Wildcat. He was apprehensive and that's when they goaded him to man-up when they saw me with my dad. They asked my dad if I was going to ride and when he said yes, it was all the prodding the young man needed. My dad supposedly chose the front seat for us to ride the coaster. When the ride ended and the excited riders were leaving the ride, the young man caught up to us and said, "Little boy, you sure do drive fast!". Now at age 70, I love coasters to this day, and I still try to select the front seat.

To Coney, with Love, Sandy Dolan Schleibaum

My parents always loved Coney Island. They always went there even before they had a family. My dad was a lifeguard there when he was younger. When they had a family, we didn't get to go on vacations because there were five kids and we couldn't afford vacations. What we did get to do every year was go to Coney Island. Usually, a few times a summer. We went every year for Norwood Day at Coney Island and then a couple of other times. We would get there when the pool opened and swim until around 5:00 pm. Then we would go to the park and ride the rides. For years after we were grown, we would still go and bring our kids on Norwood Day!

To Coney, with Love, Deborah Berling

I fell in love with Coney Island in the 1960s. It was an exciting love that children have for amusement parks and sparkling pools. Every summer my parents treated the children and grandchildren to a wonderful day at Coney. It was a full day that started at Sunlite Pool. My parents said I was a fish. When I did take a break from the water, I remember standing by the fence looking at The Lost River. The rides were calling me.

We had an early dinner in the cafeteria and then headed to the Land of Oz. When I first started going to Coney Island, I was the perfect age to enjoy both sides of the amusement park. I rode one set of rides with my nephews and then the other rides with my brother and sister. The Teddy Bear and the Shooting Star will always be my favorite roller coasters.

The 70s brought changes, and I was thankful Sunlite Pool remained in operation. Good times at Sunlite Pool were shared with friends during my carefree teen years. I relived the joys of my youth through the laughter of my children. Nothing beats being a big kid as I swam, dove, and enjoyed the slides with my sons.

My love and appreciation of Sunlite Pool was at its peak. This summer, I was hoping to introduce this magnificent pool to my grandchildren. May this book enlighten my grandchildren and all future generations, to see the joys we experienced and to learn why Coney Island and Sunlite Pool are loved and will be greatly missed.

To Coney, with Love, Michael DiTomaso

I am 77 years old and have been going to Coney since I was 10. My best memory was CYO day. We would take the bus from school. No teachers. No parents — just a handful of ride tickets.

My Uncle would take us to Sunlite Pool several times a week. Upon entering you would receive a suit towel and key. To enter Coney was 10 cents. Just a great time like a yearly vacation. I learned to swim and got a great tan.

To Coney, with Love, Patricia Miller Wilfert

As a young child, I remember boarding the Island Queen on the Ohio River downtown in Cincinnati, landing at Coney Island, and walking up the hill past my favorite ride, the ponies! Fourth of July fireworks was always a favorite family time of year, sitting on my grandfather's shoulders, probably getting cotton candy in his hair!

Going to Coney's pool with teenage friends, and watching Bob Braun and Bob Lowe dive from the high boards was fun to watch but getting up there, looking so far down to the water, resulted only with us holding hands and noses before jumping!

Riding the Shooting Star and Lost River were our favorite rides along with the Ferris wheel and merry-go-round with the big sounds of music that made you not want to get off! There was no place like Moonlite Gardens, dancing to the big bands and watching the vocalists with no one crushing to get closer, was very special, as well as being with all the 'best dressed' ladies. When the band took a break, everyone went out into the park to ride the rides, in our finery, also noting that even Betsy Schott was out there having fun with all her friends too!

I'm so happy to say that our three children also grew up doing all the things that I did and share even more memories including the hot air balloons and a friend's wedding!! All in all, I guess you could say we are thankful to have a lifetime of happy memories surrounding Coney Island... lasting through January 2024, driving through the wonderful lighted holiday displays!

You can take away Coney Island, but never the lifetime of happiness we will forever enjoy remembering! The photo is of me with my best friend Joan Schneider at Sunlite Pool in 1950.

To Coney, with Love, Logan W. Shinkle

Coney Island had been my home since 2012. I worked parking for six summers, three years at the pool in Stand 20, and five years as Riverbend food service manager which Coney operated, but also, I spent some time helping other departments out when needed.

When starting out I didn't expect to stay as long as I did. When getting home from college during the summer I couldn't wait to go back and see all the wonderful people that I've encountered through my time working there. For me, it was like I was finally accepted for who I was as a person.

Throughout my life, I would probably label myself as an outcast and never fit in with the cool crowds but thanks to Coney, for once I felt accepted for being me.

If you know me personally, you'll know that I talk a lot, and when I was on my break, I sometimes would spend the majority talking with fellow employees from other departments and even with customers and sometimes I would clock in late from those breaks. That's when I knew I could not leave Coney Island. With me being a teacher and all, I knew Coney would be my summer classroom. People would always ask me why I would keep coming back, like, didn't a lot of your friends move on? The truth was yes, they did, but it wasn't all about me making friends. It was all about working with some of the newer people who became your new friends, some of the full-timers who helped me grow into a mature adult, but most importantly it was our members. Some even became friends and then moved to work with us.

In the office, I couldn't wait for Coney to open mainly to see my summer family. One of the craziest moments that may shock some people was that I spent the night in my car on the grass lot in Lake Como. I worked a concert the night before and it wasn't until after 1 am when we were done and we had to be back there by 6 am. So, I had my parents bring me a change of clothes and my toothbrush so I could get some good rest and get to work on time, I also knew if I was going to oversleep at least someone would wake me up. I'm happy to report that I was up on time.

Lastly, I wanted to spotlight an employee who has made a huge impact on me, his name was Mike Morris AKA "Big Mike." Big Mike was one of the hardest-working people I knew at Coney. One thing I liked about Big Mike was that he knew how to put up with my crazy humor and even went as far as throwing little firecrackers at me. Don't worry nobody was injured and they were the firecrackers that you would throw on the ground. I got my revenge on him by putting caution tape around his truck, and I couldn't have planned it at any better time. It was my last day of work for the summer and I put a note on the windshield saying nice working with you. But after that summer, we would still would get into our prank wars. Most importantly, we had some really good conversations about life. There are so many people I've encountered here that have made a positive impact on me but Big Mike accepted me for who I was and allowed me to keep being myself.

I'm going to end with the following note. A friend once told me many people viewed Coney Island's seasonal employees as a way to have a second income. To many of us that came back to Coney it wasn't just a second income, we returned each summer because Coney was our family. Businesses come and go, but one thing nobody can take away from us is the fun memories we've had at Coney Island.

To Coney, with Love, Donna Atha-Burdge

I have such wonderful memories of growing up there. When I was around nine years old, I was on the ten-foot diving board and changed my mind but there was no way to get off, so I jumped, *scary!* I loved riding all the rides and Moonlite Gardens and seeing my grandfather Robert Lowe who was the oldest living lifeguard.

To Coney, with Love, Alisha Yelton

This memory is for my parents. They were dating in 1954 and they visited Coney Island on one of their dates. They will be married 69 years this year in September. They have enjoyed visiting Coney Island many times throughout the years with their four girls.

To Coney, with Love, Craig Magnarini

My earliest memories start in 1963 with my mother, grandmother, and siblings at Sunlite Pool. I learned to swim there and learned what anxiety meant when jumping off the ten-foot diving board. My mother would always talk about riding the Island Queen to Coney and attending dances at Moonlite Gardens.

My summer life revolved around Coney. I remember my mother hitchhiking on Sutton to Coney with her four kids when her car would not start. She even took me out of school early on the last day of the park being opened in 1971 to enjoy the rides and nostalgia. I am 65 now my mother is gone, and the pool is gone, but I will always cherish the great times there.

To Coney, with Love, Kaylin Zoller

When I was younger, Coney Island was a magical place for me. My dad's work would rent out the place for a yearly event. The whole place was open for us, from the water park to the rides. One specific year stands out to me. My dad's friend had two daughters, one was around my age and the other was a couple years older. After sitting at the picnic tables eating with our families us kids decided we wanted to go ride some rides and swim at the water park. We took our time riding as many rides as we could. After that, we took a break and ate some pizza at the pizza place there. I think it was LaRosa's at the time. Once we finished our pizza we made our way over to the water park. We swam in the main pool for a little before we went to the water slides. We were having so much fun and just enjoying our time. After about an hour our parents found us and were so worried because they hadn't been able to find us. They didn't know we had left and thought we had been taken. Thankfully, we were safe and were just having a fun time. I always had fond memories of Coney Island.

To Coney, with Love, Gavin Hatfield

In 2020, I was working security walking around the pool, and Deborah Lee was the lifeguard supervisor. After spending a whole summer together at work and talking, what seemed like every day, all day long, we became really good friends.

At the end of the season, I was informed that she "liked" me. Being the shy guy I was, I was refusing to go and ask her on a date. It took a Hamilton County Deputy Sheriff to tell me that if I didn't ask her now, I'd regret it. So, we took two laps around the pool and I looked at her and asked her on a date.

Well, the following year 2021, I asked that same lifeguard supervisor if she would marry me, the only difference at this point was I had become a full-time supervisor for the security department.

In August of 2021, I left Coney Island to pursue my dream of law enforcement at the Hamilton County Sheriff's Office. Come May 30th of 2022, I finally got to call my best friend my wife, and not long after that in July we found out that our little family was going to be gaining a new member.

In March of 2023, we welcomed our son Kason into this world, and as you could guess as soon as we could we introduced him to the Coney Island and Sunlite water adventure. He loved the pool and even though the pool is no longer there the memories of how our family started will always remain.

To Coney, with Love, June Foster

When I was a kid, we would have family reunions every year at Coney Island. My grandma was afraid to ride the Skyride. I remember one year I convinced her to ride it. She prayed the Rosary all the way across and back. The Shooting Star was my favorite ride.

To Coney, with Love, Ruth Stevens

I learned to swim at the age of 7! I swam on Sundays and then later in the day we would go ride all the rides, and then go back to the pool. Those were good times!

To Coney, with Love, Diane Heitz Nichols

Growing up in the 50s and 60s we'd often pack lunches and head to Coney Island for a day of swimming. I have saved this 'admission tag' they put on our wrists when we entered the 60 years ago.

To Coney, with Love, Sheri Eichorn

I don't have a lot of detailed memories of Coney Island although I've been there a lot over my lifetime. I was first there as a very young child (probably 1-2 years old; I was born in December 1968) with my parents and grandparents. I've included some pictures of this time. It is crazy to look at these pictures and see what I mostly recognize as Kings Island rides, but you can clearly see the Ohio River in the background and I recall that many of the rides at Kings Island had originally come from Coney Island.

My only memory from my early visits to Coney was one from Sunlite Pool where I remember vividly calling out to my mom that I was drowning while I only had to set my feet down and stand up to save myself as the edge of the pool was super shallow where I was. I'm sure my mother laughed about that at the time. Later in life I would take my own daughter there to ride the rides (those that were left) and swim with friends at the pool (this was around 2003-2005 probably). The pool was the best thing of all. It was so large with a shallow area around most of it for younger kids as well as deeper areas for the adults and older kids. We would set up near the edge with our chairs, towels and coolers and spend the day watching our young kids have the best time ever! Having lived in Anderson Township for most of my life, it was always a fun place to visit and it will be sad not having it around for future generations. I live in Dayton, OH (Oakwood) now, but I still will feel the loss of such an iconic park.

To Coney, with Love, Mic Moore

I was a ride mechanic at Coney from 1997 to 2000. I was the main mechanic who went to New Jersey to dismantle the Cobra roller-coaster in 1997, and also the one who put it back together in 1998.

To Coney, with Love, Cherie Mick

My grandparents, Pete LaFleur and Clara "Babe" (Hartmann) spent a lot of time at Coney Island before they were married, after they were married, and once they had a family.

They both were born, raised, and lived their whole lives in Cincinnati. They went swimming at Coney Island and also went to some of the dances. Pete won "Mr. Cincinnati," a bodybuilding award around 1940. They got married in 1942. They also made it through World War II as a couple when my grandpa was drafted into the Army in 1943. He was stationed in the Philippines. My grandparents have always been my perfect example of a loving couple. I always saw love in their expressions for each other. They would always take the time to dance with each other and make each other laugh.

Mike S., Gayle L. + Erich S. + Terry L. @ Coney Island

190

To Coney, with Love, Trish Michael

My lifelong friend and I first met as employees of Coney Island; our very first teenage job. We were assigned to the "Hot Dog Barrel" as part of Coney's food service. The Hot Dog Barrel located toward the end of the Coney Island Mall was exactly what it sounds like, we were assigned to keep the hot dogs heated and ready to go for our walk-up customers. Our question was always do you want a hot dog or a chili dog? The barrel was a small, round cubicle so we worked elbow to elbow and became fast friends. As time went on, the customers were our entertainment as so many different personalities approached our little square order window. We still see each other often and many, many times we recall our days at Coney with happy memories of our time spent in our barrel. We always laugh and smile fondly. The time at Coney made for a great friendship and great summers!

To Coney, with Love, Elisia Bybee

I have many memories of Coney Island growing up, but my most sentimental came as an adult. My mom attended Woodward High School and she had an invitation for her 50th class reunion to happen at Moonlite Gardens. Due to finances, she told me she wasn't going to go. She didn't have the money for the ticket or an outfit, and didn't like to drive at night.

I wanted her to have the experience and told her that I would be her date, and buy the tickets and her outfit. The reunion was late afternoon and it was warm, but it didn't keep this group of 68(ish) old Woodward grads from having a cocktail and dancing the sparkling star-studded evening away.

Three years later, after my mom had a stroke right before her 73rd birthday and passing the year of her 80th, the beauty of that experience and all my memories of Union picnics and swimming with family resonates with me every time I look at the purple Woodward High 50th reunion coffee cup placed affectionately on my shelf.

To Coney, with Love, Mary Johnson

I have been going to Coney since I was 4. I was born in 1947. My grandmother took us up on the Island Queen. I took my kids and grandkids there. My son tells a story that he told his 4-year-old sister that there was a dead lady in the cage under the slide. He tells the story still at 56 years old. My last years have been going with my daughter and just laying on a float to tan all day. I have so many memories of that special place. Five generations of our family have gone there. I cried when I heard that it was sold.

To Coney, with Love, Joseph A Trauth

I was bartending on August 8, 1988, at the Governors Convention in Moonlite Pavilion. The featured act was Dick Clark Revue. Governor Bill Clinton stopped by my bar and asked me what was good tonight. I served him a Christian Moerlein lager. He pretty much hung out all night at my bar drinking Christian Moerlein, watching Dick Clark work, and telling stories mainly about his appearance on Johnny Carson's show a couple of weeks prior. Bill was hilarious. He had a crowd around him most of the night, he insisted I drink a Moerlein with him and signed my program.

To Coney, with Love, Sharon Buckner

My mom loved Coney so I was introduced to the park at the age of three. We would go to Sunlite Pool and spend the day. I remember the locker room key on a gold braided elastic cord she would wear around her wrist; some wore them around their ankle. The fragrance of suntan lotion pervaded the air and the beautiful blue color of the pool's water is forever in my mind's eye.

After hours at the pool, we would change and go to the park and ride some of the rides. The Ferris wheel, the carousel, and my favorite, the big rockets which flew around the hub, it was like we were in outer space or at least I could pretend.

As I grew older, I was permitted to be dropped off with friends and spend the entire day, sans mom. Coney Island was clean, safe, but most importantly, a big, wonderful adventure. The rides, the games, the food, the pool, the lake, everything you could ever want or need, all in one place. I could go on and on, the memories I have of Coney could fill an entire book. It sincerely breaks my heart that it is gone. However, when I recall all of the wonderful hours I spent there, it fills me with warmth that no one can take away. I love you Coney Island, forever and always.

To Coney, with Love, Daryl Holdeman

These pictures show the affection my parents had for the lovely World's Largest Recirculating Pool. Dad 1925-1985. Mom 1934-2022. Five children learned to love and swim at Sunlite Pool.

To Coney, with Love, Liz Kroin

My parents met at Coney Island. My father later told my husband she was beautiful. I believe when she was crowned Miss Potato Chip, it was at Coney. I never knew the brand but, in my head, I believe it was Husman's. They got married and had me, and until we moved to New York, they frequently took me to Coney. It was so much fun I couldn't sleep the night before. Twenty-five years later, we all ended up back in Cincinnati. Our family took my kids to go on the kiddie rides, some of which were still too scary for me, and play Skee Ball and putt-putt, get soft serve, and go down the big slide. After my parents died, I mixed their ashes with some of Dorothy Applegate's, my mom's best friend, and sprinkled them on a rose bush at Coney.

To Coney, with Love, Judie Limes Wilson

Hazel and Bob

Hazel was a teenager growing up on a hog farm in Southern Indiana. Bob was a Marine in WWII stationed on Peleliu Island in the South Pacific, a long way from his hometown of Cincinnati, Ohio. There wasn't much for a young, ambitious girl to do in Tell City, Indiana, so Hazel packed her bags moved to Cincinnati, and stayed with her aunt. Hazel found a typing job at the Formica Corporation. Bob came home from the war and started taking business courses at the University of Cincinnati, eventually becoming an Insurance Agent. Sunlite Pool was the place to go in the summer, so there they both were, at Sunlite Pool on a beautiful sunny day. Bob once stated he was a 'leg man' and in his words, "Hazel had gorgeous legs!" He spotted her at the pool one day and asked her to go dancing at Moonlite Gardens, back then, they had 'big bands' playing on the weekends, and their future together was put into motion. They were married on May 17, 1947. Bob and Hazel bought a modest home in Mt. Washington and had three children, one boy named Kim, and two girls, Michele and Judie.

The Limes family, like many other families, joined Coney Island pool as members, spending the summer days swimming, breaking for lunch eating picnic lunches that they packed in a large cooler, under the tree-shaded picnic area behind the concession stand. One day, Judie was initiated to the big metal slide too young, like many other children, standing at the top of the monstrous slide, too afraid to go down, and not allowed to go down the ladder, the line backing up behind her. How many times over the years did this scenario play out? The lifeguard blew their whistle, shouting, "You can't climb down the ladder, it's too dangerous, you must go down the slide." A panicked mother, wondering how her child got up there without her noticing, wading her way to the bottom of the slide, to coerce her youngster down the slide and catch them at the bottom. It always had a happy ending. Judie, approximately 5 years old at the time, remembers her mother immediately putting her in Coney swim lessons after that. The water was so cold one day her lips turned blue and Hazel grabbed her out of the class. That very large swimming pool always had cool, refreshing water, but that day it was a little too cool. Judie eventually joined the Aquanauts swim team but quickly switched over to the diving team.

All three kids went to McNicholas High School and took summer jobs at Coney. Kim, the oldest, worked the basketball hoops in the arcade at the amusement park and also worked the 'Guess Your Weight or Age' game, which he enjoyed. He was given a microphone to do his job, and stated laughing, "You should never give a microphone to a 16-year-old kid." He also said, he always tried to guess the women a little younger than what he thought they were, to make them smile. He thought it was easy to guess ages because it was plus 3 years in either direction for age, plus 10 pounds for weight. Michele was next, landing a job at the pool, handing out towels, working in the ladies' locker room, or checking membership passes at the back 'members-only' gate behind the concession stand. Finally, Judie came of age, and of course got a summer job during high school, working at Coney in 1980. She was assigned to the parking gate when it was only $1.50 for parking, or you were waved on through if you had a membership card. She remembers one evening, the night Jerry Lee Lewis was playing Riverbend, a carload of guys with pompadours drove to the gate. She told them $1.50 for parking, and they said they were with the band, they weren't, they were just fans going to the show, but they looked the part, so unknowingly at the time, waved them through. Judie started her IT career at Community Mutual Insurance Company, Blue Cross/Blue Shield., which had their corporate picnics at Coney, she represented the company soccer tournament at the picnic. After 10 years at Blue Cross, she accumulated quite a few weeks of vacation time and spent most of them hanging at Sunlite Pool in the summer.

Eventually, Kim got married, and he and his wife Carol had two children, Kristin and Randy. Kristin and Randy went to Turpin High School and of course, got summer jobs at Old Coney. Kristin, like her

Aunt Michele, was at the back pool gate by the concession stand and also worked the new back pool gate near the newer Zoom Flume slide. Kristin's third summer at Coney was Randy's first of his four-year tenure. He started at the new kiddie rides installed near Lake Como, soon becoming ride manager. A 16-year-old employee named Christina was one of many teenage employees he supervised. Randy still teases his co-manager/friend about the time his friend wrote up Christina for wearing shorts that he deemed were too short. Fast forward four years, Randy and Christina bump into each other at a bar in Mt. Adams, remembering each other from their stints at Coney, hit it off. Like Bob and Hazel, they fell in love, got married, and have twin girls named Addison and Harper, who unfortunately, because of the abolishment of Coney, will not be able to get high school summer jobs at Sunlite Pool.

"We don't stop playing because we grow old, we grow old because we stop playing."
~George Bernard Shaw

To Coney, with Love, Carolyn Meyer

In May 1968, I turned 16 and Coney Island was my first summer job.

My mother worked there, and my next-door neighbor worked there too. We worked at the refreshment stand under the sky ride and sold popcorn drinks and ice balls.

I met my husband on the ski lift. It was the only ride my little brother wanted to ride, so I took him on again and again and we would ride around and around; that's how I met my husband. He worked on the sky ride, and we were on that ride so often, eventually he would jump in the gondola with us, and always rode to the other side, which was where the refreshment stand was.

Coney Island was so beautiful with the huge trees. We would go back to the park while it was still open and look at the trees and walk around. We are still married to this day. Coney meant so much to us because it's a big part of our lives. When we were off work, he would always go to the games and win stuffed animals for me. That was always fun. We would ride the ferry across the river from Kentucky to Ohio. It was magical. Coney Island was magical and there was no other amusement park ever as beautiful and magical as Coney Island. A few years later, my dad worked at Moonlite Gardens and that was beautiful, too. We would go to some concerts and dance there. Moonlite Gardens was a magical place also.

To Coney, with Love, Trina Napier

There's no greater memory than endless summer days at Coney, filled with pizza, sunshine and swimming. I need to apologize to all the ladies of the 80s lazily floating on their long yellow, blue, and red rafts with feet tucked securely under the ropes for splashing you.

My fondest memory with my dad was our annual 4th of July family splash and dash. With the sun high in the sky, I would climb onto my dad's back and as we swam past the rows of melting sunbathers, we would deliberately make huge splashes by slapping and kicking the cool brisk water. Then we would muster our brave face and jump off the 10 ft. diving board. All day we eagerly awaited the Fireworks, while riding roller coasters and floating down the Ohio river on the Island Queen. The splashing party became a family tradition that me and dad carried on with my children. Coney was fun for everyone.

To all those sunbathers, sorry again for splashing you, and I am also sorry that Coney Island days could not last

To Coney, with Love, Colleen Thomas

When my twin boys were born, I didn't know what to do with them as I was a first-time mom. I remembered going to Coney as a child and thought, maybe I should try it. My husband worked so I had these two little globs of skin needing something to do between waking up and napping. We went to the zoo on certain days, and a season pass to Coney Island changed our lives for 11 years.

I would put the boys in their Puddle Jumpers, life vests, and put them on their bellies, and then walked them around the pool. They giggled and laughed. Kicked their fat baby feet and splashed their hands in such excitement, I couldn't be the only one to enjoy these babies' joy so I invited my father-in-law and he had a wonderful time watching them. We would continue this every summer and then our friends joined and made the summer even better. Coney Island taught them summers and summers of top-notch swim lessons.

To Coney, with Love, Kristine Norwell Bishop

We were fortunate enough to have four generations of Coney members!!! It was our "Happy Place", our peace, our slowdown place! Our safe haven from the world!

I never got to meet my dad's parents, so knowing I swam in the same pool as my grandparents was pretty neat! Coney provided so many amazing memories that we will cherish for a lifetime! I've never had a summer without Coney, 46 summers, and my daughter has never had a summer without Coney either! We are devastated that our Cincinnati treasure was taken away from our community! We were one big happy Coney family!

My dad, Egon Norwell started coming to swim at Coney in the late 1950s as a kid with his parents Biruta and Edward Norwell. They had a large family and Coney was a wonderful option for dad and his siblings in the summer. Later, my dad and mother, Beverly, took my sister Tiffany, my brother William and I and continued the tradition. We learned how to swim, dive off the boards, and play volleyball, basketball, and ping pong at Coney! Some wonderful memories are of my siblings and I jumping off the island to my dad, learning how to swim, and being on the swim team, and diving team. We would go down the Zoom Flume, the Zip, the Silver Bullet, the Twister, Typhoon Tower. I'd watch my kids run to the exploding water tower, jump off the 10 ft board, float on fun rafts, walk laps around the huge pool, the fun rides and paddle boats on Lake Como,

I remember Balloon Glow, yummy food, ice cream, and stopping by the swim shop to pick out candy with my daughter. Aunt Linda would swim her laps, family parties, and swim with my cousins. We had relaxing days with high school friends, talking to the older group of men and women we sat by, playing volleyball with our mom, and witnessing our dad dive off the top of the tower into the deep end and thank God for surviving!

We also enjoyed hearing my mom sing at Moonlite Gardens and Summerfair with several bands she was in. My siblings and I kept the tradition going and brought our families and made new wonderful memories over the years! We will hold our beloved Coney, and the friends we made in our hearts forever!

A special acknowledgment to our family and friends who have passed on. My uncles, Al Briedis and George Norwell, loved and enjoyed Coney! I will always remember our wonderful conversations.

Another Coney staple was Carl. He loved sitting under his tree by the back gate and playing chess all the time! My dad and uncles were often in long chess games with Carl, it was fun to watch! He would give candy to the kids and had a great sense of humor!

Tilly Long was known for her swimming, ping pong, biking, and dancing! Her famous phrase was "If you don't use it, you will lose it!"

Joe, Gilbert, Don, Tony, Jon, Arno, Bob, and many more of the "Wall boys" had a lot of wisdom and enjoyed watching us kids grow over the years! We enjoyed our friendships with so many!

There will never be another Coney! She was special, one of a kind and cherished by so many! I thank my dad and mom for continuing the tradition of summers at Coney! I'm grateful and fortunate for the time spent there! We love you Coney! We will never forget the largest recirculating pool in the world! Our Coney, our Sunlite! Our pool by the great Ohio River. So much history! The joy you brought us will be in our hearts forever!

You don't stop playing because you grow old, you grow old because you stop playing! Blessings and love to our Coney family always!

To Coney, with Love, JoAnn Buck

The Cincinnati Celtic Festival was held at Coney Island from 2000 to 2005. It was presented by Cincinnati Folk Life.

Each year the festival featured many international, national, regional, and local music and dance acts. There were two music stages, a dance stage, a theater stage, a harp stage, a musical instrument workshop stage, Bardic Circle, and an Irish Hedge School. Also presented were Scottish Heavy Athletic competitions, Connemara Pony rides, Scottish Highland Dance competitions, historical re-enactors, a Celtic Art Pavilion, herding dog demonstrations, rugby games, and 60-70 vendors.

Coney Island was the perfect place for this festival, and it was very popular with the thousands of people who attended every year.

To Coney, with Love, Sydney Anne Strangarity

I grew up in Hamilton, Ohio, where our closest amusement park was LeSourdsville. It was close. We had a blast there, and they had a very small admission charge. At about age 5, I slowly became aware of Coney Island, though I did not fully understand how involved I was.

My uncle, who raised me, had grown up in Addyston, Ohio. He told me stories about riding the Island Queen down the River on several occasions, and how exciting that was to do!

We did not have much money, so going all the way to Coney Island and paying $3.75 to gain admittance for the day and an all-day rides pass was only a dream. But my uncle's detailed stories were enough for me to know how amazing it must be!

Then one day, when I was nine years old, an aunt and uncle came to visit with my cousins, and invited me to go to Coney Island with them!

All the stories my uncle told me came to life! I remember the boats on Lake Como, the rides, the pool! Oh my goodness!

Coney Island amusement moved to the present-day Kings Island location. I worked there for 13 fun years.

My family and I still visited Sunlite Pool at Old Coney many times over the remaining years, something we really would love to do. But now, it will all be just a great memory.

Such great memories of an era gone by.

To Coney, with Love, Chip Pratt

I was fortunate to work at Coney from July 2003 to April 2015. I spent my entire time as both a Park Security Officer and a Park Police Officer. It was one of the best jobs I had, spending so many days and nights working both 2nd shifts and 3rd shifts. I met so many awesome people and fellow officers who became lifelong friends. The day I heard Coney was closing it was hard to believe. At first, I thought it was a joke. One thing is for sure, they can take away the park but cannot take away the memories! Whether it was working at Coney or going to the pool with my family... Coney Island will always be a part of my life!

To Coney, with Love, Jim D'Aquila

I remember the Coney Island Railroad audio. Some of what comes to my mind is, "Ladies and Gentlemen, boys and girls, welcome aboard the CILKRR, the Coney Island and Lake Como Railroad... Up ahead is Injun Country!"

To Coney, with Love, Pat Stowe Cruse

Our story started in 1965. I went to Coney Island with my best friend Donna. We were riding The Shooting Star over and over again. We were in line with a guy and his sister doing the same thing. They happened to be behind us in line every time. So, we started talking and realized that he went to Elder High School and we went to Seton. These schools are located next to each other on the west side of town. We knew some of the same people, and that is how it all began. We started dating all through our senior year of high school and graduated in 1966. We were married in 1968. We have 4 children,

12 grandchildren, and 5 great grandchildren, and another on the way. We just celebrated our 56th wedding anniversary this past April. Coney Island and The Shooting Star hold a very special place in our hearts and memories.

To Coney, with Love, Janet Meyer Perkins

I am 72 now. As a child, we never went on vacations. Our big event for summer was going to Coney Island on Riverside Day. We would pack a lunch to eat in the picnic area. We would be able to swim and ride the rides. I remember having to use tickets for each ride. I used to ride the whip over and over. It was my favorite ride until I was old enough for Wild Cat and Shooting Star. Mom and Dad would stay in the picnic area all day and we were free to do our thing until dinner. After dinner, the family would stay together and ride together.

The best part was it was a fun time for us as a family and what we considered our annual vacation.

As I got older and could drive, I would go on other days with friends at least 2 or 3 times a year.

The year they closed my now husband and I went together making new memories riding Shooting Star and Lost River. Tumble Bug and Ferris wheel were some of our favorites. I remember winning glasses with tickets from playing some games. We used those glasses for years after we were married and told our kids how we won them.

I have been to many parks, but I have to say, none will ever compare to the memories I have of growing up going to Coney Island.

To Coney, with Love, Michael Byrd

I spent many summers at Coney Island. The Shooting Star was an awesome roller coaster! The drop from the first hill would always lift you right out of your seat! For years, I resisted riding the ride in my picture; the ride that was most easily seen from the parking lot. I didn't want to go flying out of that thing! I finally rode it. Fun, but anti-climactic when compared to the Shooting Star. No need for a lap bar on The Lost River. What a great amusement park!

To Coney, with Love, Willy Corbett

Anticipation swelled; five young voices filled our family van as I drove down Sutton towards Coney. To the tune of "Here Comes Peter Cottontail," our five daughters sang "Coney Island here we come right back where we started from, no more days to wait for you, Coney Island here we come!"

Passing through the gate the girls turned their attention to searching for the right spot. No matter where we sat it was always the right spot. The cooler was filled with snacks, peanut butter, and jelly sandwiches, and drinks including the family favorite, Mt. Dew. Mom's swim bag contained diapers, shampoo, sunscreen, and everything else under the sun. The excitement raced in the girls' hearts as they raced to find their cousins. The older girls went to the island as the younger girls played in the shallow end stopping only to grab a snack or PB and J.

I thank God for my wife Teresa and her sister Katrina for watching the gang of eleven. They came home exhausted each summer afternoon, while the girls were already looking eagerly towards the next day. Loading up the van again the next day, with the five girls and all the stuff for the day, Teresa started driving down the hill towards Coney. And as always, the girls began their journey with their favorite song, "Coney Island here we come...."

To Coney, with Love, Richard Mahan

I could not think of specific stories but my dad, Jim Mahan, was manager there in the 70s and those were awesome days for me. I remember getting there before everyone and leaving last every day. I could order food and put it on my dad's charge. I got in big trouble when he found out he was paying for my friend's lunch as well. My sister and I remember when we found a warehouse full of prizes that were going to be sent to Kings Island. Dad let us each pick one. Those were great times and Coney will be missed by many!

To Coney, with Love, Cindi Watson

As a small child we went to Coney Island quite often in the summertime. We took the ferry from Fort Thomas across the river. When entering Coney from the river there was a big wizard that you walked under to get into the park. As I walked under the wizard I stopped to make my wish not telling anyone what it was. The wish never came true in the next summer when I went back to Coney I walked under the wizard and kicked it as hard as I could almost breaking my toes because my wish of giving my family a million dollars did not come true.

To Coney, with Love, Alan Zoller

My parents dated at Coney Island and Sunlite Pool in the 1920s. They returned many times over the years with their four children. It was the only place they could afford to take the whole family on a bookkeeper's salary. The Wild Mouse was their favorite roller coaster ever!

To Coney, with Love, Robert G. Masters

My history and stories begin approximately at 10 years old when we attended my father's company picnic at Coney Island. I knew someday I would work there and I did for 3 summers before being drafted into the Army. I started in the bottle room. I also help tame the horses, and fried hamburgers. I ran the rides but I had to work up to that responsibility. I was able to take lunch breaks at Sunlite Pool! I could not tell you the number of times I went down that pool's slide. I still have a collection of tickets for games and Skee Ball. Great memories!

To Coney, with Love, Laurie Hanauer

I started going to Coney as a toddler, with my mom, dad, and brother. My dad had been a lifeguard there years ago. He talked about Bob Lowe, the "legendary" lifeguard, and took swim lessons at Coney. I can't explain but I fell in love with Coney. It was summer, family, and friendship to me. I never stopped going. Each Memorial Day I would try to be the first in the pool. I finally achieved that goal in 2018. That was like Christmas Day! Coney Island was on my soul. I was, and am, devastated by the loss. It hurts deeply. I will miss it dearly, but always have wonderful memories of my days spent at Coney.

To Coney, with Love, Pam Deimling Hackett

Balloon Fest was so much fun at Coney in the '80s! We took our four kids, a playpen for the youngest, and a packed cooler, and hung out near the boat ramp entrance. When those balloons fired up and rose into the sky the kids were so excited. We'd watch and wave until they were out of sight.

My parents joined us. They loved Coney as well, both growing up on Kellogg Avenue, my mom directly across from Lake Como, and my dad on the riverside, a short walk to Coney.

As a kid, when we would visit my Grandpa Koehler, my siblings and I would sit on his front porch, looking across the street at the main entrance. We could hear the sound of the rides, see all the lights, and smell the saltwater taffy.

Every time we visited my Grandpa Deimling or Grandpa Koehler, we would beg to stop at Coney. My childhood family going to Coney Island was a special occasion — just twice every summer. One day to spend at Sunlite Pool and another day to just enjoy the rides until closing. It was MAGICAL!

My parents also shared stories of dancing at Moonlite Gardens, ice skating on Lake Como in the winter, and surviving the flood of 1937. The flood marker near the boat dock helped us understand how both of their homes were underwater, and although displaced for a long time, they were both restored, just like Coney Island was!

My love for Coney runs deep. It will always hold a place in my history and my heart. I'm 68 years old and I continued to visit Coney for decades with my children and grandchildren.

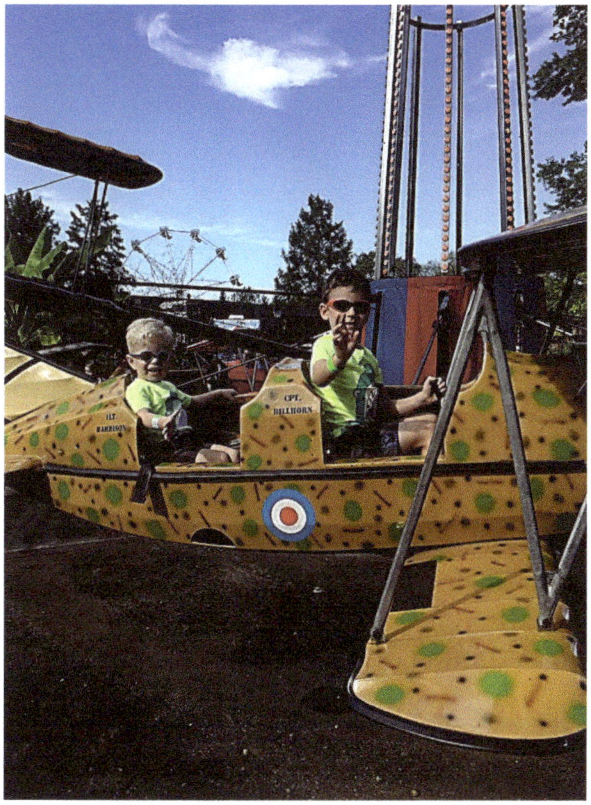
CPT.

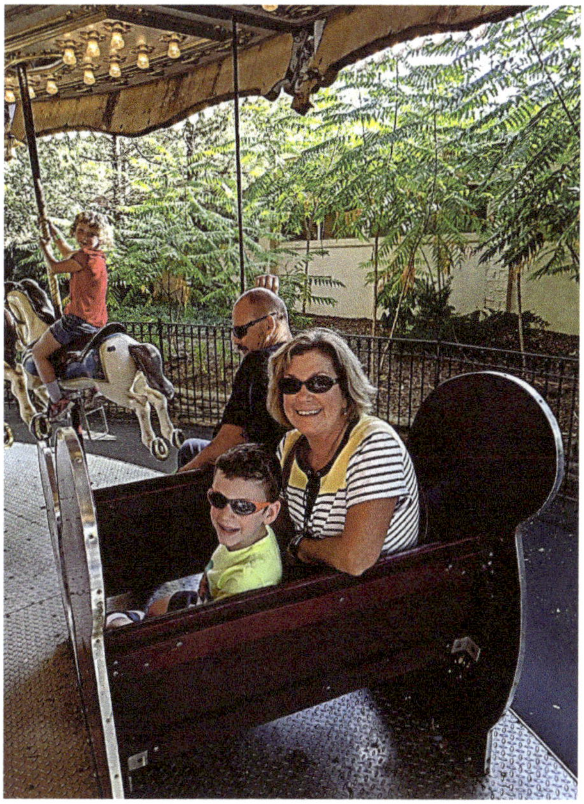

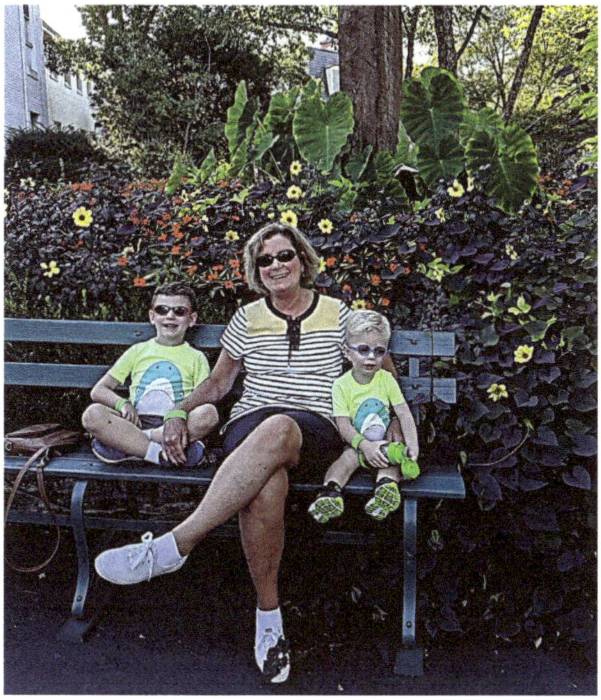

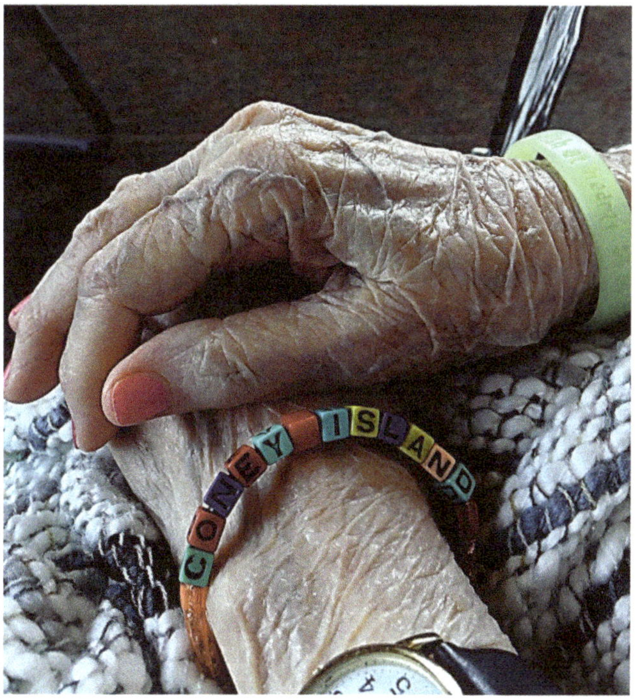
CONEY ISLAND

To Coney, with Love, Harmony Bass and the Kids- Logan, Lizzie, Lucas, and Lexi

Coney was the perfect place to create unforgettable memories with friends. We loved swimming together, taking part in Fun Fridays, and tackling the Greenie Meanie challenge.

From Logan: Coney Island Aquanauts swim team was a place to make the best memories with your best friends. We did fun Fridays, Greenie Meanies, and around the world. Some of the best memories were after practice eating donuts on Tuesdays before meets and getting to hang out with your best friends every day at practice.

From Lizzie: We all got our start at Coney with swim lessons. The best, most enjoyable moments came when my siblings and I started on the Coney Island Aquanauts swim team. My oldest brother Logan and sister Lizzie began swimming when they were 6. I began swimming with Coney when I was 5 and my other brother, Lucas began swimming on CIA when he was 4. We have been told Lucas was the youngest kid to be on Coney's swim team. He was 4 years and 6 months old exactly and swam that 50 like a champ. Coney wasn't just a pool for us. It wasn't just a place to be on a swim team. To my family, the Coney Island Aquanauts were our family. They were our summer family. Opening day of Coney for us meant we would see our swim team family again. We couldn't wait. We would meet up, practice, and have fun together as if we hadn't been away from each other. We all met some of our best friends joining the swim team and being with them 5 days a week for 6 to 7 weeks in the summer meant we would make some of the best memories. I met one of my best and closest friends because of the Coney Island Aquanauts. We don't even live close to each other. One of my fondest memories of Coney, believe it or not, is the ice-cold water of May and early June swim practices. We were in that water for practice unless it was under 60 degrees outside. If you could swim at Coney in that water during those early summer days, you could swim anywhere. I always compare other places and their water to Coney water. "Oh, you think this is cold? This is nothing. You should come swim with us at Coney at 8 am." You weren't cold unless you were "Coney cold." Some of the older kids got smart and started wearing open-water wet suits to practice. My dad was a Coney Island Aquanaut age group coach for a handful of years while my siblings and I swam at Coney. Another great memory is the SOSL relay meet where we did a Bass family Tandem relay. All four Bass siblings and Coach Eric, my dad, were on the relay together. I don't remember who won that relay, but I remember being so proud we competed together as a family. "We're from Coney, couldn't be prouder!"

From Lexi:
Some other fun memories of the CIA swim team for me are:

- Team Breakfasts
- Coaches cheering us on while sitting on the diving boards in the deep end during meets
- Fun Fridays
- Diving for donuts
- Messing up our dives on purpose so we had to bring in a dozen donuts for Tuesday
- Using Sharpie markers on our backs
- Coach Katilyn – my friends and I loved Coach Katilyn when she was our 8 and under coach
- Coach Matt's 8 and under posters – he raffled them off at the end of the season. I got the Trolls poster. It was awesome
- Swimming in the Twister Pool for 8 and under practices
- Greenie Meanies
- COLD WATER
- Dry Land
- Themed Meets – Red, White & Blue, Hawaiian, Superhero and others

- Coach Matt dressing up like a shark
- Parent vs Kid end of the Season swim meet
- Dance parties on the Island during swim meets after the pool closed
- Finishing practice and then heading to the rides with my CIA friends
- The CIA end-of-season banquet – the only time we could have floats and goggles in the deep end!
- Winning the SOSL Championships so many times– I was the girl's 25 yard, 6, and under backstroke champion when I was 6!

To Coney, with Love, Jerry S. Fry

I worked part time, when needed, at Coney at age 14 on big days, example 4th of July, GE DAY, P & G Day & holidays. At age 15 I was employed in the Land of Oz full time. My boss was Joe Cooley, a Teacher from Elder High. I learned a great deal and made many new friends. Also, my high school Superintendent Mr. Tabscott, his sons, other teachers, friends and Dennis Speigel a lifelong long friend, worked at Coney. Yes, I swam at beautiful Sunlite Pool, rode every ride in the park, canoed on Lake Como, and danced many nights at Moonlite Gardens. It was the place to be in the 1950s and 60s. Coney was my launching pad to graduate from Amelia High, graduate from Ohio State and complete a 54-year career with a company in Cincinnati. This is only a small portion of the FUN TIMES at Coney Island spent with family & friends.

To Coney, with Love, Marie Mills

Coney Island was and always will be home. Growing up, my family and I lived out our summer days at the pool. We participated in swim lessons, midnight pool parties, purposely getting stuck on the Zoom Flume, and finding money in the deep end, all because we could. We will forever cherish our time there.

As I grew up, my childhood memories of Coney were passed down to my kids. With every visit home, I would gladly take my kids several times to Coney. We had just as much fun each time. With races down the Twister Slides, and Silver Bullet, and jumping off the island only to settle back in the grass eating whatever we could sneak in while playing cards. It was the one summer activity we always looked forward to. A song that my family would sing as we drove down Sutton towards the pool was, "Coney Island here we come, right back where we started from. No more days to wait for you, Coney Island here we come!!" We were always so excited to sing that song! It never got old. Coney Island may be gone, but not forgotten.

To Coney, with Love, The SunBurners — Manager, Dave Waterson

We had the privilege of being the house band for Sunlite Pool for over a decade before its closing. The SunBurners were founded in May of 2011 and we had no idea that this Coney Island "gig" that we landed later that summer would become the cornerstone of our band's development into Cincinnati's #1 Island Party Band. From 2011 until 2023 (including 2020), we played over 75 SunBurner Sunday Funday shows - quite possibly one of the longest-running house band gigs in the city in recent memory. Cincinnatians would regularly see a band member elsewhere throughout the year and exclaim "You're in that Coney band, aren't you?!" We didn't even care that they didn't know the band name, but more that we were connected to them somehow through the magic of Sunlite Pool.

As the years went by, Sunlite Pool became less of a gig and more like a home away from home for the band. Fresh LaRosa's pizzas and complimentary frozen daiquiris from the tiki bar helped the band recharge each week. Yes, there was no better poolside gigs in the city. But it was always the people, especially the regular members and dedicated Coney staff, that made it such a great spot and kept the band coming back for so many years in a row. It's difficult to describe what made Sunlite Pool so one-of-a-kind, but we think it was the people. To the Coney Island staff and Sunlite Pool visitors — thank you for allowing us to entertain you, poolside, for over a decade!

Thank you Coney!
We enjoyed the ride(s)!

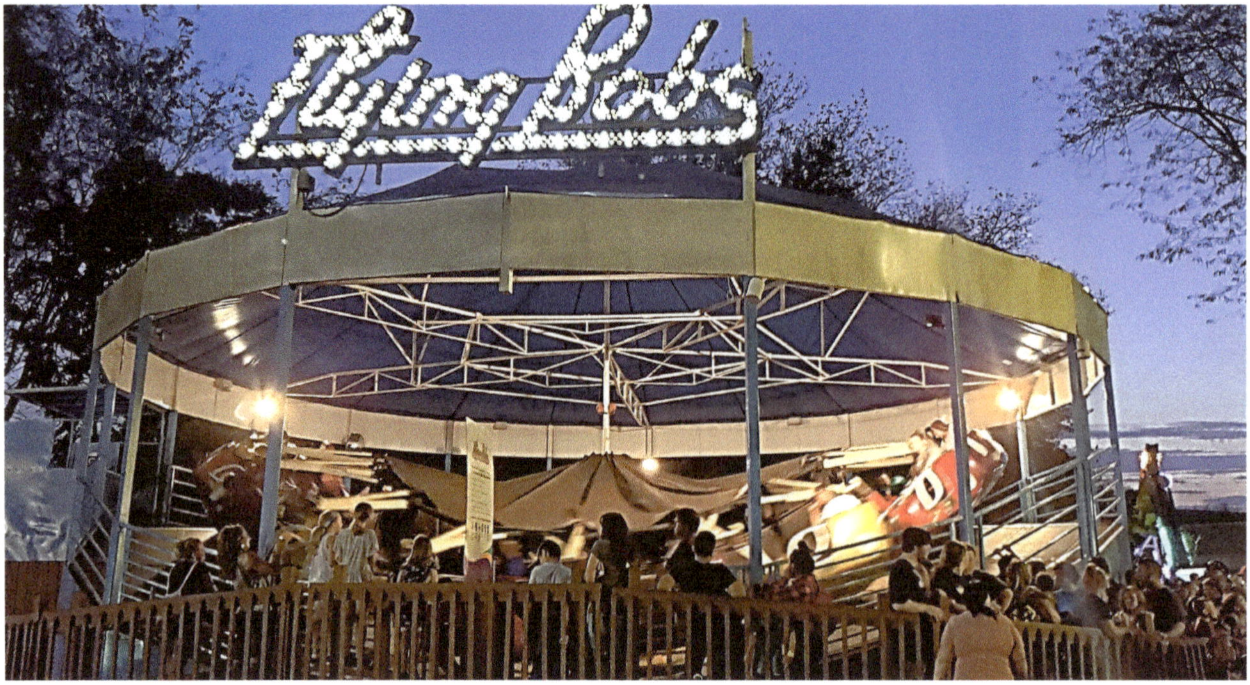
Flying Bobs

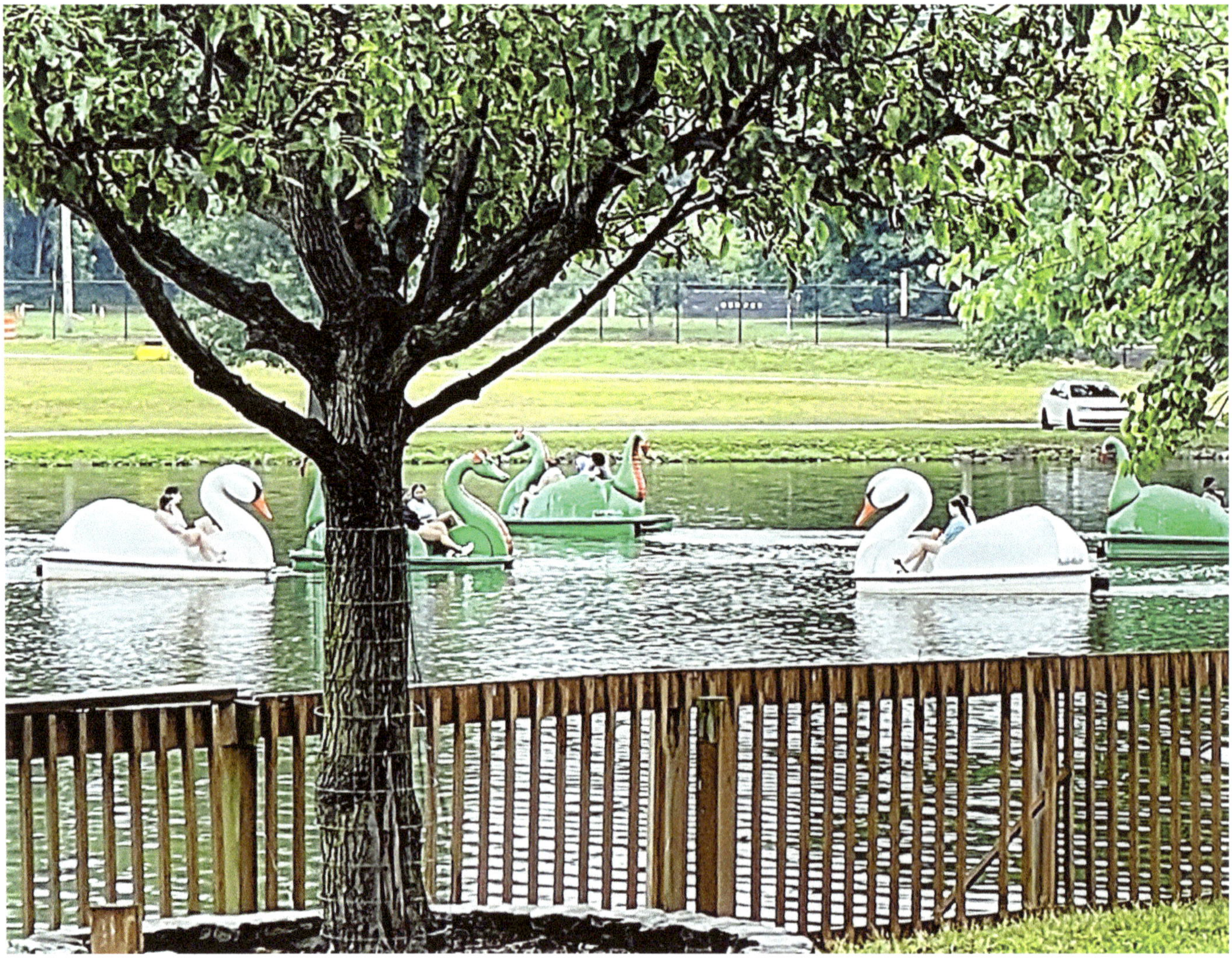

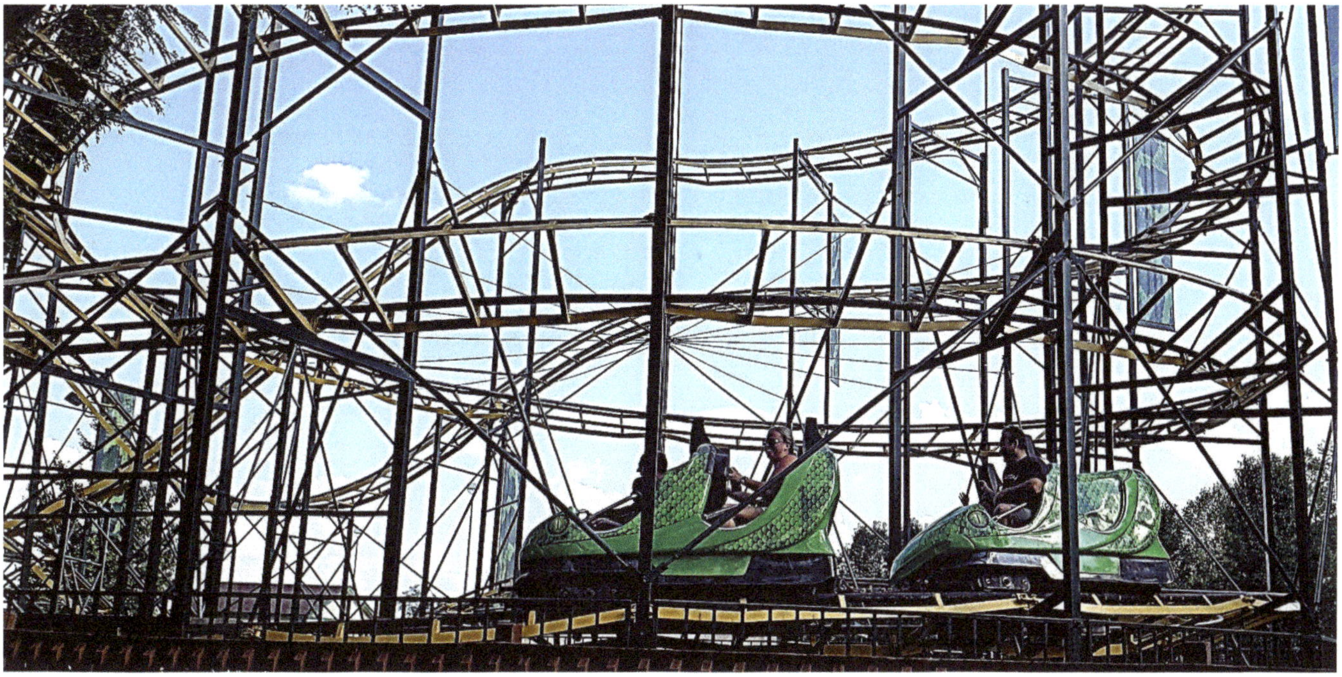

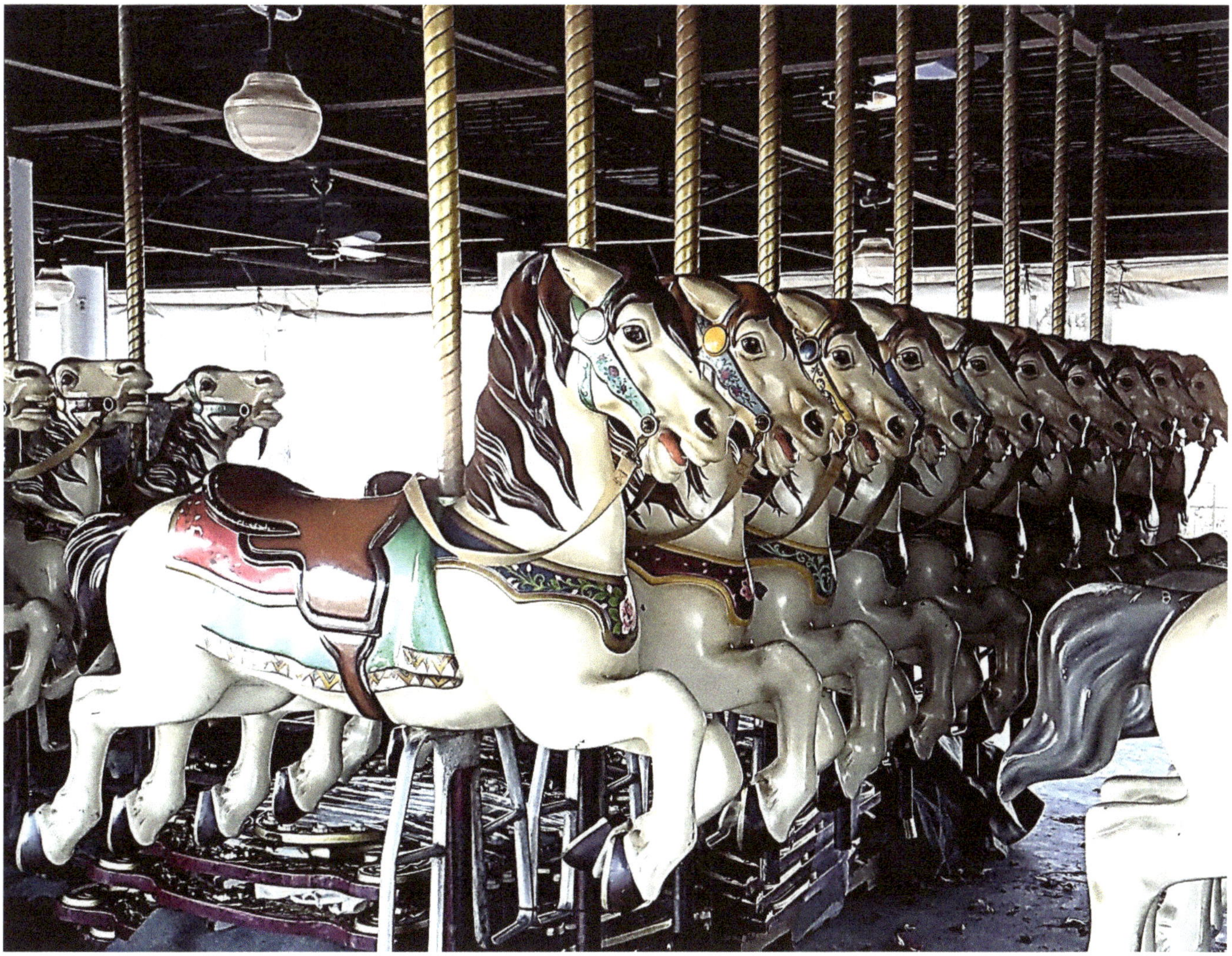

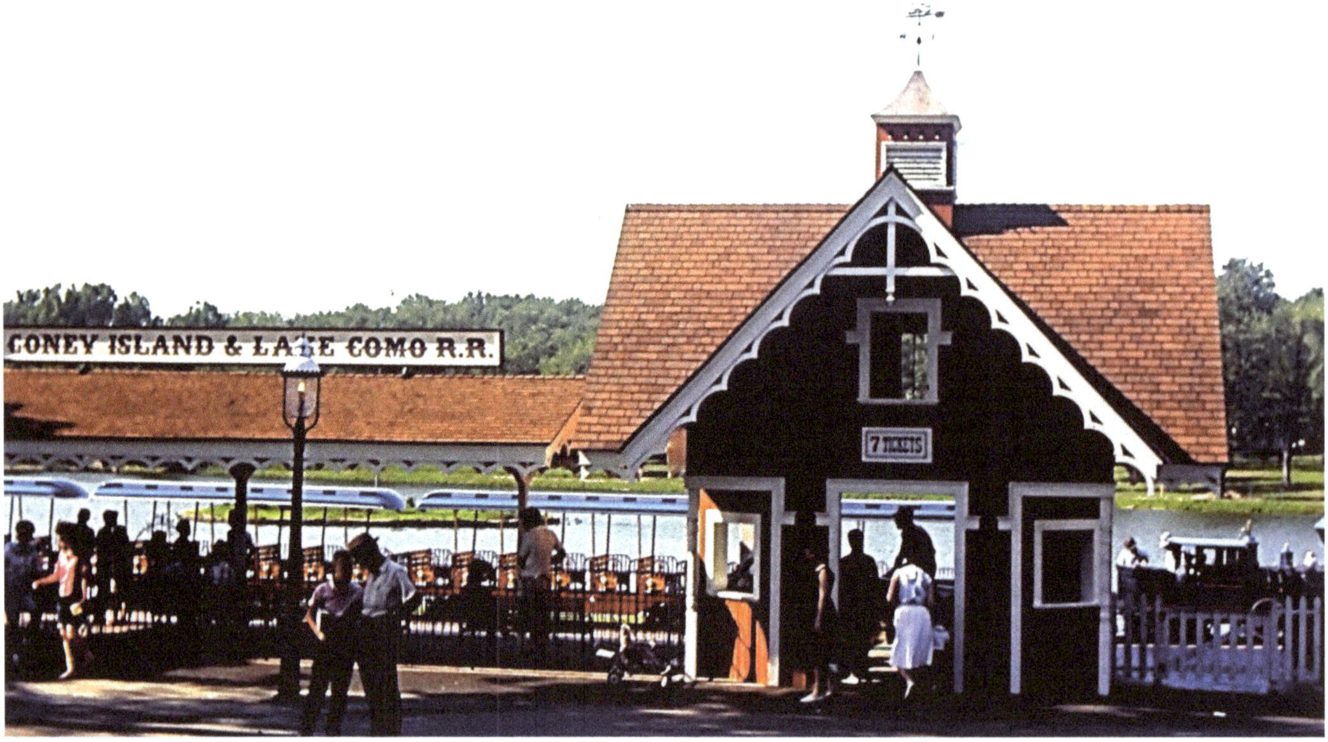
CONEY ISLAND & LAKE COMO R.R.
7 TICKETS

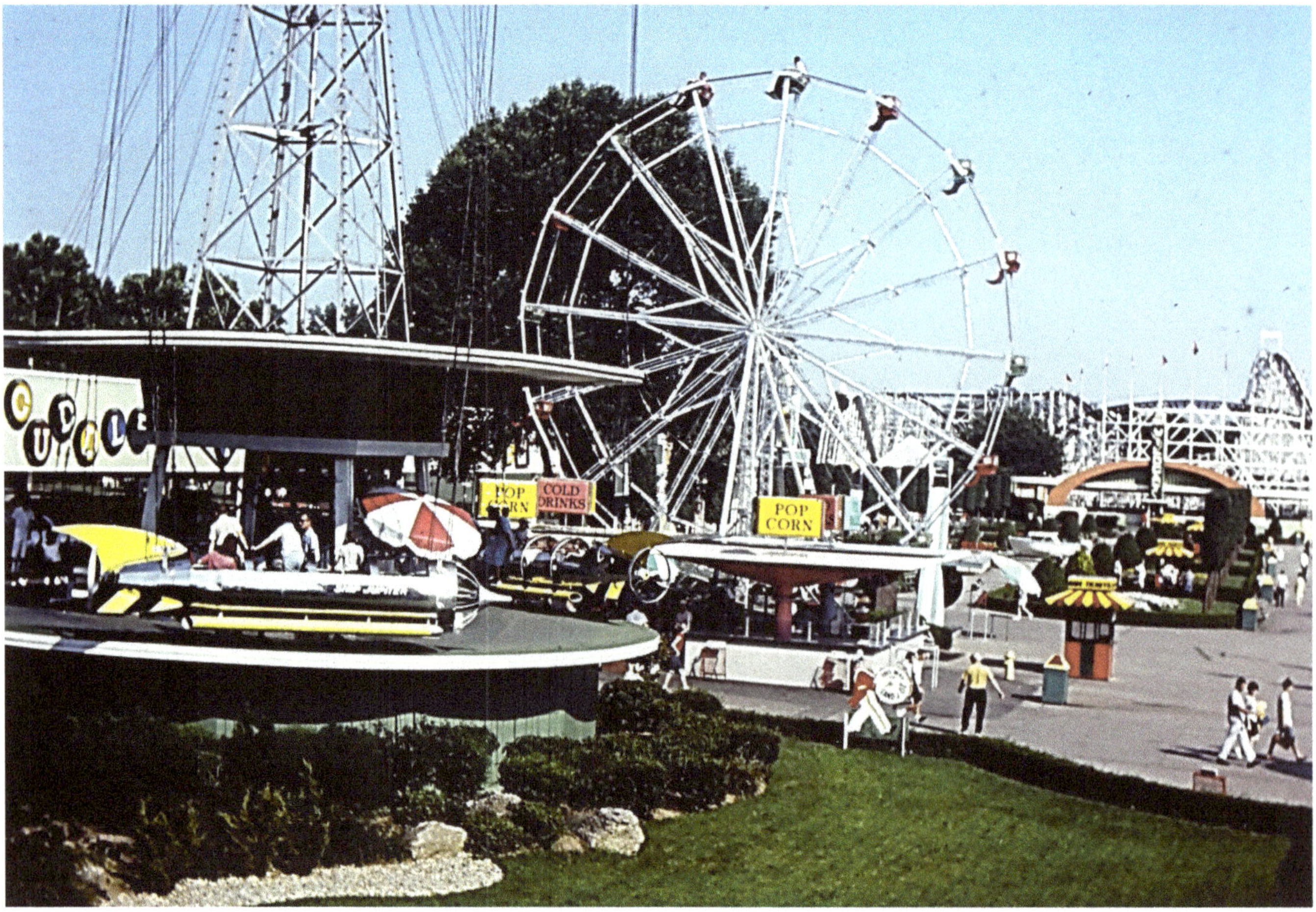
COLD DRINKS
POP CORN

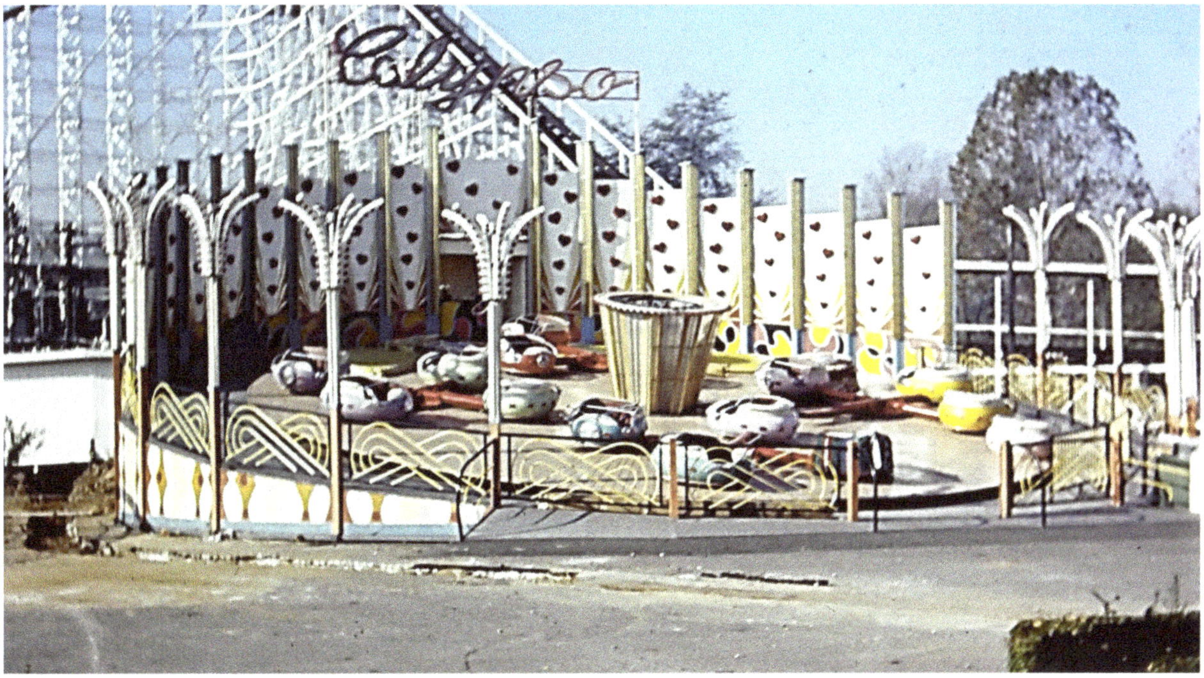
Calypso

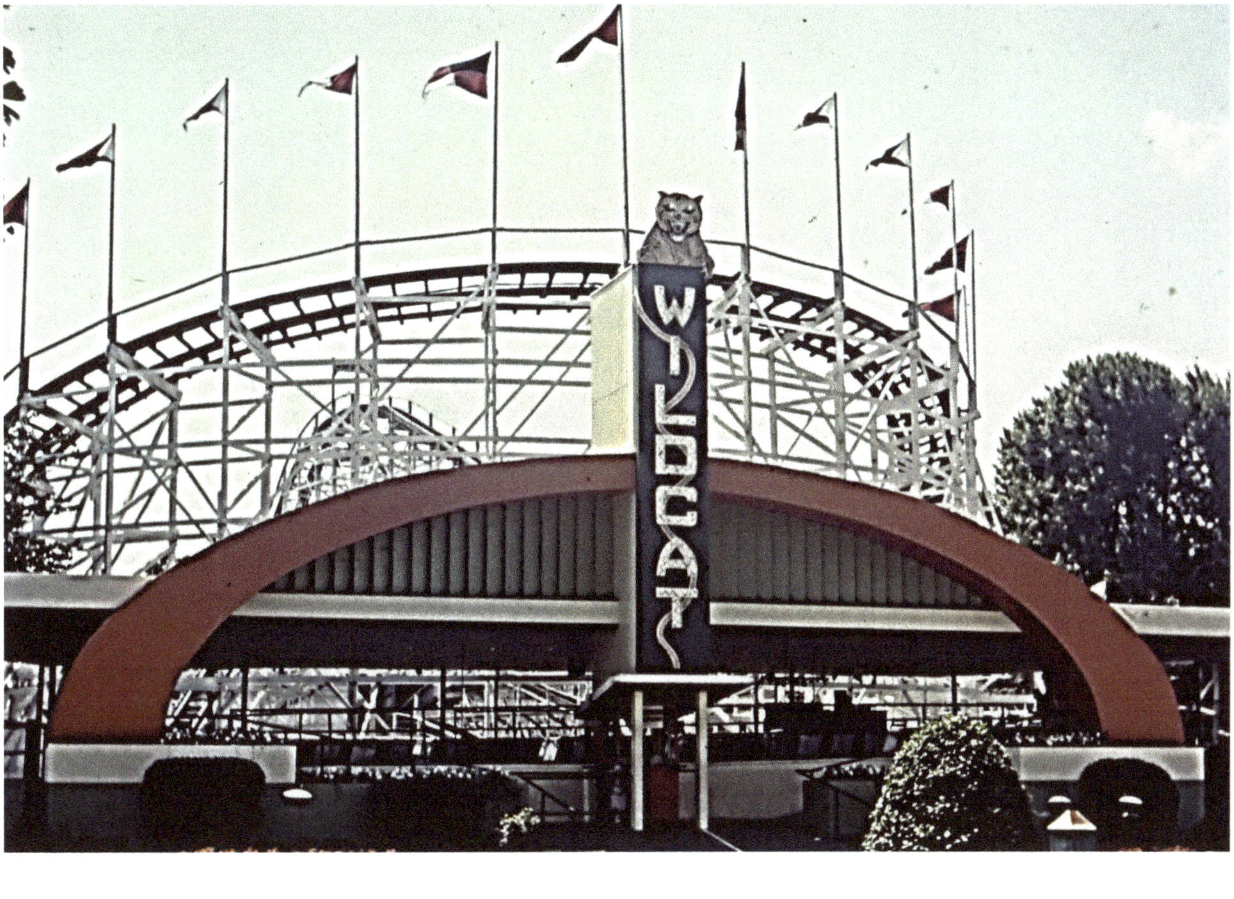
WILDCAT

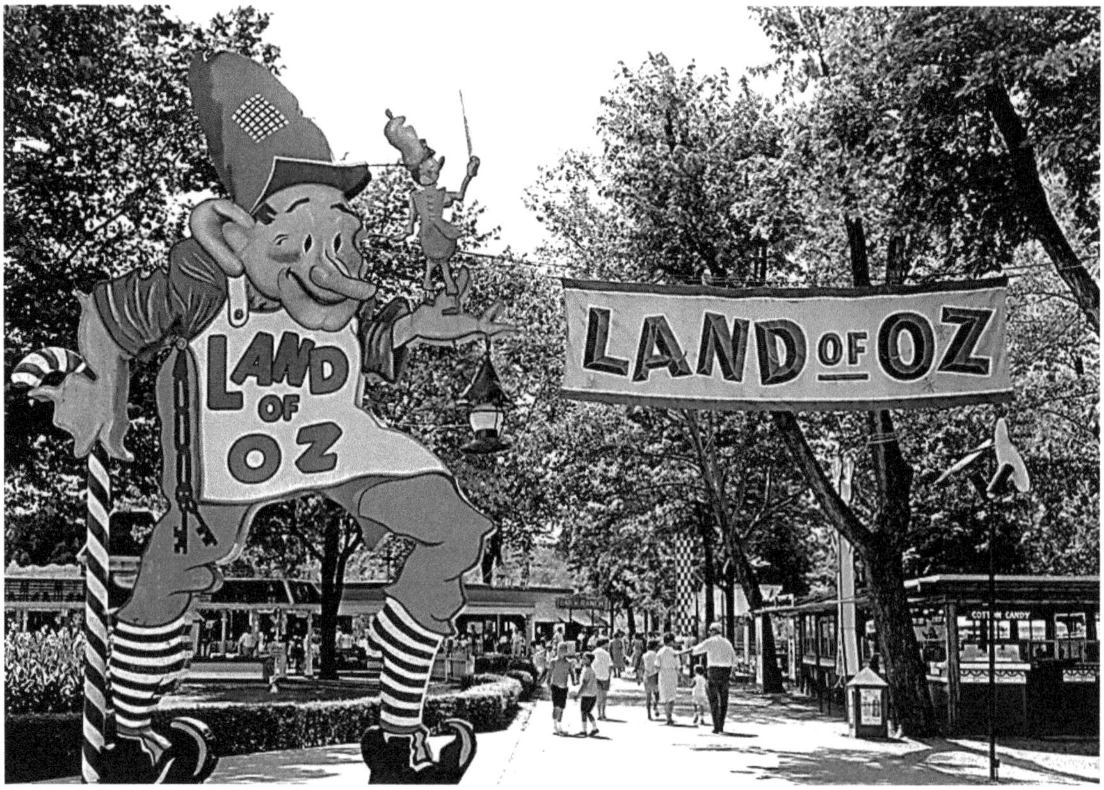
LAND OF OZ
LAND OF OZ

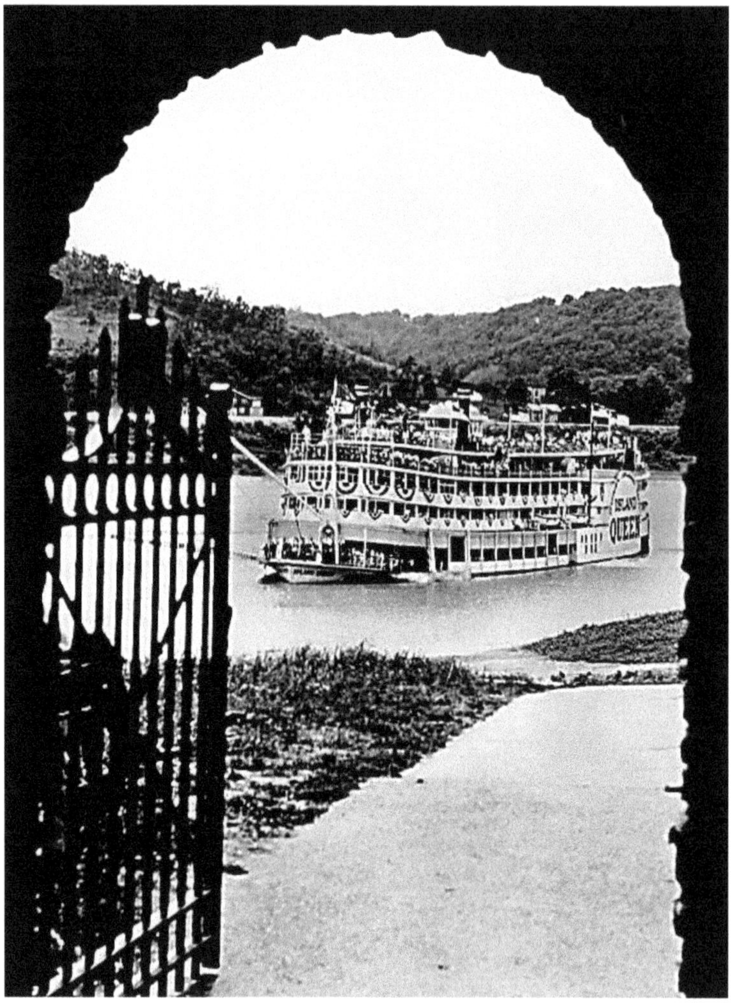

Milton Keynes UK
Ingram Content Group UK Ltd.
UKHW052141011124
450603UK00006B/67